CRISTINA Fí
2015

CULTURE AND WELL-BEING

Anthropology, Culture and Society

Series Editor:
Dr Jon P. Mitchell, University of Sussex

Recent titles

Claiming Individuality:
The Cultural Politics of Distinction
Edited by VERED AMIT AND NOEL DYCK

Anthropology and the Will To Meaning:
A Postcolonial Critique
VASSOS ARGYROU

On the Game:
Women and Sex Work
SOPHIE DAY

Slave of Allah:
Zacarias Moussaoui vs The USA
KATHERINE C. DONAHUE

A History of Anthropology
THOMAS HYLLAND ERIKSEN
AND FINN SIVERT NIELSEN

Ethnicity and Nationalism:
Anthropological Perspectives
Second Edition
THOMAS HYLLAND ERIKSEN

Globalisation:
Studies in Anthropology
Edited by THOMAS HYLLAND ERIKSEN

Small Places, Large Issues:
An Introduction to Social and Cultural Anthropology
Second Edition
THOMAS HYLLAND ERIKSEN

What is Anthropology?
THOMAS HYLLAND ERIKSEN

Corruption:
Anthropological Perspectives
Edited by DIETER HALLER AND CRIS SHORE

Control and Subversion:
Gender Relations in Tajikistan
COLETTE HARRIS

State Formation:
Anthropological Perspectives
Edited by CHRISTIAN KROHN-HANSEN
AND KNUT G. NUSTAD

Youth and the State in Hungary:
Capitalism, Communism and Class
LASZLO KURTI

Locating Cultural Creativity
Edited by JOHN LIEP

Cord of Blood:
Possession and the Making of Voodoo
NADIA LOVELL

Fair Trade and a Global Commodity:
Coffee in Costa Rica
PETER LUETCHFORD

Cultivating Development:
An Ethnography of Aid Policy and Practice
DAVID MOSSE

The Aid Effect:
Giving and Governing in International Development
Edited by DAVID MOSSE AND DAVID LEWIS

Ethnography and Prostitution in Peru
LORRAINE NENCEL

Witchcraft, Power and Politics:
Exploring the Occult in the South African Lowveld
ISAK NIEHAUS WITH ELIAZAAR MOHLALA
AND KALLY SHOKANEO

Power, Community and the State:
The Political Anthropology of
Organisation in Mexico
MONIQUE NUIJTEN

Negotiating Local Knowledge:
Power and Identity in Development
Edited by JOHAN POTTIER, ALAN BICKER
AND PAUL SILLITOE

Class, Nation and Identity:
The Anthropology of Political Movements
JEFF PRATT

Ethnic Distinctions, Local Meanings:
Negotiating Cultural Identities in China
MARY RACK

The Cultural Politics of Markets:
Economic Liberalization and Social Change in Nepal
KATHARINE NEILSON RANKIN

Bearing Witness:
Women and the Truth and Reconciliation
Commission in South Africa
FIONA C. ROSS

Landscape, Memory and History:
Anthropological Perspectives
Edited by PAMELA J. STEWART
AND ANDREW STRATHERN

Terror and Violence:
Imagination and the Unimaginable
Edited by ANDREW STRATHERN, PAMELA J. STEWART
AND NEIL L. WHITEHEAD

Anthropology, Art and Cultural Production
MARUSKA SVASEK

Race, Nature and Culture:
An Anthropological Perspective
PETER WADE

Learning Politics from Sivaram:
The Life and Death of a Revolutionary
Tamil Journalist in Sri Lanka
MARK P. WHITAKER

CULTURE AND WELL-BEING
*Anthropological Approaches to
Freedom and Political Ethics*

Edited by
ALBERTO CORSÍN JIMÉNEZ

Pluto Press
LONDON • ANN ARBOR, MI

First published 2008 by Pluto Press
345 Archway Road, London N6 5AA
and 839 Greene Street, Ann Arbor, MI 48106

www.plutobooks.com

Copyright © Alberto Corsín Jiménez 2008
The right of the individual contributors to be identified as the author of this work has been asserted by them in accordance with the Copyright, Designs and Patents Act 1988.

British Library Cataloguing in Publication Data
A catalogue record for this book is available from the British Library

ISBN-13 978 0 7453 2680 1
ISBN-10 0 7453 2680 3

Library of Congress Cataloging in Publication Data applied for

This book is printed on paper suitable for recycling and made from fully managed and sustained forest sources. Logging, pulping and manufacturing processes are expected to conform to the environmental regulations of the country of origin.

10 9 8 7 6 5 4 3 2 1

Designed and produced for Pluto Press by
Chase Publishing Services Ltd, Fortescue, Sidmouth, EX10 9QG, England
Typeset from disk by Stanford DTP Services, Northampton, England
Printed and bound in India

CONTENTS

Acknowledgements   vii

Introduction: Well-Being's Re-Proportioning of Social Thought   1
Alberto Corsín Jiménez

Part I   Distributive values

1. The Impossibility of Well-Being: Development Language and the Pathologisation of Nepal   35
Ian Harper and Bryan Maddox
2. Good Ways and Bad Ways: Transformations of Law and Mining in Papua New Guinea   53
Eric Hirsch

Part II   Persons

3. Well-Being: In Whose Opinion, and Who Pays?   69
Wendy James
4. Primed for Well-Being? Young People, Diabetes and Insulin Pumps   80
Griet Scheldeman
5. On Well-Being, Being Well and Well-Becoming: On the Move with Hospital Porters   95
Nigel Rapport

Part III   Proportionalities

6. Measuring – or Practising – Well-Being?   115
Michael Lambek
7. 'Realising the Substance of Their Happiness': How Anthropology Forgot About *Homo Gauisus*   134
Neil Thin
8. The Intension and Extension of Well-Being: Transformation in Diaspora Jain Understandings of Non-Violence   156
James Laidlaw

9. Well-Being in Anthropological Balance:
   Remarks on Proportionality as Political Imagination   180
   Alberto Corsín Jiménez

Notes on contributors   199
Index   202

ACKNOWLEDGEMENTS

This volume came out of a conference held at the University of Manchester in September 2004 on the topic of 'Well-being: anthropological perspectives'. I would like to thank all those who attended the conference, and in particular the speakers whose original papers make up the material of this book, for their participation and enthusiasm. Laura Rival's paper could not in the end make it to the volume, but I would like to thank her for her active participation during the event.

Very special thanks are due to James Carrier, who helped shape the proposal for the conference at its earliest stages. Although he was unable to attend the conference, much of the original impetus for the organisation of the event came from his support. Thanks also to Wendy James, who appreciated the relevance of the topic and provided encouragement at the time when it was most needed.

Finally, I want to express my gratitude to the following institutions, which provided funding for the event: the British Academy, the Royal Anthropological Institute and the Social Anthropology department at the University of Manchester.

INTRODUCTION: WELL-BEING'S RE-PROPORTIONING OF SOCIAL THOUGHT

Alberto Corsín Jiménez

Man is apolitical. Politics is born in the *in-betweenness* of men, hence wholly *outside* Man. There is no political substance as such. Politics emerges in the in-between and is established as a relation. (Arendt 1997 [1993]: 46)

... liberal political theory should shape its account of itself more realistically to what is platitudinously politics. (Williams 2005: 13)

What would happiness be that was not measured by the immeasurable grief at what is? For the world is deeply ailing. (Adorno 2005 [1951]: 200)

In describing the Nuer of the southern Sudan, Evans-Pritchard describes Nuer happiness as 'that in which a family possesses several lactating cows, for then the children are well-nourished and there is a surplus that can be devoted to cheese-making and to assisting kinsmen and entertaining guests' (1940: 21). This is in line with the Nuer's larger interest in cattle. Men are addressed by names that describe the colour and shape of their favourite oxen; women and children often take their names from the cows they milk. Cattle names also figure profusely in songs and poems; and it is cattle, too, that are used to prescribe marriage payments, and to define kinship rights and obligations. Moreover, men establish contact with the spirits of their ancestors through cattle. Kinship and genealogy are thus expressed through the movement, transference and circulation of cattle.

The focus of Evans-Pritchard's famous monograph is not, however, cattle, but the organisation of political institutions, which amongst the Nuer were structured around the alignment of territorial, lineage and age-system segments. At different orders of social organisation (homestead, village, clan, tribe, etc.), the principles triggering these segmentary alignments create different moments of political cohesion. In the absence of formal government and legal institutions, the principle of segmentation worked as a principle of structural politics: it brought disparate people together in a unified political project. As a second-, third- or fourth-order alignment of kinship-genealogical connections, then, 'the political' thus became the expression of the Nuer 'hypertrophy of [their] single interest' in cattle (Evans-Pritchard 1940: 41).

In his work Evans-Pritchard did not address the topic of well-being directly. He is not alone in this in anthropology, where the topic has never been the focus of explicit attention. But, as I hope the above vignette illustrates, his extraordinarily rich descriptions of the social and political forms of life in Nuer country provide an alternative route into the political and theoretical imagination of well-being, one that takes ethnography as its point of departure. In this line, this book is about the social theory of well-being, and about anthropology's contribution to the sociological imagination of such a theory. Its main aspiration is to show the relevance of *ethnography* for thinking through questions of political morality, and to do so by trying to engage in an original and innovative way with the literature on the economic, political and philosophical dimensions of well-being. As the first integrally anthropological contribution to the growing literature on well-being and the quality of life, the volume amounts to an effective exploration of the possibilities of an anthropology of political and ethical forms.

The concept of well-being has emerged as a key category of social and political thought in recent times, especially in the fields of moral and political philosophy, development studies and economics (for example, Clark 2002; Crisp and Hooker 2000; Dasgupta 1993, 2001; Griffin 1986; Sen 1999; Sumner 1996). It has been used by United Nations Development Programme (UNDP) in the construction of its Human Development Index (UNDP 1990, 1994, 1998, 2002) and the World Health Organization (WHO) in devising its quality- and disability-adjusted life-year metrics (Cummins 2005; WHO 2001; WHOQOL Group 1993, 1998). In this sense, well-being has rapidly become a standard currency in economic and political models of welfare and development: the methodological and epistemological building block for theories of cosmopolitan and global justice (for example Nagel 2005; Nussbaum 2006). As a toolkit for policy-making, well-being has helped to cut through and unify cross-cultural understandings of what it means to be a capable person, bringing together ideas about health, education, political empowerment (political and civil rights), gender relations, human rights, the natural environment, and individual freedom and opportunities. Associated with the notion of well-being, and perhaps more insidious for what they have of a global morality dictum (Strathern 2005), are parallel discussions about the 'quality of life' (Nussbaum and Sen 1993; Offer 1996) and discursive generalisations about what constitutes a 'good life'.

This book takes a critical look at the notion and discursive field of well-being, exploring its valency and analytical purchase for social theory from the vantage point of cross-cultural comparison. By examining what well-being means, or could mean, to people living in a number of different regional and ethnographic contexts (Sudan–Ethiopian border, Nepal, Papua New Guinea, India, Israel, the UK), the collection takes issue with some of the presuppositions behind Western conceptions of well-being, at a time when discourses about what characterises a 'good life' are being subjected to far-reaching scrutiny under the influence of globalisation and the widespread reach of models of liberal welfarism and development. The book thus intends to open new territories in the anthropological study of political and distributional systems of values and ethical imaginaries, and hopes to establish a major point of departure for those wishing to research the social life of ethics. The volume also makes a contribution to social theory at large by volunteering new analytical models with which to make sense of the changing shapes of people's life and ethical projects.

The rest of this introduction is concerned with reviewing the recent rise of well-being as a category of political and economic thought, and with disentangling its place in, and consequences for, anthropological and social theory. Though I hope to cover sufficient ground to understand the significance of well-being for political theory and social ethics, my review of the literature here is necessarily swift, given the vast number of works that have dealt with the topic. My remit is social theory, narrowly defined to cover political and moral philosophy, as well as economics, but not, for instance, psychology, despite the latter's sizeable contribution to the 'quality of life' literature (for example Skevington 2002; WHOQOL Group 1993). I have concentrated on the former fields because it is in dialogue with these disciplines that I believe anthropology's ethnographic edge can make the greatest contribution (though see Thin's remarks in this volume on the relation between anthropology and psychology in this respect).

The review is divided into three sections. In the first section I review the place of well-being in contemporary theories of political morality and distributive justice, where, especially since the appearance of John Rawls's *A Theory of Justice* (1999 [1971]), the concept has gained prominence in political thought. Here we take a closer look at how well-being figures in contemporary political and moral philosophy, and how it has made its way into economic and development theory at large. The section aims to show some of the assumptions behind politics and social distribution in modern political theory: about what is 'political' and how 'society' divides itself up for distribution.

The second section focuses on the naturalisation of the 'political' in social thought. It reviews some well-known, both classic and modern, approaches to well-being (or surrogate conceptions, such as 'the good life') to draw out some general conclusions about the kinds of displacements the notion of well-being has effected in our political imagination. The notion of displacement, and especially the size or proportions of such movements, is important here, and will stay with us for much of the rest of the introduction, because my concern is to focus on how political morality levers social theory. We are looking here to understand how 'politics', 'society' and 'ethics' become objects or proportionate forms for one another.

The last section brings ethnography into the argument, and does so by setting the chapters that make up the rest of the volume in perspective, and outlining the general contribution that ethnography and anthropological theory can make to our better understanding of social ethics. Here I make profuse use of the idea of 'proportionality', introduced earlier in the text. This relates to another concept, that of the 'limit'. Building on these two concepts, my conclusion intimates that well-being is a holder of limits: an unstable and fragile resting place for the political, upon which press the disproportionate shadows of a (variously conceived) outside world.

EQUALITY AND JUSTICE

All forms of social organisation work, among other things, as institutional systems for the distribution of social justice (Douglas 1986). What makes up the fund of social justice (say, moral values, such as equality, fairness or obligation; resources, primary goods or basic needs; marginal or total utility, etc.), how it gets distributed and which institutions do the allocation, and how the various elements come together into a system, if one may speak of a system at all, are of course matters of difference and dispute. Political philosophy and social choice theory deal in these matters, and do so with a view to finding the most reasonable, rational, efficient and/or egalitarian ways of organising the distribution of justice.[1]

Variously defined, well-being has always been at the centre of such debates about the social organisation of justice. As a surrogate of, or proxy for, justice, the term has been used and invoked to telescope the individual into the social; it has allowed economists, political philosophers and policy-makers to collapse sociological differences onto a rational template. Different schools of thought have disaggregated this moment of rationalisation into different units of measurement, such as 'income', 'utility', 'standard of living', 'quality of life', 'human development' or 'intergenerational welfare' (for a comparison and economic valuation of each, see Dasgupta 2001). As one would expect, each unit yields different results of what counts as justice and of where to look for it. More importantly, every method has derivative effects on our political imagination, affecting the way we come to think of the 'persons' that inhabit our theories (Douglas and Ney 1998), and of the institutional arrangements through which these imaginary persons organise their social and political life. For there is little doubt that the theoretical semblance of the kinds of people that aim for, say, utility maximisation is not and cannot be the same as that of those who aspire towards human flourishing – or so our theories say.[2]

Today debates about matters of political ethics and distributive justice are very much framed by the terms laid out by John Rawls in his *A Theory of Justice*, published in 1971 and described by Bernard Williams as the 'most powerful contribution to Anglo-American political philosophy' in the twentieth century (2005: 29). Rawls's starting premise shares the foundational assumptions of the classic contractarian philosophies of Hobbes or Rousseau: the idea of an 'original position' or primordial state of affairs, where people who do not know how they fare in life today, nor what kind of tomorrow awaits them, have to negotiate and choose the institutions that will regulate their social lives thereafter. In this scenario, individuals reason behind what Rawls famously called a 'veil of ignorance', an analytical device coined to make sure that people remain considerate of the possible interests of their fellow men, for these could turn out to be not unlike their own 'plans of life' once the veil is removed.

Rawls maintained that individuals in the original position would all share similar kinds of aspirations, and in particular that they would all want to work towards designing a basic social structure whose institutions would always and everywhere maximise the well-being of the worst-off, because this could well be the social position they found themselves in once the veil was removed. In this regard, Rawls reasoned on the assumption that an individual's intuitions and decisions regarding rational prudence could provide a route for solving the larger problem of choosing society's basic institutional structure (a telescoping of the individual into the social not without its problems, see Nagel 1973). In staging such an inaugural moment for the design of our institutions of distributive justice, Rawls made it clear that the idea of the right had to take priority over the good, for individuals must concede to an idea of society premised on fairness, where the good of society as a whole cannot be advanced if it presses against the interests of any one individual. The social structure of fairness summoned here is thus founded on two principles of justice:

First principle: Each person is to have an equal right to the most extensive total system of equal basic liberties compatible with a similar system of liberty for all.

Second principle: Social and economic inequalities are to be arranged so that they are both: (a) to the greatest benefit of the least advantaged, consistent with the just savings principle, and (b) attached to offices and positions open to all under conditions of fair equality of opportunity. (Rawls 1999 [1971]: 266)

Rawls articulated this vision for a 'system of equal basic liberties' in terms of a list of 'primary goods'. These were defined as 'things which it is supposed a rational man wants whatever else he wants.... The primary social goods ... are rights, liberties, and opportunities, and income and wealth', as well as 'a sense of one's own worth' (Rawls 1999 [1971]: 79). Throughout his later work, Rawls has insisted that the focus on primary goods is necessary as a minimum legislative requirement, and that those aspects of political morality that fall outside the immediate scope of the primary goods list (which are not few, as we will see below: they touch on matters to do with personal differences in physical and mental needs and abilities, as well as variations in power and capabilities, between persons and communities) are to be settled in a post-original position consensus.

Rawls's emphasis on the 'priority of liberty', and his fleshing out of this inaugural principle in terms of a basic list of primary goods, has been challenged on a number of fronts. Critiques have come from all quarters of the political philosophy spectrum. Although I do not have the space to dwell in detail on the different types of critiques, a cursory review will be useful, because they touch on questions which go to the very heart of the anthropological enterprise. Utilitarians like John Harsanyi, for example, criticised Rawls for the narrow-minded conservatism of the rational actors he chose to populate his theory with. Harsanyi (1975) argued that risk-taking is part of everyday rational decision-making, and suggested that it could be quite feasible for Rawls's 'original position' citizens to decide not to invest in the kind of institutions that would accommodate a worst-case scenario; people often do things that go against their long-term interests because of the prospect of considerable short-term benefits. Robert Nozick's famous libertarian theory (1974), on the other hand, challenged Rawls's model for its focus on the procedural *outcome* of distributive justice and thus its neglect of the various *processes* through which redistributions are effectively and regularly brought about by society. Nozick's argument is important because it points to the role and mode of appearance of the state in distributive politics, thus bringing attention to the fact that other social agencies are often just as involved in matters of justice. In this sense, Nozick's theory further signals the importance of 'entitlements' to justice: for Nozick, certain rights, and most famously the right to property, are inalienable, and the state certainly has no role to play in their distribution.

Perhaps it is the so-called 'communitarian' critique that most resembles the kinds of reservations that anthropologists would have of Rawls's work, although I myself find Bernard Williams's own variation of the communitarian project (a label he did not endorse) more in line with how anthropologists think. (Williams [2005: 37] coined the wonderful term 'Left Wittgensteinianism' to label his own political philosophy; I will return to his views later.) Communitarian critiques of the Rawlsian project tend to converge on a rejection of the theory's conception of personhood, which they see as too abstract. Michael Sandel (1982), for example, noted that Rawls's agents are put in the position of having to make a decision about their future with no knowledge of who they are; in this sense, their theoretical appearance as 'unencumbered selves' is utterly meaningless: people's reasons for doing things are always embedded, part and parcel of their moral biographies, and it makes no sense to provide an account of rational decision-making which is dislodged from the moral communities wherein these biographies take shape. For if moral reasoning is not the accounting of the obligations, debts and ties of solidarity that weave us into a community, then it is nothing.

We can see, therefore, that the debate around Rawls's theory of distributive justice generated a lively discussion which, though philosophical in principle, was deeply informed by issues and categories central to social theory. Questions of personhood, of the distribution and entitlements of agency, of the structure, responsibilities and appearance of the state, of the make-up and remit of moral communities, have all been raised in contestation, or qualification, of Rawls's arguments, and in the attempt to provide a more robust theoretical description of the mode in which justice ought to appear

Introduction

in society. In dialogue with these philosophical debates, anthropology's historical corpus of ethnographically informed theoretical contributions should therefore certainly be able to help us clarify the conceptual place of well-being in social experience.[3]

I will return to the question of social theory, and in particular the way in which theories of political morality put certain social imaginaries to work, in due course. But first I would like to return to Rawls's work because it is in dialogue with his notion of justice as a distributed fund of 'fair equality' that Amartya Sen developed his extremely influential view of human development in terms of *capabilities*, perhaps the most prominent of all theories of well-being today.

One aspect of the communitarian critique of Rawls's work noted above was that the design of institutions of distributive justice cannot be carried out in ignorance of the concrete social and historical conditions of a community: justice cannot be a matter solely of *procedural* arrangements; it needs to have a regard for concrete or *substantive* matters of social life too. (This element of the critique echoes the famous formalist vs. substantivist debate of the 1950s and 1960s in anthropology.) Thus, the critique had it, having outlined what the architecture of social well-being would look like in terms of 'fair equality of opportunity', Rawls failed to note that if equality is to operate as a principle of justice, its hold over the social organisation of 'offices and positions' must also be substantive and not just a matter of procedural justice; in other words, primary goods, in Rawls's definition, cannot in themselves accommodate the right type of advantage, if and when inequality is at stake, because inequality is never formal but always takes concrete shapes. Said differently, to those for whom disadvantage is a given (for example, disabled people), access to a set of primary goods provides no remedial mechanism to help overcome their systemic disadvantage. The point was famously made by Amartya Sen in his Tanner Lecture on Human Values (1980), who observed that such resourcist or commodity (that is, primary goods or basic needs) approaches to the question of distributive fairness failed not only to account for the disadvantages in well-being of (say) disabled people, but more generally fell short of addressing the very real question of human diversity. As Sen succinctly put it, 'Rawls takes primary goods as the embodiment of advantage, rather than taking advantage to be a *relationship* between persons and goods' (1980: 216, emphasis in the original). Sen's point is that a focus on primary goods, or indeed on other commodity or utilitarian approaches to well-being, is necessarily deficient, because it draws on what people do with these goods (for example, they use them to expand their use or quota of liberty, or to purchase certain rights, or to increase their marginal or total utility), or on how agents react to their using them (for example, they feel an increased sense of freedom, contentment, pleasure, happiness, etc.) rather than on 'what goods do to human beings', which would serve to emphasise instead how the distributional fund empowers people to do the things and be the people they want to be (1980: 219). Sen's alternative proposition was to develop a theoretical programme that considered the types of provisioning and social arrangements that need to be in place for people to share an equal fund of *basic capabilities* – for people to be capable of functioning as others do.

Over the years, Sen's call for a 'basic capabilities' approach to human well-being has become the most famous of all theories of political ethics, not least because of Sen's own involvement in designing UNDP's 'Human Development Index'. It has also inspired a return to Aristotelian virtue ethics in political philosophy, because of its affinities with Aristotle's metaphysical conception of human flourishing as personal self-fulfilment (Crisp 1996; Nussbaum 1988, 1993). To give the gist of it, Sen's view of well-being is founded in a robust analytical programme that holds a view of human development in terms of the expansion of 'substantive freedoms', which are both the means leading to, and the ends resulting from, the instrumental use of political freedoms, economic facilities, social opportunities, transparency guarantees and protective securities (Sen 1999: 38–40). For Sen, freedom is both constitutive of, and instrumental in, human development.

An important element in Sen's conception of human *well-being as freedom* is the analytical distinction he makes between 'functionings' and 'capabilities'. As he puts it, a person's functioning 'reflects the various things a person may value doing or being ... [which] may vary from elementary ones, such as being adequately nourished and being free from avoidable disease, to very complex activities or personal states, such as being able to take part in the life of the community and having self-respect' (1999: 75). A person's capabilities, on the other hand, reflect the substantive freedoms that she enjoys or has access to in making realisable the functionings of her choice. The well-known example with which he illustrates the difference is that of the fasting affluent person, who achieves the same functionings as the destitute person who has no option but to starve yet has access to a very different set of capabilities (1993: 40, 1999: 75). The distinction is important because it allows Sen to make a second-order distinction, that between the respective places of 'achievements' (functionings) and the 'freedom to achieve' (capabilities) in both our well-being and, more generally, our agency towards our life goals, which may or may not have to do with our well-being. This allows Sen to come up with a four-fold classification, that includes: (1) agency and (2) well-being achievement, on the one hand, and (3) well-being and (4) agency freedom, on the other (1993: 35). This perspective emphasises as much the *opportunities* that people have to bring about changes in their lives, as the *processes* that allow them to realise such visions. In *Development as Freedom*, for instance, Sen develops this point in relation to the question of the social status and agency of women. Women's freedom to pursue and achieve goals other than their own personal well-being, Sen argues, has important consequences for, among other things, community, family and children's development. Fostered by the provision of female education, employment and property rights, women's agency can, for example, play a crucial role in the reduction of birth-rates, as widely shared observations on the relationship between literacy and fertility rates attest. It can also make an important contribution to changes in the patterns of distribution of resources within families, with women playing a leading role in household decision-making; or in children's welfare, often promoting a reversal of the gender bias against the survival of young girls; or in attitudes towards environmental conservation, when women acquire rights to land and become involved in agricultural work (Sen 1999: 190–203).

Sen's nuanced philosophical anthropology carries its own social theory. Albeit it is not Sen's concern to make this explicit, some aspects of his sociological imagination are informed by an analytical finesse that one seldom finds in the work of anthropologists or sociologists. His theory of personhood is a case in point. Here people's agency and location in a structure of reflexive choices is described as being conditioned and oriented by a set of functionings and capabilities; inflected by instrumental and constitutive factors; and qualified by a temporal horizon of achievements and freedoms. Such a broad and yet nuanced conception of how a person makes her appearance in a political and social field is impressive. Moreover, all such analytical distinctions are operational, readily available to policy-makers for public action – a formidable achievement by all accounts.

There is an aspect to Sen's programme, however, where his social theory starts to become problematic.[4] This is best illustrated if we ask of his work the question that Bernard Williams (2005: 54) demands be put to all political philosophies: what does a theory do to the circumstances that summon it? The question would not, of course, come as a surprise to Sen, who is a self-declared rationalist and universalist (Sen 2002). But it does beg the question of how a political philosophy (indeed, any theoretical programme) relates to its field of action: how a description of the world embeds itself in that world. Williams's critique of the discipline of political philosophy holds that all its different versions stand discursively *outside* the world. They are not part of the world, and certainly not written in the language of sociological *contrasts* that make ethical practice substantively real (see also Castoriadis 2002 [1999]: 166). Political philosophy is not political, and it is not political because it lacks sensibility to historical particularities (cf. Mouffe 2005 [1993]).

Williams makes one exception to such characterisation of political philosophy: what he calls, with Judith Shklar, 'the liberalism of fear' (Williams 2005: 52–61). Shklar makes a distinction between the liberalism of fear, the liberalism of natural rights and the liberalism of personal development (1989: 26–28). For Williams, who shares Shklar's view on this score, the liberalism of fear is the only truly universal form of political thought, because it is the only philosophy whose 'materials are the only certainly universal materials of politics: power, powerlessness, fear, cruelty, a universalism of negative capacities' (Williams 2005: 59) It is the only form of political thought that keeps the political inside. And it is this aspect of the embeddedness of politics that brings the limitations of Sen's rationalist programme to light.

For Williams, the asymmetry of power that the liberalism of fear takes to be the basic category of political life provides no ultimate reference point for what 'unfreedom' may look like, except that it entails being in someone else's power. All conditions of coercion and unfreedom are local and historical. In these circumstances, it is not 'freedom' that is of political value, but the 'condition of life without terror' (Williams 2005: 61). This is the first requirement for political life. It may be followed, indeed it ought to be followed, by the gradual securing of other rights, but these cannot be prescribed by philosophy, and can only emerge through local processes of political and historical discovery.

Following Williams's insistence on a mode of political reasoning that captures, and takes recursive advantage of, its own sociological contrasts, the next section takes a closer look at some of the social and political objects that have been made to inhabit, and animate, classical political thought on well-being. Its focus is on how politics has been 'displaced' from political argument (Williams 2005: 58), made to appear in a place 'outside' the political, in what I will call the naturalisation of political reasoning, or its autarkic justification.

THE DISPLACEMENT OF THE POLITICAL

Appeals to nature, or justifications of a natural kind, are well known in institutional theories of political justice, the classical case being natural rights and law. Norberto Bobbio puts it bluntly when he says that the 'philosophical presupposition of the liberal state ... is to be found in the doctrine of natural rights developed by the school of natural rights (or natural law)' (2005 [1988]: 5). In anthropology, Mary Douglas once glossed these sociological or moral arguments under the banner of the so-called 'principle of coherence'. She observed that 'the principle of coherence must ... be founded on accepted analogies with nature. This means that it needs to be compatible with the prevailing political values, which are themselves naturalized' (1986: 90). Thomas Scanlon has used the term 'teleology' to make a similar point: the idea that certain 'states of affairs' have intrinsic value, that is, a value that naturally belongs to the state of affairs, and where the state of affairs thus lends itself to an end-based conceptualisation of the ethical (1998: 79–87). Well-being is no different. In the literature, well-being often evokes an image of (basic) closure, a *minima moralia* represented by roundedness or completeness. We have seen some examples above: in the foundational self-sufficiency of primary goods (Rawls), the natural inalienability of property rights (Nozick) or the appeal to a conception of freedom as the capability to function (Sen).

Appeals to autarkic justification, however, have an old pedigree in the humanities. They are the expression of natural thought's settled and balanced appearance in the political organisation of the human condition. From Aristotle's idea of happiness as *eudaimonia*, the perfected life, where

Introduction

the accomplishment of the supreme good of rational self-sufficiency is informed by a metaphysics of natural growth, that is, where only the exercise of contemplative reason realises human's functional capacities to their full (Kenny 1992), to Hannah Arendt's famous conception of the 'human condition' as 'the modes in which life itself ... makes itself felt' (Arendt 1998 [1958]: 120), of which the metabolic vitalism of 'labour' figures as its first moment of expression; throughout Western political thought, then, one finds an urge to locate a resting place for politics in (some form of expression for) nature's wholeness, and in particular to make some variant of autarkic morality a central category of political life.

The manner in which ideas about autarkic wholeness have circumscribed and shaped contemporary political thought have, therefore, in this sense, been determinative of our larger conceptualisation of 'society', and of the ways in which different people make their own articulations of social ethics appear. As we have seen above, enfolded in the notion of well-being one finds competing social models about the organisation of, and articulations between, the public good and private life. Said differently, different theories of well-being produce different versions of how and when society appears as a whole, under the banner of social justice, the state or cosmopolitanism; and how and when it appears as a part, under the labels of individualism, rights or moral claims;[5] about, also, the legislative instruments and formations of such parts-and-wholes assemblages, as in human rights law or the responsibilities of states or international agencies for structural poverty (Williams 2006); and, furthermore, about the movements and orientations of reason, which sometimes hold people together in moral communities, welded by ties of solidarity, obligations or debts, and sometimes keep them separate, sanctioned as autonomous and rational agents (Overing 1985). In other words, all theories of well-being carry a social theory within them, that works to naturalise a programme of political morality, where all kinds of problematic social objects and categories clash in a confrontation that threatens to tear apart the stability of the programme.

In this section I want to examine how the autarkic tendency of political thought has created its own social objects of inclusion, first and foremost 'society', but also other ethical artefacts, such as 'life', 'politics', the 'economy', and that complex hybrid of all of the above which is 'well-being'. A good place to start to understand the work of this type of political naturalism is Aristotle's *Nicomachean Ethics* (NE), because it is here that he develops a political argument around virtue ethics, and because it is virtue ethics, as noted above, that some political philosophers have turned to in recent times (for example, Nussbaum 2005, 2006; see also Lambek, this volume).

Aristotle's view on the perfect life rests on a biological paradigm, where all things tend towards their teleological functional end. And human happiness, Aristotle tells us, is no different. In fact, for Aristotle happiness is the supreme good, the end towards which other activities tend: 'the complete good is thought to be self-sufficient ... the self-sufficient we now define as that which when isolated makes life desirable and lacking in nothing; and such we think happiness to be' (Aristotle 1984 [*c.* 4 BCE]: I.7.1097b5–17). Jonathan Lear has examined in detail the movement of Aristotle's thought in the *NE*, and concluded that what one sees at play in Aristotle's ethical and political thought is the development of a 'structure of trauma' (Lear 2000: 45). Happiness is defined throughout the *NE* as a state of self-fulfilment, the highest of the virtues, or 'goods', of practical life. What Aristotle means by self-fulfilment, however, is never clear; or rather, the definition is always on the move, self-effacing itself. According to Lear, the process is first set in motion when Aristotle introduces his definition of 'happiness': this should be read as an 'inaugural instantiation' (2000: 8), where Aristotle both injects the concept into our life *and* prefigures the structural shape that our *life itself* will need to take for happiness to occur inside it (2000: 26). The gist of Lear's argument is that Aristotle is a 'seducer' (2000: 22), someone who never quite ties his subject down because he keeps shifting attention to new objects of ethical curiosity: happiness is a matter of *practical virtuousness*, which when looked at closely turns out to be a matter of *self-sufficiency*, which suddenly makes problematic the question of *life as a whole*, which on second reflection opens up a new perspective on the relationships we have to others in life, and thus on solitude and *contemplation*, which is ultimately something that only the gods can do full time, and is thus a reminder of our mortality and of the very limited nature of happiness, wherever it turns out to reside. Every one of Aristotle's intellectual movements aims therefore at 'remaindering' itself out: at creating a surplus or space 'out there' from which things look different; or, as Lear puts it, 'any form of life will tend to generate a fantasy of what it is to get *outside* that life' (2000: 48, emphasis added).

Lear's is a psychoanalytic take on Aristotle's ethical project, although his insights into the remaindering tendencies of his thought have sociological validity too. Indeed, Lear himself notes how, in a last and desperate movement, Aristotle tries to save his ethical edifice, which crumbles from the pressures that keep displacing it, by resorting to the *political* principle of law enforcement (2000: 58). Politics is Aristotle's last desperate attempt at safeguarding the integrity of his ethics. We need politicians and legislators to guarantee our peaceful existence, to provide us the time of leisure necessary to lead a life of contemplation. In this light, politics becomes both a means and an end; at once the vehicle and goal of political life, the impetus behind, and the constraining system of, political organisation.

Now the appearance of politics as the regulatory mechanism of ethical life suddenly creates its own sociological forms. Aristotle's own thought contains some clues: *outside* political life, we have seen, only contemplation can deliver ethical sovereignty; *inside* politics, however, this now obtains through the work of friendship, for Aristotle believed that, amidst the frenzy of practical life, only in friendship can one come close to experiencing the 'complete' goodness of happiness (Marías 1989: 67–89). Friendship and contemplation

Introduction

become, in this light, reversible forms: one achieves in social intercourse what the other obtains in solitude.

In his essay, Lear makes the point that, in postulating an outside for political life in contemplative activity, Aristotle appears to be valuing death, for only in a deathlike state do we find ourselves properly removed from the pressures of practical life (2000: 53). This is a convincing argument, and Lear has good reason for pursuing it, for his interest is in elucidating the contribution that psychoanalysis can make to virtue ethics. But here I want to focus on the sociological dimensions of Aristotle's thought instead. And though death might indeed be an appropriate *outside* for politics in psychoanalytic terms, there is also a case to be made about its sociological counterpart. Said differently, if we focus our analysis *within* the political, the play of reversibilities noted above (friendship:solitude) casts its own sociological 'outsides' or remainders.

As it turns out, the remaindering moment of political life *inside politics* is given by tyranny. In a remarkable essay on the 'shadows' of Western political thought, Eugenio Trías (2005) has observed that the Aristotelian virtue of friendship is in fact obtained, in the classical context, as the figure-ground reversal of tyranny. Using Plato's description of tyranny as the *hostis* or public enemy of the republic, Trías shows that for the tyrant any and all forms of social mobilisation are potentially threatening to the *status quo*. To uphold his mantle of dominance, the tyrant must of necessity exercise violence over the social body *as a whole*: there must be no place outside, or remainder over, the reach of the tyrant's power (2005: 134–35). Only the tyrant can stand *outside* society. Tyranny thus makes 'society' appear in an inverse relation to what friendship and its social ethics enables. More importantly, this moment of appearance makes ethics in turn a residue of a form of proportional sociality, where the tyrant's need for unlimited or *disproportionate* political violence creates a total social object ('society'), which leaves no or very little space for ethical action. Classical Greek thought, then, effected a set of displacements between 'ethics', 'politics' and 'society', whose sociological imagination was essentially incommensurable,[6] and where ethics thus appeared as a leftover of political organisation.

The question of the *size* or proportional forms that 'society' takes in politics, only vaguely noticeable in Aristotle, makes a central appearance in Hannah Arendt's *The Human Condition* (1998 [1958]). Arendt wrote *The Human Condition* in the wake of the Hungarian Revolution of 1956 and, like many of her works, it is an attempt to make sense of the political predicament of humankind in the aftermath/presence of totalitarianisms and unprecedented state violence. The classic locus is Auschwitz, which for Arendt brought about the collapse and confusion of society 'over elementary questions of morality' (Arendt 2005 [1963]: 125). Margaret Canovan has said of the book that it is an attempt to grapple with the 'miraculous openness and ... desperate contingency' of political action (1998: xvii), a view that contrasts sharply with Aristotle's explicit, if flawed, teleological framework.

Arendt's vision for humanity is intrinsically possibilistic, embedded in a rich and recurrent world of beginnings, from the birth of a new human being to the 'space of appearance' which characterises pure political life, and to which she gives the name *vita activa*, the 'life devoted to public-political matters' (1998 [1958]: 12). Elsewhere Arendt described this life of action and recurrent nativity as 'miraculous', and 'the political' as the place where one can hold out and hope for miraculous happenings (1997 [1993]: 66). The institutional organisation of such assemblies of hope has taken different shapes at different historical times, and Arendt dedicates much of *The Human Condition* to contrasting classic and modern modes of convention. Effectively, what Arendt attempts in this book is an archaeology of the different ways in which ethics, society and politics have been conjoined or separated in Western political thought, and does this by exploring the different modes of articulation of the categories that she calls 'labour' (as we will see, contemporary political thinkers – like Sen – would call this 'well-being'), 'work' (sociality) and 'action' (politics).

Central to our interest here is the way in which Arendt makes the concept of 'society' appear as a proxy for understanding the very functioning of the life process, in a way not unlike how Aristotle makes 'politics' the end-point of a teleological process. For Arendt, the rise of 'society' as a concept of theoretical significance in the modern age marked the moment when 'the life process itself ... [had] been channeled [sic] into the public sphere' (1998 [1958]: 45). There are two movements to this conceptualisation. First, we need to understand that Greek thought lacked a concept of society. Social life, as we understand the term today, was circumscribed to the realm of the household (*oikonomia*). Social relationships inside the household were conducted to provide for the biological necessities of survival, what Arendt called the life of labour. Outside the household, on the other hand, men encountered one another in the reality of the *polis*, where the space and possibility for political life effectively took shape.

We come to the second movement. The Greek situation, Arendt observed, is starkly different from our own. She insisted that our contemporary equation of the public with 'society' is a peculiarly modern phenomenon, characterised by the movement of 'life' (that is, labour) out of the realm of the household and into the public sphere. The new public sphere is thus a *political economy*: a household (*oikonomia*) gone public, where the routines of everyday survival, the labours previously hidden in the privacy of the household, have now acquired public status.

In typically poignant and lucid style, Arendt concludes that this new 'society' is 'the form in which the fact of mutual dependence for the sake of life and nothing else assumes public significance and where the activities connected with *sheer survival* are permitted to appear in public' (1998 [1958]: 46, emphasis added). In this world, the political organisation of survival amounts to, and in effect requires no more than, its economic organisation. This is why, for Arendt, contemporary political philosophy falls short of fulfilling its intellectual project unless it takes charge of the analysis of the economics of industrial labour and the new regimes and organisation of technocratic work; and why, when she described our modern world as a 'society of laborers' (1998 [1958]: 46), she was in fact making a profound metaphysical statement about the sociology of our contemporary human condition.

Well-being is not a term that Arendt uses, although if we were to endorse the current interest in biological functionings her notion of 'labour' would play an analogous sociological and political role. In this sense, what Arendt's analysis brings to the imagination of well-being as a political category is her insistence that the appearance and disappearance of sociological categories (the rise and death of the 'household', 'society' or 'the public') is fundamentally entangled with the political organisation of the life-process.

The point has in fact been recently brought home by Giorgio Agamben in his analyses of the structures of sovereignty and the modern state. In *The Open* (2005), Agamben suggests that our historical and ever-shifting sense of humanity entails, at its very heart, a debate with its own animal condition. Agamben's definition of our human nature dwells on the idea of opening or caesura, the very movement and debate through which the human condition takes stock of its ever-displaceable limitations: in other words, how people constantly push their de-finitions (their limits) outside (2005: 28, 77). For Agamben, this historical conversation with ourselves about the possibilities of our own animal nature makes for one of the most fundamental categories of political life. Historically, we have come to define our politics through consciousness of our humanity's natural limits.

Today, however, Agamben argues, the place of this most basic political-cum-metaphysical relation (between our human and animal conditions) has been displaced (2005: 53); the relationship has disappeared from our political vocabulary, the human and the animal reciprocally hollowing each other out from our existential equation (2005: 36). No longer a central aspect of how we define ourselves, the disappearance of our human-animal openness from our existential consciousness has left us historically homeless; the structure of human life has been evacuated of its historical condition and been left nude of itself. Today, humanity is 'bare life' (see also Agamben 1999).

Like the social organisation of Arendt's 'sheer survival', 'bare life' carries a political moment of its own and Agamben's *oeuvre* at large is dedicated to the task of fleshing out its sociological episteme (see Agamben 1996, 2000, 2004). In *Means without Ends* (2001), for example, Agamben criticises the moment of *spectacular* politics through which the modern state takes its form (cf. Debord 1995 [1967]). All modern political communities, states included, endorse a vision of, and become institutional guarantors for, a foundational programme for the 'good life' or 'sufficient life' of the community.[7] This substantive approach to political life has been corrupted in modern government, where politics has become an autarkic goal in itself, no longer a means to an end (Agamben 2001: 97). We are witnesses here to politics' consummation of its own teleological end: having arrived at its historical *telos*, humanity has become *animal* once again, realising the exhaustion of the human project (Agamben 2005: 98). The point is a simple one: politics, Agamben suggests, is no longer about managing the understanding of our human-animal condition. The relationship has been cancelled and a final definition of what we are – sheer life – stabilised. In our present conjuncture, then, humanity is left with no task other than the management of its own biology, a return to the *oikonomia* or life of labour that Arendt ascribed to the pre-political (that is, the household). With Foucault, however, Agamben believes that this moment of epochal self-consumption is nevertheless capable of re-politicisation, indeed, it is a political moment itself, and he identifies three domains where this is happening: bioethics, the global economy and the new political economy of well-being or humanitarian assistance (2005: 99).

Stephen Collier and Andrew Lakoff (2004) have recently furthered this line of thought from an anthropological perspective. They have explored the global appearance of what they call 'regimes of living', by which they mean the coming together of political, technical and moral forces in the creation of temporarily stable funds of ethical reason: where 'ethics' emerges as a signpost to the kind of new questions about human nature and the life process that have been opened up by technological reason and biopolitics (see also Ong and Collier 2005). Regimes of living are, in this light, anthropological artefacts of 'bare life', for which there appears to be no shortfall of examples: the liberal ethics behind the regulation of new human reproductive technologies (bioethics); alternative legal and appropriative modes of intervening in or generating capital flows (global economy); and the counter-politics and claims to citizenship of the urban disenfranchised (global humanitarianism) (Collier and Lakoff 2005). These and other developments, Collier and Lakoff argue, are calling for a new formulation of the question 'How should one live?', where the means of techno-political practice (how), the protocols and models of evaluative behaviour (should) and the subjects of ethical reflection (one) are cast anew for every new regime of life.

In the notion of 'regimes of living' we find thus an analytical device with which we can start mapping both the displacement of the political *and* its substantive reappearance in concrete claims for ethical recognition. Arendt and Agamben's critical reading of the taking over of the political by the economic offers support to such a view of political morality as a moment of fugue. Comparing their views with Aristotle's insights into the development of ethical life provides further evidence of the location of political justice in its outside or remaindering spaces. In reviewing the writings of these authors I have therefore hoped to serve two purposes. First, I hope to have shown that there is no single space where one may look for well-being. Liberal political philosophy provides us the means to analyse the ways in which modern society makes questions of justice and equity appear (to itself); it does not provide us with a recipe for isolating well-being as a universal value. For modern plural society, questions of distributive justice become questions of state sovereignty, where political morality is a matter of the legislative

Introduction

administration of biological life. But this account of how well-being ought to be distributed arrives already a political moment too late: it is supported on an architecture of social institutions that finds no empirical counterpart in how society recognises and assembles its different parts together.

A second purpose of my selective review has been to bring attention to the way in which political philosophy creates its own sociological imagination. I have attempted to provide a sense of the way in which 'society', 'politics' and 'ethics' (or their absences) are assembled in different proportions every time human nature or the human condition are invoked to legitimate a political programme for the sustenance of life. Another way of saying this is to note that political categories take different proportional sizes; that they create a lever for themselves by distributing their own contrasts or remainders from other categories. Not to attend to these contrasts is therefore to mistake the distribution of justice for a decision about resource allocation: to think of politics as a one-sided gesture rather than as a continuous displacement in the 'terms of recognition' of society itself (Appadurai 2004).

THE DISTRIBUTION OF CONTRASTS

I want to turn now to some concrete examples of how people create their own spaces of recognition by re-proportioning the imagination of the 'social wholes' to which they belong. I do so by providing a critical commentary to the chapters that follow. I do not review my own chapter, which is but a theoretical reformulation of the argument I have been developing in this introduction.

The comments, and the chapters, are organised around three themes: 'Distributive Values', 'Persons' and 'Proportionalities'. The chapters themselves, however, should not be read as examples or elaborations of the themes that I ascribe to them. They touch on these issues, but they certainly touch on many more too. My choice simply reflects the introduction's narrative strategy, and my own theoretical interests.

Distributive values

Justice and equality are, still to this day, political philosophy's classic distributional values. Theories abound on how they ought to be conceptualised, where to look for them and how to distribute them; we have looked at some of them in this introduction. Distributions, however, should not simply be seen as moments in the institutional allocation of values.[8] We can lend more purchase to the notion of 'distribution' if we think of it as a social moment too. What is given away is always an index of what is left behind. How people make themselves available to others, or, in Thomas Scanlon's sober phrasing, what we owe to each other (Scanlon 1998), is therefore always already a distributional moment: an expression of society's dislodgement of itself into the parts that it values. This is what social life amounts to: the ongoing re-evaluation and re-distribution of sociality itself. To attend to these social moments of evaluative redistribution is to attend to the configuration of the political.

The focus of Ian Harper and Bryan Maddox's chapter is precisely the ordering of 'the political' in Nepal, with particular attention to its mode of disappearance in development discourse and practice. Their argument revolves around two examples: public health interventions and literacy programmes, which they candidly gloss as 'the view from the clinic' and 'the view from the classroom', respectively. Health and literacy are, of course, fundamental constituents of well-being; they are both dimensions of the Human Development Index, and both contribute a central set of functionings in Sen's capability approach. Both are values, then, that have been institutionally sanctioned for distribution.

Public health interventions in Nepal have been guided by what Harper and Maddox call an ideology of 'pathologisation', where the body politic is medicalised and benchmarked against normalised (bureaucratised, fiscal, chartered) conceptions of the diseased and afflicted. Examples abound and include the introduction of the Disability Adjusted Life Year (DALY) analysis, the Directly Observed Therapy Short-course programme for the treatment of tuberculosis, or the vitamin A capsule distribution programme. These programmes are designed to leave politics 'outside'. The recipients or beneficiaries of these programmes are counted as 'bodies', whose well-being directly correlates with the distribution and delivery of medical treatment. The social context of intervention is thus neutralised. Health problems are the problems of 'individuals'; the structural inequalities and social conditions that make life for these individuals 'problematic' (from a normalising perspective) is rarely, if ever, considered. And when they are considered, the bureaucratic logic tends to pathologise them too, part of a discursive field of 'social pathologies' that includes terrorism, corruption, crime, violence and human rights violations. The view from the clinic thus polarises the world into pathological beings and 'well beings'. Under such conditions, the moment of appearance of the political takes the form of what Harper and Maddox, following Finkielkraut, call 'humanitarianism'. Their analysis echoes on this point Agamben's diagnosis of the governance of 'bare life'.

The view from the classroom presents a contrasting scenario which comes to confirm the distressing realisation of a view of development predicated on the absence of politics. As they argue, literacy is nothing if not a political affair. A long tradition of anthropological scholarship on literacy has shown that the shaping of literacy practices is deeply embedded in social contexts that are always complex and burdened with inequalities. To fetishise literacy as development agendas do is therefore, once more, to uproot the political from the social moment of action to which it belongs.

Eric Hirsch takes up the question of comparing *institutional* and *social* perspectives on the distribution of values. His chapter offers a rich description

Introduction

of two different 'distributional logics' at work in Fuyuge responses to state welfarist policies in contemporary Papua New Guinea (PNG). PNG is the focus today of very significant resource extractive operations (mining, for the most part), which have already had a massive impact on the local ways of people. The scale of the operations has surpassed the cultural capacity of the Fuyuge (and other PNG) people to accommodate their sense of well-being to the new situation (see also Rumsey and Weiner 2004). It has turned them into 'patients' rather than 'agents' of development, to use two terms that Hirsch adapts from Sen's work. To understand how this has happened Hirsch contextualises his argument by first outlining the historical conditions under which the state made itself present to Fuyuge and other PNG people during colonial times, and by relating these to Fuyuge understandings of what they call *mad ife*, the good ways or, we would say, well-being.

The Fuyuge notion of 'good ways' carries a number of corollaries. It is supported on the presence of an *amede* or 'chief', a person who can summon and unify all Fuyuge productive relations (productive, that is, of other relations, not just goods). In colonial times, the good ways of the *amede* were contrasted with those of *ha u bab*, men with a renowned capacity for instilling fear. With the advent of colonial government the ways of *ha u bab* disappeared, and people today speak appreciatively of 'the law' for having furnished an environment where they can walk around without fear of attack, and for providing also the means (for example, money) with which to make relational life yet more productive.

Fuyuge appreciation of 'the law', however, is contrasted with their reaction to resource extractive operations. Mining corporations require a legislative framework to carry out their projects: they need landowners to compensate for the use of land; they need provincial, national and governmental stakeholders (schools, local elites, ministers, officials) with whom to negotiate the terms of access and exploitation. These are not categories that Fuyuge relate to. Coerced to participate in a distributional game the scale of which exceeds them, the Fuyuge have had a hard time 'converting' the wealth of their land resources into a valuable set of relational capacities. Whereas the introduction of 'the law' allowed the Fuyuge to act as both agents and patients with regard to one another (that is, to reciprocally augment their relational capacities), resource extraction demands from them an orientation towards redistributive exchanges where the form of their human capacities has no value. Hirsch's elegant analysis is therefore significantly poignant because it carries the implication that not all distributions, and certainly not the wholesale distribution of wealth (Hirsch uses the term 'quality of life'), contribute to our well-being. Running through his argument we find thus the suggestion that certain distributive processes (that is, Fuyuge exchanges of relational capacities) are in fact antecedent to what we have come to know as the sanctioning moments of institutional distributive justice.

Persons

It has become a commonplace in anthropology to describe the Melanesian model of personhood as a 'distributed' or 'fractal' person.[9] Hirsch's description of Fuyuge's relational exchanges of capacities, and their coercion and concentration into one visible ritual (*gab*) appearance, provides a partial illustration of this: people bringing together their relations into a unified (whole) appearance for a *gab* ritual; and, inversely, people disaggregating land relations into (partial) claims for resource compensations.

This distributed (parts and wholes) view of the person is not wholly foreign to political philosophy. The communitarian school, with its emphasis on the holistic understanding of moral and biographical agency, holds a similar view, though its analytical framework, and certainly its social theory, is very different. What both approaches have in common, however, is the underlying appreciation that if the notion of well-being carries any moral meaning whatsoever, it must in principle reflect people's ownership over its description. Well-being must be carried through persons. An analytic of well-being that does not contribute to a more robust theory of the person is therefore already lacking.

Keeping the whole of the person in view is what Wendy James reminds us about in her account of the modern discursive use of well-being in the context of development. Her critique resonates with Bernard Williams's call to historicise our liberal notions of justice. Like Williams, James finds in the current use of the rhetoric of well-being a fastidiously modernist and a-historical presumption about how individuals ought to fare in life – and like Williams, too, she finds R.G. Collingwood's philosophical conception of history instructive, especially in regard to how people construct their evolving sense of self. She reminds us, for example, of the classical Azande conception of the enhancement and protection of personal capacities via magic. Under such circumstances, she asks, how are we to make sense of the notion of 'well-being', when the capacity of agents to carry out their plans is enmeshed in complex structures of potential and hidden forces? The point echoes Hirsch's analysis of the relational coercion of capacities, and is extended to suggest that if well-being is to retain its purchase as an analytical category it needs to be mobilised into a more robust (historicised) theory of personhood.

A final aspect of James's sober argument that I would like to comment on is the distinction she makes between 'welfare' and 'well-being', and her intimation that worked into the distinction is a heavy baggage of assumptions about the interrelations between state provision, individual enhancement and the modern political economy of liberal justice. This is a set of assumptions that we need to remain sceptical of, especially if, as her own history of ethnographic fieldwork in North East Africa attests, 'the "normal" background of people's lives [is] a theatre of conflict'. Her description of refugee camps in Ethiopia tells us of the absurdity of looking for well-being in situations where a community's historical sense of purpose has been evacuated – where people are told, and slowly come to realise, that they will never return to their old ways of livelihood. These people, James reminds us, are surely in desperate need of welfare provision; but who will ever deliver or return to them their well-being, and how?

In her account of how three teenagers describe the hold that diabetes has over their lives, Griet Scheldeman provides a partial answer to James's question: in her ethnography, well-being emerges as the process of satisfactorily managing the incorporation (literally, into the body) of a relational complex, at the heart of which is one's sense of ownership over one's life. Scheldeman offers us an extraordinarily thick description and elucidation of how capabilities are existentially performed and brought to life; where a medical condition (diabetes) suddenly foregrounds the functioning of the body as the ultimate determinant of how life is faring for oneself, rather than how one fares in life.

For the teenagers that Scheldeman worked with, though varying in their satisfaction with the use of an insulin pump to control their affliction, *freedom* was the Aristotelian conception of the good that defined whether life (with the insulin pump) was good or not. They wanted to regain the freedom they once enjoyed (and that they saw in fellow adolescents) to do as they pleased – to do the things teenagers do, go to the places teenagers go to, without an obsessive concern for the care of their bodies. Well-being became thus about the staging of the right conditions (learning to live with an insulin pump, or without one: to play with its control panel, to count calories, to think of a corresponding insulin dose and administer it) to make life itself invisible: to accomplish the transition from a situation where life itself has hold over one's freedom to one where one is freely in control of one's life.

It is at this juncture that the 'quality of life' discourse takes over. What does it mean to make the conditions of life invisible, to hide them behind the veil of freedom? (Is the veil of freedom not what Rawls invited us to think with when placing us behind a 'veil of ignorance'?) This is no rhetorical question. Quality of life in the Scottish city of C, where Scheldeman carried out her fieldwork, is hardly something one can turn a blind eye to. Characterised by 'financial hardship, third-generation unemployment, teenage pregnancies, violence, broken families, [and] unhealthy diets', the notion of 'empowering' adolescents to live the life they want to live takes a rather disconcerting turn. Scheldeman's chapter invites us to reflect about our own existential categories, and to seriously reconsider how and where (in which social contexts) we decide to place them when conjuring the notion of well-being.

Another richly ethnographic description of the emplacement and living of well-being in action is to be found in Nigel Rapport's many-layered account of 'professional well-being' amongst a group of hospital porters at Constance Hospital in Easterneuk, Scotland. I can hardly do justice to the ethnography with a brief summary here. What I would like to draw attention to is Rapport's insistence on the need to open our analyses to the 'aesthetics' of people's ongoing appropriations of their selves and their life-worlds; or, as he gracefully puts it, the need to constantly actualise 'the connection between the rhythms of selfhood and the shapes and forms of its environments'. This is of course a holistic enterprise, although for different people we can attempt to discern the different aspects of its institutional, social and personal manifestations. Rapport does this by focusing on four aspects of the life-rhythms of porters' professional lives: movements around the hospital site; movements between the hospital and the outside world; moving between being a porter and a patient; and the existential fragility of the life-rhythm itself, thrown into relief by the maximal antithesis of what well-being is, namely, death. Central to Rapport's rich experiential analysis of how porters take on the rhythmic thrusts of every one of these existential and environmental pressures is the notion of proportion or balance. At various points he observes that the porters' sense of well-being is evinced in a feeling of balance: 'Just as well-being called for a balance or proportion to be achieved between work and play, health and sickness, and so on, so there was a proper proportion to the way the claims one staked should be recognized.' The balancing metaphor should not, however, be interpreted for what it has of stability or repose. Rapport's focus on 'movements' is in this sense a crucial analytical insight: to be well one needs an appreciation of the 'proportionate movement' through which one becomes and grows into a person. This is the 'aesthetics' of which he speaks in his introduction: well-being as the artful covering-up of our future remainders.

Proportionalities: the remaindering movement of life

When people give themselves to others, and to themselves, in different distributive guises, we can describe such efforts in terms of proportional give-aways. We have seen an example in Rapport's account of the rhythmic accommodations of porters' life-projects to their institutional surroundings. Proportionality has of course long been a dominant metaphor and explanatory paradigm in philosophical descriptions of moral reasoning and theories of ethics at large. One need only recall the image of Dike, the Greek goddess of Justice, holding level the scales of justice in her hand. My own chapter in this volume takes up this issue of the image and ideology of proportionality in our ethical thought, tracing some of its earlier uses in economic and political thinking, and attempting to unpack some of the analytical consequences that are borne out from making the idea of proportionality explicit in and to our social theory.

There is an echo here with Slavoj Žižek's psychoanalytic philosophy (for example, Žižek 2006). Although Žižek has not directly addressed the question of well-being, he develops an interesting and analogous position with regard to the concept of 'human rights' (Žižek 2005). Žižek argues that what the rhetoric of human rights accomplishes is to cover-up the elision that universal human rights proclamations effect over concrete political economic conditions. What is interesting is thus not what is universal and what is particular, but the political movement through which this 'gap' is opened up in the first place. What we ought to be paying attention to instead, then, is how political interventions remainder our communities into particulars (parts) and universals (wholes). In other words, how we re-proportion our social thought.

Proportionality, however, is also an indigenous category. What gets balanced and taken 'into account' is always a matter to be elucidated ethnographically. Michael Lambek, for instance, explores in his chapter how the notion of well-being, as a political and experiential category, is evinced through the fragile and not always easy *balancing* of social and personal alternatives. He offers us a profound reflection on the possibilities of anthropology as ethical practice; that is, on the contribution that ethnographic description can make to what he calls, with Alexander Nehamas, the 'art of living': the internal variations in people's practical engagement and evaluation of the lives they are living. Staging a dialogue between C.B. Macpherson's notion of human capacities and Sen's capability approach, and exploring the purchase of the Aristotelian conception of virtue ethics as practical moral development, Lambek draws some important conclusions about the liberalist habit of economising the process and practice of living. Of the many important points he makes, I would like to draw attention to two that relate directly to what has been said in this introduction. The first is his intimation that whatever well-being is, we always need to remember that, once summoned, the concept will come with its own social context. Echoing Bernard Williams's criticism of scale-free liberal political theory, Lambek reminds us that 'the well-being of any given social unit ... must always be contextualized with reference to the well-being of the social unit at the next levels of inclusion'. There are thus two outsides to well-being: an outside to its scale (outside its level of inclusion) and an outside to the concept itself. This relates to the second of Lambek's points that I would like to mark here. Throughout the chapter, Lambek observes that the idea of well-being appears to be inherently escapist: communities change and, with them, the generational perception of social well-being; values and goods once internal to life become commoditised and externalised, turned into objects of consumption rather than of self-realisation; the passions that once animated these aspirations become routinised or suppressed into our unconscious. Happiness and unhappiness emerge thus as mutually determinative, forever displacing each other in a continuous reversible movement (Corsín Jiménez and Willerslev 2007). Or, echoing Lear, whom Lambek cites, forever remaindering each other out.

Happiness is the topic of Neil Thin's chapter. Thin offers us a comprehensive review of anthropology's astonishing silence in matters of happiness, despite the discipline's avowed commitment to the holistic understanding of indigenous worldviews. Emphatically, he insists throughout that not engaging with the study of happiness is irresponsible, because it is an indirect way of endorsing a non-evaluative stance on human conditions: anthropology needs to outgrow its relativist frame, and to define a new political space for itself.

In a beautiful book called *La espera y la esperanza: historia y teoría del esperar humano* (Wait and Hope: The History and Theory of Human Expectations) published in 1957, Spanish philosopher Pedro Laín Entralgo wrote a reconsideration of Heidegger's philosophical anthropology by using as his point of existential departure, not *angst* as Heidegger had done, but *hope* (Laín Entralgo 1957). Although by no means a political manifesto, the exercise proved illuminating because it cast in a new light the politics of possibility in Franco's Spain: an anthropology of hope opens up very different political spaces to one that is based on anxiety, let alone violence or revolutionary struggle (cf. Miyazaki 2004). (I recall here Arendt's description of the political as the space of *hopeful* or miraculous appearances.) In his chapter, Thin criticises those studies of the existential condition of humanity that have a preference for focusing on what he calls 'negative minimalisms', to wit, suffering, violence, deprivation, destitution, etc. In this sense, I believe Thin would converge with Laín Entralgo in thinking that our conceptual point of departure for describing human experiences is fundamentally determinative of how we allow people to represent to themselves their own capacities for action. This is why I take it to be that both negative minimalisms and (let us call them) hopeful maximalisms work in fact as *political limits* (Trías 2005): they delimit the social theory that is built around them, re-proportioning in their wake the size of the political. It is for this reason intriguing that our politics today is constructed out of the minimum common denominator of 'sheer survival' and 'bare life'. In this perspective, it would seem that the only hope for the good life today would be to press against its *minima moralia*, to stand as liminal morality. For as Adorno put it, 'Exuberant health is always, as such, sickness also. Its antidote is a sickness aware of what it is, a *curbing of life itself*' (2005 [1951]: 77, emphasis added)

The question of the curbing and delimitations of life is elucidated in James Laidlaw's chapter on the contemporary redistributive practices of diasporic Jains, where he explains how Jainism's social ethic is today shifting from a commitment to virtuous self-fashioning to an utilitarian (aggregate) conception of well-being in terms of the alleviation of suffering.

Jainism is a religious tradition of renunciatory asceticism. The world, for Jains, is a space of relational predation, where all living organisms are continuously exercising violence on all others. We kill the creatures that inhabit the water we drink, when we drink it and when we take a bath; we kill the food that we eat, when we eat it and when we cook it; we kill the creatures that populate our surroundings, when we take a walk or when we roll over in our sleep. The world is tensed with immanent violence. Jainism thus cultivates a pedagogy of negation, what Laidlaw calls an 'ethic of quarantine': disciplining the self into a regime of renunciation, learning not to harm the world by separating one's own being from the world, and devaluing one's own being.

Now the ideology of renunciation remains at some level a canonical representation of Jainism's ascetic soteriology; it is not an ethnographic description

Introduction 25

of how Jain communities live their everyday lives. But, Laidlaw observes, it does provide an ethical and aesthetic counterpoint to quotidian affairs. In this sense, the ideal of renunciation provides a point of reference against which Jains re-proportionate their own understanding of what, at different junctures, is appropriately austere or opulent. 'Well-being and the ascetic pursuit of release', Laidlaw writes, 'are contrasting but mutually supporting.'

The imagery of 'juxtaposition and movement' between self-destructive temptation and disciplined asceticism conjures its own forms of existential *limitation*, its own coordinates for what Adorno called the *curbing of life*. In particular, the image of life as liminally tensed in a fragile and proportionate accomplishment is thrown vividly into relief if we attend to Laidlaw's comparison of Jainism's soteriological tradition with modern diasporic re-interpretations of non-violence.

Traditional Jain emphasis on non-violence and the potential interconnectedness of all life forms, Laidlaw tells us, has found a cohort of friendly contemporary interlocutors in the environmental and animal rights movements. Laidlaw observes how some commentators, especially among Jain diasporic communities, are presenting Jainism as an ancient precursor of these movements. These eco-reinterpretations of Jain philosophy have, however, profoundly distorted the original ethical orientation of Jainism. In the tradition of renunciatory Jainism, ethical consciousness emerges from one's realisation of the world's inherently disgusting nature. Here asceticism's capacity for ethical conduct is cultivated through the virtue and praxis of world-distanciation, where ascetics' striving for release from their bondage to the world is held as the highest aspiration. This is profoundly different from eco-Jainism's novel sympathetic appreciation of nature. Violence and suffering, far from being intrinsic qualities of the world, qualities that should indeed be conducive to our self-motivated worldly-cum-ethical liberation, are instead seen here as inductive to further engagement with the world. Eco-Jains build on their conceptualisation of the connectedness of all life forms to advocate the proactive alleviation of suffering as a way to improve the aggregate, collective well-being of us all. However, as Laidlaw boldly observes, such a reorientation of Jainism towards ecological ethics works only insofar as it effects a profound hollowing out of the terms of relational violence that made Jainism eco-friendly in the first place. Violence and sympathy are not equivalent reversibles in traditional Jainism. Only non-violence, that is to say, non-worldliness, is conducive to ethics.

An ethics predicated on the absence of life, or on a life that is the existential precipitate of disciplined renunciations, renunciations that use the *limits of the world* (Trías 1985) to curb life's virtuousness; such a life casts its own sense of magnitude-in-the-world in terms that are disproportionately different from the eco-Jains' vision of the world as an integrated and holistic totality. How people delimit the world for themselves and for others – how, that is, they re-proportion their sociological imagination[10] – thus becomes a central question for understanding the making of collective and personal life-projects, including the delineation of projects of well-being. Stephan Feuchtwang (2006), in a recent article on the interlacing of political and cultural idioms of the exceptional (*pace* Agamben) and the ambivalent in the realisation of the imagery of the 'sub-human', has made an interesting observation to this effect. For Feuchtwang, the political condition of the sub-human finds a fitting resource for its imagination in the language of *asymmetries* and *imbalances*, for example, cannibalism, sacrifice, bestiality or exorcism, images all of 'extreme forms of imbalance or blockage of bodily intakes and flows' (2006: 259). In this context, he opts to exemplify the political governance of the spaces of humanity through the image of the 'king at death: the asymmetry between the power of life and the powerlessness of the body that is almost a corpse. It is the sovereign power over life and the power to abandon life to death' (2006: 268). Here the human as a political project – the king and his royal purchase over life and death – casts its own shadow as an effect of the disproportionate: of excess and surplus, of self-consumption and exhaustion, of the 'limits of the world' that circumscribe the human condition as, in the words of Castoriadis, a figure of the thinkable (2002 [1999]). It is not life or death, then, biology or eschatology, that singles out and determines what well-being is, but the various sizes of the political worlds that we inhabit and that furnish our human condition with a sense of our own proportionate possibilities.

* * *

I conclude with a brief word about the conceptual purchase of the notions of the 'limit' and the 'proportion' for social theory.

My use of the concept of the limit takes inspiration from the work of Spanish philosopher Eugenio Trías (1983 [1969], 1985, 1991, 1999, 2005). Over the years, Trías has developed an ontological programme for understanding the human condition as a liminal condition, where the moment of openness to the creativity of action, as Arendt would put it, is given by our inhabiting the threshold of meaning. Here the world that we know reveals itself as a moment of tension, where the order and organisation of our place-in-the-world is provided for by a fragile and extreme alignment of ontological happenings. By signalling the place where our world exhausts itself, where the alignment is evinced and the world reaches its end, the concept of the limit thus further helps to break up and displace the world for us.

It is this facility to bring into focus or identify the *displaceable* that I take to be the limit's potentially valuable contribution to social theory. In this perspective, limits are useful to think with, because they signpost society's own model of self-consciousness: how society redistributes its own social moments. They mark the cleavage point at which one social proportion remainders itself away from another, thus casting a shadow over the social body – and giving the social body a 'size'. 'Individuals' and 'society' are the

Introduction

classic example: their size is given by their own remaindering-away from their opposite.

Using the imagery of the *gigantic*, James Weiner has recently appealed to a similar conceptualisation of the limits and proportionate remainders of life in the following terms:

> What is gigantic in human life? If we consider nature itself as only a social construction, we lose the sense of a domain that lies *beyond the power and limits of the human* and that is therefore large in comparison to it. We might then want to ask, what confronts human life with something that exceeds it? What lies beyond human life but nevertheless exerts an influence on it? (Weiner 2001: 163–64, emphasis added)

Following Weiner's call for an anthropological imagination of the gigantic, we can start to think of well-being as a liminal category: a holder of limits. What existential pressures induce the curbing of life? When and how does life start to displace and resize itself: when does it become larger-than-life, and when does it contract its own powers, become something disgusting or embarrassing? Where, in sum, does the gigantic lie for different people: how do people re-proportion their life-projects, and how do they cement and put limits to them?

Using an epistemology of the gigantic, of limits and proportions, the anthropology of well-being could thus be re-described as the anthropology of residual politics: a theoretical vision for political theory that works with an idea of society as a remaindering polity; a social theory that looks for the *politeia* or community in the movements through which it outgrows itself, pressing its own limits, gaining a sense of its own proportions. A theory, then, that keeps its own social objects of description (society, ethics, politics, well-being) within purview – at a variable and yet proportionate distance.

This is of course a project for comparative social theory, for all limits are Janus-faced, constraining on one side, expansive on the other; and a proportion is by definition a relation of magnitude, a relation to something of a different order than itself. It is thus a project that reaffirms ethnography's unique analytical value. Only through the insights gained from ethnographic comparison can we open up social theory to new forms of what Williams called realist or platitudinous politics. Seen in this light, it makes of course all the sense in the world that Evans-Pritchard decided to focus on cattle as the idiom through which to re-describe the Nuer's political organisation of well-being. For it was relations established through cattle that held in proportion Nuer political life.

ACKNOWLEDGEMENTS

My thanks to Michael Lambek for reading a first draft of the text and asking some pertinent but crucial questions regarding its clarity. The conclusion has also greatly benefited from James Weiner's comments, who kindly contrasted my argument against his own interests in the generation of social knowledge in a generous email exchange, making in passing some most pertinent observations about the irrelevance of anthropology for some important questions of political theory. Karen Sykes and Stef Jansen read the paper, provided encouragement, and helped tighten its structure at a time when it was close to running wild; my warmest thanks to them.

NOTES

1. Anthropologist Michael Blim has recently written a very elegant book arguing for a view of human well-being in terms of the value of (political, economic and social) 'equality' (Blim 2005). Blim's conception of equality is broad enough to accommodate social and cultural differences, although I think I do justice to his account if I say that his interest is not *social theory*. His challenge is how to arrive to a robust enough conception of equality that will allow its endorsement as a global value.
2. This a limitation of theory, because people are of course known for giving different reasons for pursuing one and the same action; some reasons may be rendered as 'utilitarian', some 'communitarian', some 'existential', etc.; some are accounted for in terms of desires, preferences, even behavioural inclinations or instinctual predispositions. It is at this level that political philosophy is at its analytical messiest. On 'kinds of persons', and the implications of different categorisations and classifications of personhood for policy-making, see Hacking (2002, 2006).
3. On the category of the person, see, for example, Bird-David (1999), Carrithers et al. (1985), Collins (1982), Corsín Jiménez (2003), Douglas and Ney (1998) and Strathern (2004); on the distribution and entitlements of agency, see, for instance, Gell (1998), Hann (1998), Strathern (1999), Verdery and Humphrey (2004) and Wilson and Mitchell (2003); on the anthropology of the state, classic and recent contributions include Cohen and Service (1978), Ferguson and Gupta (2002), Geertz (1980), Navaro-Yashin (2002) and Taussig (1997); on the place of solidarity, obligation and debt in the making of moral communities, the list is as extensive as the discipline itself; some classic references include Fortes (2004 [1969]), Mauss (2002) and Mauss and Hubert (1964); for some recent scholarship see Godelier (1999), Komter (2005), Laidlaw (2000), Strathern (1988) and Sykes (2005).
4. A caveat is in order: the following critique of Sen's social theory applies to economic theory at large (see also Gudeman 1986). In all truth, Sen has probably done more than any other scholar to make both his economic modelling and his social theory sensitive to one other. (Partha Dasgupta's efforts in this regard are also worthy of praise [1993, 2001].) The question remains, though, whether there is an inherent limit to how much social theory economics can take into account. I do not mean to be flippant: the problem is how to design *institutional models of resource allocation* that are reflexive and thus responsive to *sociality's own redistributive orientations*; for economics needs to pre-empt sociality's own redistributive moments for its institutional allocations to take effect.
5. On parts and wholes configurations, see Strathern (1991, 1992) and James (this volume).
6. There is no 'sociological' thought in Aristotle, as we have come to understand the term today. The closest he comes to developing a 'sociology' is in his *Politics*, but even here he produces an analysis of the *politeia* as 'community life' (Marías 1951: xlix). The point is important because it gives a sense of the extent to which 'ethics' and 'the good life' were conceptualised within the political, but never within society. On the relation between 'the political' and 'community', and the evacuation of the former from the latter in modern social life, see Esposito (2003 [1998]) and note 7, below.
7. A point that echoes Roberto Esposito's argument that modern political thought is organised around the 'immunisation' of life (2003 [1998], 2005 [2002]). For Esposito,

Introduction

the modern conception of a political *community* depends crucially on the disassembling of the social into 'immunised' individuals. Thus, there is no social life proper in modern politics: *immunitas* is the basic condition for all associative life, a diagnosis that situates Shklar and Williams's 'liberalism of fear' in harrowing historical perspective.

8. However, institutions can also be seen as redistributional movements; see Corsín Jiménez (2007) for an outline of a theory of redistributive institutional life; see also Douglas (1986).
9. Marilyn Strathern's work is the classical referent here; a recent exposition of her thought in relation to the topic of medical health (well-being) is Strathern (2004).
10. 'If there is any value in carrying the discussion forward,' Marilyn Strathern has written of social theory's prospects, 'it is because the question of *proportionate description* remains in the anthropological account' (1991: 53–54, emphasis added)

REFERENCES

Adorno, T.W. 2005 [1951]. *Minima Moralia: Reflections on a Damaged Life*. London and New York: Verso.

Agamben, G. 1996. *La comunidad que viene*. Valencia: Pre-textos.

—— 1999. *Homo sacer: el poder soberano y la nuda vida*. Valencia: Pre-textos.

—— 2000. *Lo que queda de Auschwitz*. Valencia: Pre-textos.

—— 2001. *Medios sin fin: notas sobre la política*. Valencia: Pre-textos.

—— 2004. *Estado de excepción. Homo sacer II*. Valencia: Pre-textos.

—— 2005. *Lo abierto: el hombre y el animal*. Valencia: Pre-textos.

Appadurai, A. 2004. The Capacity to Aspire: Culture and the Terms of Recognition. In V. Rao and M. Walton (eds) *Culture and Public Action*. Stanford, CA: Stanford University Press.

Arendt, H. 1997 [1993]. *¿Qué es la política?* [Spanish translation of *Was is Politik? Aus dem Nachla*], trans. R.S. Carbó (Pensamiento contemporáneo 49). Barcelona: Ediciones Paidós.

—— 1998 [1958]. *The Human Condition*. Chicago: University of Chicago Press.

—— 2005 [1963]. *Eichmann and the Holocaust*. London: Penguin Books.

Aristotle. 1984 [c. 4 BCE]. *Ethica Nicomachea*. In *The Complete Works of Aristotle: The Revised Oxford*, trans. L.W.D. Ross and J.O. Urmson. Princeton, NJ: Princeton University Press.

Bird-David, N. 1999. 'Animism' Revisited: Personhood, Environment, and Relational Epistemology. *Current Anthropology* 40, S67–S91.

Blim, M. 2005. *Equality and Economy: The Global Challenge*. Walnut Creek, CA: AltaMira Press.

Bobbio, N. 2005 [1988]. *Liberalism and Democracy*, trans. M. Ryle and K. Soper. London and New York: Verso.

Canovan, M. 1998. Introduction. In *The Human Condition*. Chicago: University of Chicago Press.

Carrithers, M., S. Collins and S. Lukes. 1985. *The Category of the Person: Anthropology, Philosophy, History*. Cambridge: Cambridge University Press.

Castoriadis, C. 2002 [1999]. ¿Qué democracia? In *Figuras de lo pensable (las encrucijadas del laberinto VI)*. México: Fondo de Cultura Económica.

Clark, D. 2002. *Visions of Development: A Study of Human Values*. Cheltenham: Edward Elgar.

Cohen, R. and E.R. Service (eds). 1978. *Origins of the State: The Anthropology of Political Evolution*. Philadelphia, PA: Institute for the Study of Human Issues.

Collier, S.J. and A. Lakoff. 2005. On Regimes of Living. In A. Ong and S.J. Collier (eds) *Global Assemblages: Technology, Politics, and Ethics as Anthropological Problems*. Malden, MA: Blackwell Publishing.

Collins, S. 1982. *Selfless Persons: Images and Thoughts in Theravāda Buddhism*. Cambridge: Cambridge University Press.

Corsín Jiménez, A. 2003. Working out Personhood: Notes on 'Labour' and its Anthropology. *Anthropology Today* 19, 14–17.
—— 2007. Introduction: Re-institutionalisations. In A. Corsín Jiménez (ed.) *The Anthropology of Organisations*. Aldershot: Ashgate/Dartmouth.
Corsín Jiménez, A. and R. Willerslev. 2007. 'An Anthropological Concept of the Concept': Reversibility among the Siberian Yukaghirs. *Journal of the Royal Anthropological Institute* 13, 527–44.
Crisp, R. (ed.). 1996. *How Should One Live? Essays on the Virtues*. Oxford: Clarendon Press.
Crisp, R. and B. Hooker (eds). 2000. *Well-being and Morality: Essays in Honour of James Griffin*. Oxford: Clarendon Press.
Cummins, R.A. 2005. Measuring Health and Subjective Wellbeing: *Vale*, Quality-adjusted Life-years. In L. Manderson (ed.) *Rethinking Wellbeing*. Perth: API Network.
Dasgupta, P. 1993. *An Inquiry into Well-being and Destitution*. Oxford: Clarendon Press.
—— 2001. *Human Well-being and the Natural Environment*. Oxford: Oxford University Press.
Debord, G. 1995 [1967]. *The Society of the Spectacle*, trans. D. Nicholson-Smith. New York: Zone Books.
Douglas, M. 1986. *How Institutions Think*. Syracuse, NY: Syracuse University Press.
Douglas, M. and S. Ney. 1998. *Missing Persons: A Critique of the Social Sciences*, Aaron Wildavsky Forum for Public Policy, 1. Berkeley, CA: University of California Press.
Esposito, R. 2003 [1998]. *Communitas: origen y destino de la comunidad*. Buenos Aires: Amorrortu Editores.
—— 2005 [2002]. *Immunitas: protección y negación de la vida*. Buenos Aires: Amorrortu Editores.
Evans-Pritchard, E.E. 1940. *The Nuer: A Description of the Modes of Livelihood and Political Institutions of a Nilotic People*. Oxford: Oxford University Press.
Ferguson, J. and A. Gupta. 2002. Spatializing States: Toward an Ethnography of Neoliberal Governmentality. *American Ethnologist* 29, 981–1002.
Feuchtwang, S. 2006. Images of Sub-humanity and their Realization. *Critique of Anthropology* 26, 259–78.
Fortes, M. 2004 [1969]. *Kinship and the Social Order: The Legacy of Lewis Henry Morgan*. London: Routledge.
Geertz, C. 1980. *Negara: The Theatre State in Nineteenth-century Bali*. Princeton, NJ: Princeton University Press.
Gell, A. 1998. *Art and Agency: An Anthropological Theory*. Oxford: Clarendon Press.
Godelier, M. 1999. *The Enigma of the Gift*, trans. N. Scott. Chicago: University of Chicago Press.
Griffin, J. 1986. *Well-being: Its Meaning, Measurement and Moral Importance*. Oxford: Clarendon Press.
Gudeman, S. 1986. *Economics as Culture*. London: Routledge & Kegan Paul.
Hacking, I. 2002. Making Up People. In *Historical Ontology*. Cambridge, MA: Harvard University Press.
—— 2006. Kinds of People: Moving Targets. In *The Tenth British Academy Lecture* (pre-publication version). London: British Academy.
Hann, C.M. (ed.). 1998. *Property Relations: Renewing the Anthropological Tradition*. Cambridge: Cambridge University Press.
Harsanyi, J.C. 1975. Can the Maximin Principle Serve as a Base for Morality? A Critique of John Rawls's Theory. *American Political Science Review* 69, 594–606.
Kenny, A. 1992. *Aristotle on the Perfect Life*. Oxford and New York: Clarendon Press.
Komter, A.E. 2005. *Social Solidarity and the Gift*. Cambridge: Cambridge University Press.
Laidlaw, J. 2000. A Free Gift Makes No Friends. *Journal of the Royal Anthropological Institute* 6, 617–34.
Laín Entralgo, P. 1957. *La espera y la esperanza: historia y teoría del esperar humano*. Madrid: Revista de Occidente.

Lakoff, A. and S.J. Collier. 2004. Ethics and the Anthropology of Modern Reason. *Anthropological Theory* 4, 419–34.
Lear, J. 2000. *Happiness, Death, and the Remainder of Life*. Cambridge, MA: Harvard University Press.
Marías, J. 1951. Introducción. In *Política [de Aristóteles]*. Madrid: Centro de Estudios Políticos y Constitucionales.
—— 1989. *La felicidad humana*. Madrid: Alianza Editorial.
Mauss, M. 2002. *The Gift: The Form and Reason for Exchange in Archaic Societies* (Routledge classics). London: Routledge.
Mauss, M. and H. Hubert. 1964. *Sacrifice: Its Nature and Function*, trans. W.D. Halls. London: Cohen & West.
Miyazaki, H. 2004. *The Method of Hope: Anthropology, Philosophy, and Fijian Knowledge*. Stanford, CA: Stanford University Press.
Mouffe, C. 2005 [1993]. *The Return of the Political*. London and New York: Verso.
Nagel, T. 1973. Rawls on Justice. *Philosophical Review* 82, 220–34.
—— 2005. The Problem of Global Justice. *Philosophy and Public Affairs* 33, 113–47.
Navaro-Yashin, Y. 2002. *Faces of the State: Secularism and Public Life in Turkey*. Princeton, NJ: Princeton University Press.
Nozick, R. 1974. *Anarchy, State and Utopia*. New York: Basic Books.
Nussbaum, M.C. 1988. Nature, Function, and Capability: Aristotle on Political Distribution. *Oxford Studies in Ancient Philosophy* suppl. vol., 145–84.
—— 1993. Non-relative Virtues: An Aristotelian Approach. In M.C. Nussbaum and A. Sen (eds) *The Quality of Life*. Oxford: Clarendon Press.
—— 2005. Wellbeing, Contracts and Capabilities. In L. Manderson (ed.) *Rethinking Wellbeing*. Perth: API Network.
—— 2006. *Frontiers of Justice: Disability, Nationality, Species Membership*, Tanner Lectures on Human Values. Cambridge, MA: The Belknap Press of Harvard University Press.
Nussbaum, M.C. and A. Sen (eds). 1993. *The Quality of Life*. Oxford: Clarendon Press.
Offer, A. (ed.) 1996. *In Pursuit of the Quality of Life*. Oxford: Oxford University Press.
Ong, A. and S.J. Collier. 2005. Global Assemblages, Anthropological Problems. In A. Ong and S.J. Collier (eds) *Global Assemblages: Technology, Politics, and Ethics as Anthropological Problems*. Malden, MA: Blackwell Publishing.
Overing, J. (ed.) 1985. *Reason and Morality*, ASA Monographs 24. London and New York: Tavistock Publications.
Rawls, J. 1999 [1971]. *A Theory of Justice*, revised edn. Cambridge, MA: The Belknap Press of Harvard University Press.
Rumsey, A. and J.F. Weiner (eds). 2004. *Mining and Indigenous Lifeworlds in Australia and Papua New Guinea*. Wantage: Sean Kingston Publishing.
Sandel, M. 1982. *Liberalism and the Limits of Justice*. Cambridge: Cambridge University Press.
Scanlon, T.M. 1998. *What We Owe to Each Other*. Cambridge, MA: The Belknap Press of Harvard University Press.
Sen, A. 1980. *Equality of What?* The 1979 Tanner Lecture at Stanford. In S.M. McMurrin (ed.) *Tanner Lectures on Human Values*, vol. 1. Salt Lake City: University of Utah Press.
—— 1993. Capability and Well-being. In M.C. Nussbaum and A. Sen (eds) *The Quality of Life*. Oxford: Clarendon Press.
—— 1999. *Development as Freedom*. Oxford: Oxford University Press.
—— 2002. *Rationality and Freedom*. New Delhi, Oxford: Oxford University Press.
Shklar, J. 1989. The Liberalism of Fear. In N. Rosenblum (ed.) *Liberalism and the Moral Life*. Cambridge, MA: Harvard University Press.
Skevington, S.M. 2002. Advancing Cross-cultural Research on Quality of Life: Observations Drawn from the WHOQOL Development. *Quality of Life Research* 11, 135–44.
Strathern, M. 1988. *The Gender of the Gift: Problems with Women and Problems with Society in Melanesia*, Studies in Melanesian Anthropology 6. Berkeley and London: University of California Press.

—— 1991. *Partial Connections*. Savage, MD: Rowman & Littlefield Publishers, Inc.
—— 1992. Parts and Wholes: Refiguring Relationships in a Post-plural World. In A. Kuper (ed.) *Conceptualizing Society*. London: Routledge.
—— 1999. *Property, Substance, and Effect: Anthropological Essays on Persons and Things*. London and New Brunswick, NJ: Athlone Press.
—— 2004. The Whole Person and its Artifacts. *Annual Review of Anthropology* 33, 1–19.
—— 2005. Resistance, Refusal and Global Moralities. *Australian Feminist Studies* 20.
Sumner, L.W. 1996. *Welfare, Happiness, and Ethics*. Oxford: Clarendon Press.
Sykes, K. 2005. *Arguing with Anthropology: An Introduction to Critical Theories of the Gift*. London and New York: Routledge.
Taussig, M.T. 1997. *The Magic of the State*. New York and London: Routledge.
Trías, E. 1983 [1969]. *Philosophy and its Shadow*. New York: Columbia University Press.
—— 1985. *Los límites del mundo*. Barcelona: Ariel.
—— 1991. *Lógica del límite*. Barcelona: Editorial Destino.
—— 1999. *La razón fronteriza*. Barcelona: Editorial Destino.
—— 2005. *La política y su sombra*. Barcelona: Editorial Anagrama.
UNDP. 1990. *Human Development Report*. New York and Oxford: Oxford University Press for UNDP.
—— 1994. *Human Development Report*. New York and Oxford: Oxford University Press for UNDP.
—— 1998. *Human Development Report*. New York and Oxford: Oxford University Press for UNDP.
—— 2002. *Human Development Report*. New York and Oxford: Oxford University Press for UNDP.
Verdery, K. and C. Humphrey (eds). 2004. *Property in Question: Value Transformation in the Global Economy*. Oxford and New York: Berg.
Weiner, J.F. 2001. *Tree Leaf Talk: A Heideggerian Anthropology*. Oxford and New York: Berg.
WHO. 2001. *International Classification of Functioning, Disability and Health*. Geneva: World Health Organization.
WHOQOL Group. 1993. The World Health Organization Quality of Life Assessment (WHOQOL): Position Paper from the World Health Organization. *Social Science and Medicine* 41, 1403–09.
—— 1998. The World Health Organization Quality of Life Assessment (WHOQOL): Development and General Psychometric Assessment. *Social Science and Medicine* 46, 1569–85.
Williams, B. 2005. *In the Beginning Was the Deed: Realism and Moralism in Political Argument*, selected, edited, and with an introduction by Geoffrey Hawthorn. Princeton, NJ: Princeton University Press.
Williams, L. 2006. Towards an Emerging International Poverty Law. In L. Williams (ed.) *International Poverty Law: An Emerging Discourse*. London and New York: Zed Books.
Wilson, R. and J.P. Mitchell (eds). 2003. *Human Rights in Global Perspective: Anthropological Studies of Rights, Claims and Entitlements*, ASA Monographs 40. London: Routledge.
Žižek, S. 2005. Against Human Rights. *New Left Review* 34, 115–31.
—— 2006. *The Parallax View*. Cambridge, MA: MIT Press.

Part I

Distributive Values

1 THE IMPOSSIBILITY OF WELL-BEING: DEVELOPMENT LANGUAGE AND THE PATHOLOGISATION OF NEPAL

Ian Harper and Bryan Maddox

Phenomena, which in the normal state are almost effaced because of their tenuousness, appear more palpable in extraordinary crises because they are exaggerated. (Renan 1890 [from Canguilhem], quoted in Young 1995: 39)

Central to this chapter is attention to how Nepal, and the well-being of its people, are represented. Nepal has long occupied multiple discursive spaces within which the country has come to signify both more and other than it really is. In these representational spaces and disciplinary forms, ideological and political sensibilities delineate what can be said, intersecting with and diverging from its multiple realities. What links these diverse representations and circulating statements of the requirements for a modern Nepal is that, within their contested truths, Nepal is never allowed to *be as it is*. Change is the rationale for government and for development institutions, the justification for missionaries' presence and for the increasing involvement of the private sector and civil society and all their prescriptions. Nepal in need of greater commodification in all spheres of activity; Nepal requiring greater centralised state powers; Nepal in need of fewer state powers; Nepal in need of Maoist and republican revolution; Nepal in need of redemption; Nepal in need of the elimination of disease, superstition and corruption – multiple diagnoses; multiple prescriptions. But an overarching form, we suggest, seems to link these, in that they constitute Nepal's reality as needy and lacking in significant ways. In short, to run with the medical metaphor – the implications of which we explore here – Nepal is pathologised. Frequently divergent causal relations for Nepal's multiple pathological states are articulated and divergent discursive cures proposed. Like the shamanic practitioner, the *jhankri*, chanting *mantras* – these consistently repeated and always discursively *excessive* realities create and seek to inscribe the subjectivities necessary for a modern Nepal to exist.

This chapter emerges from a number of conversations we have had over the years, evolving from our experiences and research in which we were trying to articulate some of the points of contact for what, in development discourses, are frequently separate, namely health and literacy programmes and practices.[1] After many discussions we alighted on the striking fact that the language used about these programmes is markedly similar; and we develop the implications of how these discursive representations generate certain truth effects. We argue that certain representations of Nepal within policy circles, particularly those that pathologise Nepal's multiple realities, carry greater political weight than others; that is, they circulate more widely in certain political circles, and thus have greater commodity value and fundability. We are concerned to highlight how these tropes are institutionalised in practice, and to critically pose questions regarding the implications of this way of constituting Nepal in development discourse. As such, we are aligning ourselves here with those scholars who are concerned with examining an 'analytics of the modern', drawing on a Foucauldian line of analysis that 'draws attention to the heterogeneous forces – forms of knowledge, types of authorities, and practical mechanisms – that seek to shape the conduct of individuals and populations to effect certain ends' (Inda 2005: 17).

Throughout this chapter we are conscious that well-being, however defined, is linked to notions of agency and having some degree of control over one's life course. As such, we continually pay attention to the potential difference between being a patient and an agent, and the slippage between these modes of being. To quote Sen (2004), whose work we look at more critically and in greater detail in the last section: 'we are not only patients, whose needs demand attention, but also agents, whose freedom to decide what to value and how to pursue it can extend far beyond the fulfilment of our needs'. As Thin (2005, this volume) points out, part of the difficulty of articulating ways of being other than the pathological and the patient is that there has been a systematic bias in the social sciences, and in development discourse, to focus on the exceptional, on suffering and the 'pathological'. Well-being tends to be the unarticulated default setting that will appear once disease and pathology have been eliminated. This effacement has considerable implications as we discuss.

The chapter, then, is divided into two sections. We start by looking at 'health' itself, and then at the application of metaphors of health and pathology in other sectors. We focus on literacy as a particularly trenchant example of how this metaphor is put to use, as well as the limits of its utility.

HEALTH IN NEPAL

'Health' in Nepal, as elsewhere, is one of the key arenas of focus for the 'techniques of government'. Since the 1950s, following the ending of its isolationist policies, Nepal has embarked wholesale on development and scientific progress as the rationale for government. As such the treatment and prevention of sickness and disease has been the object of governmental evolution – through five-year plans – as well as the object of concerted

The Impossibility of Well-Being

international pressure and activities, and a key focus of the burgeoning non-governmental organisation (NGO) industry. Health remains probably the primary arena of modernisation programmes. It is beyond the scope of this chapter to look at the multitude of practices that make up this arena, or to attempt to systematically excavate a genealogy of the policies and practice involved. Rather, we focus on ethnographic snippets – small nodes of focus – to act as implosion points for our analysis.

In 1999 the small town of Batase was little more than a collection of shops in Palpa district, on the dusty road heading out west towards Arghakhanchi district and beyond, areas from which stories of increasingly violent Maoist activity and its effects were being more frequently heard.[2] A school, a health post, a private Ayurvedic clinic, three private pharmacies and several NGO offices were to be found here, amongst the other small shops selling commodities to the travellers discharged from the buses or Trax jeeps that ferry passengers to and from Tansen, the district centre and beyond. The United Mission to Nepal's (UMN) Community Health and Development Programme (CHDP) office was five minutes up the hill overlooking the town, and it was to this office that Ian Harper came in February 1999. Like many of the other participants coming for this 'traditional healers' training, Ian had walked for several hours to get there on the first morning of the three days. As Stacey Pigg (1997) has demonstrated in her analysis of training programmes aimed at 'traditional healers', these are focal points where 'problems' articulated around people's health are translated into solutions. She points out that these are the spaces where the gaps between top-down planning, the need for 'community participation' and the importance of local socio-cultural information in appropriately tailoring implementation to local conditions can be bridged.

Outside the room where the training would take place, there was a drawing of a candle throwing off light, under the painted cloth sign welcoming the participants to this training, to which six healers in total had come. Above the candle was written: 'Primary Health Care Training for traditional healers'. The objectives of the training were as follows: to give information on primary health care; to develop the traditional healers as good referral workers; to develop better communication between healers; and to encourage those working in health to provide better health services. The training started, after introductions, with an anatomy and physiology lesson and developed from this biological and biomedical body. It is crucial, said Shiva, the main trainer, to understand this or you won't understand the rest.

Thus reduced, this non-phenomenal, non-experiencing, medically objectified body formed the basis of the entire training. He pointed out bones, nerves, the brain – described as a central office, like Kathmandu to the body of Nepal – from where nerves travel downwards to all parts of the body, like to the eyes, and then back to the brain, which tells us what we are seeing. The brain is also responsible for making decisions and manages, for example, what the legs do and how we walk, we were informed. Bones were named and how muscles work highlighted. Thus reorienting the healers' knowledge to one starting from the anatomical body, it became possible to begin to list the diseases and illnesses that needed to be located within it.

What are the implications of Shiva's comment, on that cold winter's day, that if the healers did not understand the idea of the anatomical body, they would not understand anything else? Here we have a very good example of how knowledge and power intersect. Not only is the anatomical body used as a way of understanding the functioning of the state, and vice versa, but here the state's actors work at reorienting the knowledge of the traditional healer. Shamanic knowledge is seen as little more than superstition and frequently represented as one of the major reasons why Nepal fails to develop (Harper 2003) – one of an array of practices that make up biopower, the drive to power over life and death of the species body.

It has long been recognised in anthropology that the body is a powerful metaphor for thinking with, particularly in relation to the social (Douglas 1966, 1970). In their now classic essay highlighting the interaction between the three bodies – individual, social and political – Lock and Scheper-Hughes argued that the body in sickness offers a model for social disharmony, while the body in health offers one of wholeness: 'Ethnoanatomical perceptions ... offer a rich source of data on both the social and cultural meanings of being human and on the various threats to health, well-being, and social integration that humans are believed to experience' (1996: 56). Emily Martin (1994), too, has demonstrated how an understanding of the internal workings of the body – she looked at the immune system – is developed by the metaphorical imposition of evolving ideas of the nation-state onto the internal workings of the body. There is a relationship between how the internal machinations of the body – be it the undissected, or dissected body (Davis 2000) – and the external body of society are understood. Similarly, as Gupta (1998) has suggested (following Nandy and Munzo), life stages of personal growth serve as a metonym for the growth of the nation. The life stages of the development of humans are superimposed on the life stages of the nation-state. Nations are 'newly born', economies 'grow', political systems 'mature' (towards capitalist systems). 'Here is a discourse that explicitly maps the bourgeois individual subject of the west onto the nation-as-subject', suggests Gupta (1998: 41). One consequence of such language, argues Gupta, is that Less Developed Countries occupy the role of children in relationship to the 'developed' northern nation-states.

One meta-history of medicine can be read as a positivist enterprise that creates the idea of the body existing as an object outside of human relations, the product of Enlightenment thought and the societal transformations occurring then (Samson 1999). The contours of disease are then delineated and constituted as being within this objectified entity, as the relations and conditions of production of this knowledge construction are effaced (Foucault 1988). Concomitantly, we see the growth of the idea of the normal as perhaps the most powerful ideology of the nineteenth and then twentieth century

(Hacking 1990), and the growth of the idea of the pathological defined as aberration from an idealised norm (Canguilhem 1991). The dichotomous thinking of disease/non-disease – more broadly reflected in our Enlightenment metaphysical inheritance – is intimately linked to utilitarian discourses, to the functioning of the state, and to programmatic and institutional goals more broadly defined. However 'developed' these states, their own planning regimes are dependent on a 'narrowing of vision' necessary for project implementation (Scott 1998). Scott demonstrates how, for this to occur – and he uses forestry as an example – much falls outside of its frame. 'Fiscal forestry' is dependent on a utilitarianism confined to the direct needs of the state. The vocabulary used to organise nature demonstrates how it is oriented towards its uses – as 'natural resources'; 'crops' are useful, 'weeds' are not useful; livestock is useful, predators are not. The narrowing of vision allows the state to impose its logic.

These links between disease and the state are clearly seen in the realm of health economics. There has been resurgence since the late 1980s of the need for proven economically justifiable interventions in the health sector – part of a process of (neoliberal) reform. Economic concerns and cost-effectiveness have become the primary driving forces in the health sector. The World Bank has rapidly defined the baseline for debate, and the methodologies that it promotes are hegemonic, even if contested (Zwi 2000). 'Selective' primary health care became the buzz term, a shift away from socialist experiments in health care (institutionalised in the idea of Alma Ata) that had attempted to broaden out the definition of health. A number of vertical, disease-oriented programmes became the focus of attention. A new method of analysis was introduced by the World Bank which, it is suggested, can be used to prioritise any possible intervention in a 'developing' country's health delivery services. This combines epidemiological and economic analysis to establish a league table of priority health interventions, ranked by health gain per dollar spent (Paalman et al. 1998; World Bank 1993). It evaluates the extent to which populations suffer from disease, the so-called 'burden of disease', and the cost-effectiveness of any intervention known to reduce that burden. The unit of analysis introduced was the Disability Adjusted Life Year (DALY) and interventions became judged in terms of cost per DALY saved. This approach is highly dependent on economics grounded in national GNP figures, and there have been sustained and prolonged critiques of it, both on grounds of questionable economics and its ideological positioning. The weightings and value judgements implicit in what is 'health' and who defines it have also come under question (Paalman et al. 1998).[3] Nonetheless, these reductionist economistic analyses have become very influential, both in marking the return of the disease model, and vertical single-disease programmes, a move away from the 1978 dream of Alma Ata.[4]

While Nepal's ills proliferate along with the demise of the state and the increasing violence, within this frame of reference a few public health successes are promoted as being high status, and are widely supported and viewed as successful. Among these are the vitamin A capsule distribution and the Directly Observed Therapy Short-course (DOTS) programme for tuberculosis treatment. These two programmes, highly medicalised, vertical and bureaucratic, have become examples of what can be done – exemplars of the possible within a Nepal in 'crisis'. Both vigorously exclude the political from their frames of engagement (except for 'political commitment' to get the programmes on the health agenda), seeing themselves as technical and scientific interventions in the realm of life itself. Let us assume that the rise of these programmes as exemplars of success, and the proliferation of Nepal's crises is not a coincidence. Our focus now becomes how this relates to how well-being is understood in the context of Nepal and its developmentalist discourses. The conflation of health and disease – the focus on eliminating tuberculosis and providing vitamins – makes more intelligible the sublimation of well-being to disease and lacks, within these particular states, neoliberal and ideological manifestations.

Several more examples of the conflation of practices, and of discourses and interests, illustrate these points further. Since the late 1980s Nepal has witnessed a spectacular mushrooming of private pharmacies and clinics (Harper 2002). Amongst this proliferation of new pharmacies and private clinics, in 2003 the government increased the tax on imported drugs. Within days the Nepal Chemists and Druggists Association announced that no more drugs would be imported until the tax was removed. Since Nepal is totally dependent on drug imports, as the imports dried up the government had no choice but to withdraw their excise. The interests of what amounts to a cartel of pharmaceutical companies have far more power to influence policy than the state at present. As a worker for one of the companies suggested to Ian in an interview in August 2004, we need to ask ourselves why the logic of the free market – that is, that drug prices should drop when more companies compete to distribute these drugs – doesn't actualise in practice in Nepal. At the same time, the vitamin A programme – which turns the capsule into a fetish for public health – is supported and sponsored by a particular and powerful 'assemblage': USAID, Roche, Johns Hopkins and a range of interests external to the Nepal state (Harper 2002). Broader political framings have no place in the scientific literature, nor in the advocacy for the positive effects of this minimalist intervention.

In a series of interviews Ian Harper undertook with drug shop owners in 1999, the rise of the distribution and use of drugs was highlighted as being necessary to deal with the perceived increase in depression. Despite poverty being described as the cause of much suffering, and consequent rise in rates of depression by these practitioners, at least, it was suggested, with anti-depressant drugs there was something that could be done (Harper, 2003). We recognise that the growth of 'depression' is linked to poverty, but at least we can do something with these drugs, was how it was put to Ian in one interview. Medicine is efficacious because it is able to clearly delineate the pathology and, crucially, do something about it. To what extent does this efficacy translate into other realms?

SOCIAL PATHOLOGIES AND THE BODY POLITIC

The photo on the front cover of Hari Bahadur Thapa's *Anatomy of Corruption* (2002), one of a number of new books highlighting the corruption proliferating in Nepal, depicts a man lying on an operating table. A large bundle of money is being removed from an incision in his side by a team of surgeons. To the side of the operating table lie the other symbols of corruption that have been removed from the incision: a luxurious cushion, a pajero jeep, further bundles of notes, some gold bars. 'Our country is blighted by unemployment, poverty, and ignorance.... Corruption is everywhere and our government has reached the terrible state of having repeatedly to stretch out its hands to donors for aid', states the introduction.

As Gywali has pointed out – reflecting on the rise of discourses on corruption in Nepal within development discourses – the current way of looking at 'corrupt' behaviour, is to label it as an aberration, a pathology, or as he phrases it, 'a fall from the garden of Eden' (2004: 192). Corruption, or rather the capacity to root it out and eliminate it, has become a key indicator of the functioning of a healthy democratic polity. A significant aspect of 'good governance' is the development of anti-corruption legislation and institutional mechanisms to deal with it. This has also become a key component of what is described as the 'new architecture of aid': the focus on reform, rather than projects; on promoting economic liberalisation and privatisation linked to new aid packages resulting from Poverty Reduction Strategies, Sector Wide Approaches and the like (Mosse 2005).

Most of those who indulge in 'corrupt' practices (which must include nearly all public service workers in Nepal, as their basic wage is unable even to feed a family of five in most urban areas) do not perceive their practices as pathology but strategies of survival. As such their social surroundings must be pathological too, Gywali (2004) further suggests, and so we are led interpretively through this frame into suggesting the social surroundings are also pathological: the answer then becomes one of sweeping reform, or revolution, or most likely into the proliferation of rules and regulations that do little more than create a smokescreen for further corruption. The use of medical metaphors here for describing the social environment, and the narrowing of vision entailed within it, has very considerable consequences.

As those who work in the public sector come to rethink their own survival strategies as pathological, then, so too many of the young adults who train to be health workers come to rethink their own cultural and family values in new ways.

Community Medical Assistants (CMAs), for example, are workers who are trained for one year after their school leaving certificates to work in the health posts. Currently, thousands are being produced from the mushrooming privately run institutions. One of the prescribed texts, a book on 'health management' by Shivaprasad Sapkota, has an entire section dedicated to 'community health diagnosis', which contains a section on the 'function of a community pathologist' (Sapkota 2005: 231). This involves being trained to do the following:

1. Study of community anatomy such as topography, social structure and political structure
2. Study of function and regulation physiology
3. Identification of unfavourable community behaviour pertaining to health and disease/signs and symptoms
4. Identification of specific community health disease problems (diagnosis), recommending a plan of action to overcome these community health and disease problems (prescription). (2005: 231)

Through such representations, and other texts and trainings, trainee health workers come to perceive many of their own 'cultural' practices as superstitious and as barriers to the attainment of 'health'. Consider this interview Ian Harper conducted in 1999 with one of the trainers at the 'traditional healers' training. Along with her hopes and desires, Ms X explained to Ian her position on local healing practices. There is a very strong faith/belief in the traditional healers, she explained. Her mother, she told Ian, still believes in them; she uses them for small problems and she still gets better. In the 'community' this is what it is like, Ms X continued. She did not feel that people visiting the healers was a good idea, as it delays them from going to the hospital when they are really ill. All the healers say is that it is the 'spirits' and 'witchcraft' and so the Community Health Development Programmes Ms X was working in give training to the healers and teach them about health. She told Ian how she would like to see more education in the community, more awareness. People don't send their children to school and their faith in these practitioners is too strong, she stated. They hide their diseases because of dishonour, or shame. They have no 'outside knowledge' and are very traditional with 'old thoughts', she explained to Ian. He asked her if nothing about the old ways was any good? Some are OK she replied, like not mixing meat and milk, as this gives an excess of protein, or rubbing oil into children and putting them in the sun, as this increases the production of vitamin D. She was using her understanding of medicine and science to filter 'the traditional' for good and bad practices. And when Ian interviewed a number of trainee health workers in July 2004, they further reflected that their future work would be opening small drug shops in the rural areas to bring medicines to the people, as health-related practices were being conflated with drug consumption.

There has been a recent growth in discourses globally, and in Nepal, around questions of mental health. This has been accompanied by a profound shift in how mental health is understood. From a concern with more psychoanalytic ideas around health and well-being, when the *Diagnostic Statistical Manual* was revised in 1980 (to *DSM III*), it became much more focused on the delineation of specific pathological states and diseases (Healy 1999; Luhrmann 2001; Young 1995). A form of 'diagnostic' psychiatry started to emerge (see Horwitz 2003: 72–73). This medicalisation process has long been in the offing: Young (1995) also reflects on how the past was medicalised in the years leading up to the First World War. 'Traumatic memory' was seen as a kind of 'parasite', and as a form of mimesis inscribed in the body. This was coupled with the normalisation of pathology – pathology as a loss or displacement of normal functions – and the notion that the normal could only be seen through the pathological (Young 1995). In many ways it was the physicians and health workers and their vision, who reflected the deep-seated societal tensions and processes at work, suggested Young. We argue that this is similarly the case in Nepal today.

Today, the International Consortium for Mental Health Policy and Services has produced a Mental Health Policy Template.[5] Its intention, as with much US-produced policy, is that it should be 'generalizable across countries and regions and ... include what is common to all countries'. As with all templates, it acts as a framing device (as do logframes, for example), which delineates certain essential categories for thinking through the issues at stake. The introduction states that:

The Template uses language, concepts and terminology consistent as possible with mainstream health sector reform and aims to be consistent with the World Health Report 2000 Health Template.... While countries may wish to use terminology that is country specific, the generic terminology, consistent with the World Health Organization, will provide a common language that may facilitate communication between countries, regions, and organizations associated with mental health policy and servicing.[6]

The list of 'social pathologies' included on the Consortium website is as follows: substance abuse, violence, abuses of women and children, crime, terrorism, corruption, criminality, discrimination, isolation, stigmatisation and human rights violations. This again refers to the global nature of these problems and that social pathologies 'often lead to a flood of social, economic and psychological problems that undermine well-being'. This is directly referred to in the 1995 Harvard-produced volume *World Mental Health: Problems and Priorities in Low-income Countries* (Desjarlais et al. 1995). While defining mental health not simply as the absence of mental disease, but 'a state of well-being in which the individual realises his or her own abilities, can work productively and fruitfully, and is able to contribute to her or his community' (1995: 7), the book remains focused on the reasons for the overall increased production of mental health problems. The lens onto well-being remains firmly based on the view from the clinic, the space where pathology is diagnosed and dealt with. The chapters themselves are revealing in this regard; they discuss the global context of well-being (economic and political welfare); suicide; substance abuse; violence; dislocation; children and youth; women; the elderly; behaviour and health. The book ends up as a political manifesto and agenda for change.

In the introduction, there are overlapping clusters of problems, which include 'social pathologies', like substance abuse, violence, abuses of women, child abuse – these link in a circular way with 'health problems' and 'exacerbating conditions, like high unemployment, poverty, limited education, stressful work conditions, gender discrimination' (1995: 7). This view from the clinic, which extrapolates from diseased bodies requiring mending to the diseased body of society, also lends itself to activism as, for example, in the work of Paul Farmer, who works very much within the medical frame, but puts it to political and activist use. For him, those with multi-drug resistant TB in Russian prisons, or HIV in New York or Haiti and the desperate lives that unfold on the pages of his book, *Pathologies of Power*, are all 'symptoms and signs of structural violence' (2003: 255). It is the pathology of the abuses of power that needs to be eliminated, and he tries to rectify the (neoliberal) hijacking of human rights discourses, turning these discourses back towards a true concern for the poor and their health, as they come in through the doors of his clinic, bearing the stigmata of their alienation from the neoliberal order. He follows a long tradition of physicians in the mode of Virchow, seeing 'politics as medicine writ large'.

While Farmer provides a political narrative to the attempts to engage with what Agamben has dubbed 'bare life', Finkielkraut criticises the growth of 'doctors without borders'. Applying the Hippocratic oath to the global village must be applauded, he suggests, but:

... things break down, however, when we look at the world with the eyes of a doctor, when our interest in others focuses on just saving lives, when those unable to rise and speak for themselves, gain our sympathy for being, as Régis Debray put it, 'the target of any place and of anything,' and for nothing more. Things break down when, with our eyes completely open, we can no longer see the difference between accident and aggression and describe the multiplicity of catastrophes with the same narrative theme, as interchangeable victims. (2001: 90)

He suggests that humanitarian man, focused on the universality of suffering in its medical forms, 'offers the unanticipated possibility of unloading the terrible burden of political morality' (2001: 94).

It is hard not to read this in the light of the bombing of the Red Cross in Iraq in 2004, and the shock this gave to our humanitarian sensibilities. While we have vigorously, but at great cost, kept the realms of humanitarianism and politics as military intervention separate, the view from the 'pathological' terrorists recognises the complicity. We have effaced history and politics from the notion of the alleviation of suffering, yet this effacement is something that those 'terrorists' in Iraq have not done. They all too clearly see the connection between war, aggressive interventionism and humanitarianism. As, indeed, it might be argued do those 'terrorists' – the Maoists – in Nepal, who increasingly target US-funded international non-governmental organisations (INGOs) and their work, and who feed off discourses of anti-Americanism and anti-neoliberalism. We witness in Nepal the rise of the success of certain public health interventions that also serve to 'unload the burden of political morality'. To put this another way, there is a conflation of biopolitical interventionism as medical practice, humanitarianism and neoliberal reform.

Well-being as medical intervention, then, remains the most powerful organising principle and its metaphorical slippage into education is the focus of our final section.

ILLITERACY (ILL-LITERACY) AS SOCIAL PATHOLOGY

... the challenge of illiteracy is an unresolved issue in Nepal. (NFEC 2003)

This pathological trope is not limited to conventional spheres of medicine. Just as Illich (1971) argued that society is 'schooled' through education, one can add, following Foucault (1973), that the clinic has also become a dominant institutional form. A literacy promotion poster produced by UNESCO Asian Cultural Centre (1981) nicely illustrates this point. The poster depicts a rural scene divided by a river, with the caption 'Let's Read'. It is a fine example of exaggeration, discursive excess and the 'prescription of subjectivities' (Harper 2005). On the left (interestingly), is the land of illiteracy – one fraught with disease, snake bites, accidents and ill-health. On the right, the land of literacy is portrayed as an orderly and healthy space. The right portrays a hospital (clinic) and a school as its key images. The sick and injured are driven or carried on a stretcher from the land of ill-literacy to the hospital. They are represented here as the passive recipients of humanitarian aid.

Despite Paulo Freire's (1972) insistence on the political character of literacy and illiteracy, the depoliticising trope of the pathological continues to be evident in the approach of some of the larger INGOs and bilateral organisations. Illiteracy is constructed as a disease, a 'plague' (Ritzen 2000), that is 'endemic' in developing countries (Chowdhury 1996). The task of the world community is therefore the 'eradication' of illiteracy, a trope commonly used for infectious diseases such as polio, tuberculosis and malaria following the defining moment in global public health when this became a possibility, on the elimination of smallpox.

A web search for 'illiteracy/Nepal/eradication' reveals over 4500 hits in which literacy is framed as forms of social pathology together with a series of other social ills; child and infant mortality, disease, war. This often repeated scenario of pathology and ill-being of the social body functions to legitimise humane interventions. What is implied is that the disease of illiteracy makes well-being impossible. Nepal, it suggests, cannot be developed, or modern, while illiteracy is endemic.

The pathological trope constructs illiteracy as an attribute of the individual, rather than encouraging an examination of the social forces that reproduce such inequality. Literacy, like medicine becomes disembedded in its uses and meanings, and is separated from the factors that reproduce illiteracy. Literacy programmes are designed and evaluated according to a biomedical model. Individual illiterates are isolated, counted and treated in special groups. A single course of six months, if properly 'delivered', should be sufficient to remove illiteracy entirely from their being, much in the same way that a treatment course of anti-tuberculous drugs will eliminate the disease tuberculosis from infected bodies. Poor-quality programmes and those that lack follow-up 'post-literacy' programmes run the risk of 'relapse'. The emphasis is on the complete removal of ill-being rather than the promotion of a literate society.

It should, of course, be noted that illiteracy is one of the most significant developmental challenges in Nepal (about half the adult population is non-literate according to the 2001 census). If these figures are disaggregated in terms of gender, caste and regional differences, they reveal massive inequalities of opportunity, particularly within the poorest and most socially excluded communities (NFEC 2003). This situation has received scant attention from the Nepali government, the donor community and the social elite, many of whom seem to believe that such inequality is either acceptable or unimportant. Discourses of 'development' and modernisation seem to be entirely compatible with such inequality.

As Richard Burghart suggested in his discussion of state formation in Nepal, the Nepali political elite integrated aspects of the modern nation-state with Nepali institutions and elite values in a way that produced somewhat syncretic localised forms and values: 'In this changing field of intracultural and intercultural relations, one may recognise the features of the modern nation-state as the Nepalese government legitimises itself on native terms but through foreign eyes' (1996: 260).

One might wonder, therefore, whether representations of illiteracy as pathology invite a similar syncretism, where universal literacy is accepted as a universal right (whereas it was not before the 1950s), but in terms that dissociate the state from ultimate responsibility for such inequality. The state is presented either as an innocent bystander (the illiterate poor are a barrier to development), or a benign actor ('the country's national target is to eradicate illiteracy' (UNESCO 2000)). One commentator on the rhetoric of illiteracy has asked whether it is possible 'to eradicate illiteracy without eradicating the illiterates' (Fasheh 2002). In the case of Nepal this question must surely be considered – and has actually been considered by some educationalists in their strategies for tackling illiteracy. One prominent Nepali educationalist Bryan spoke with in 2002 argued that it would be better to focus the government's attention on primary education, since the low life expectancy of adult illiterates would reduce their number relatively quickly in any case. A more diplomatic view, more commonly expressed, is that

The Impossibility of Well-Being

primary education is a more efficient means of increasing literacy rates: 'It is more pragmatic to strive for increased efficiency of the primary education system than to provide literacy education to a more dispersed and diversified adult population' (NFEC 2003: 68). Even allowing for such a body count, it seems likely that the inequality that reproduces high levels of illiteracy would remain. This becomes apparent when we look at the nexus between literacy and language in Nepal.

Despite the pervasive multilingual nature of Nepali society, and the commitment to multilingualism in the 1990 Constitution, the Panchayat ideology of monolingual nationalism remains dominant in areas of education and governance (Gurung 2002; Maddox 2003). Within such an ideology Nepali is produced as the language of the state and of education, and the medium of written interactions with government and non-government organisations.[7] This language policy was the cornerstone of educational language policy in the 1950s: 'If the younger generation is taught to use Nepali as the basic language then other languages will gradually disappear, the greater the national strength and unity will result' (National Education Planning Commission 1956: 97, cited in Gurung 2002: n.p.).

This view arguably remains the dominant, if implicit, policy on language in Nepal. The pervasiveness of this inequality has been commented upon by Gurung: 'In the context of Nepal, before talking about equality one has to first observe the obstacles of inequality. The traditional, ethnic, linguistic differences, which have a direct impact on literacy and education' (2002: n.p.).

During a workshop on language and literacy in the Tarai that Bryan attended in 2002, the participants (NGO workers, educationalists and government officials) became split over the thorny question of language choice. During discussions on the nature and scope of multilingualism in Nepal, some of the participants echoed the Panchayat view, arguing that local languages should not be encouraged, and that there should only be one language (Nepali) in Nepal. The local languages (often described as dialects), they argued, were a barrier to development and should be allowed (and encouraged) to die off. The consequences of such a view are felt daily in the structural violence (to use Farmer's term) of interactions with government and non-government organisations. With this policy of monolingualism in governance, development policy and education, and little political commitment to adult literacy programmes, it is hard to envisage a situation where greater levels of literacy might emerge.

* * *

What alternatives are there then, to this trope of illiteracy as social pathology and ill-being? Amartya Sen promotes literacy as a key function and a universal aspect of well-being. Illiteracy and innumeracy, Sen argues, 'are forms of insecurity in themselves' (2002: 22); as such, literacy can be regarded as an essential human freedom: 'the ability to be well nourished, to avoid escapable morbidity and mortality, to read, write and communicate, to take part in the life of a community, to appear without shame' (Sen 1990: 126). Sen's apparently Aristotelian-inspired approach to universal characteristics and values of well-being leaves little scope for relativist notions of oral culture. As Dreze and Sen have argued: 'Literacy is an essential tool of self defence in a society where social interaction includes the written media' (1995: 143). This view of literacy is also reflected in Nussbaum's (1993, 2006) discussions of well-being and capabilities, which, like the medical discourses discussed above, seem to promote a vision of humanitarianism without borders. Literacy is indeed a pervasive global phenomenon and has so many social functions that it is difficult to envisage a scenario where being literate would not bring with it some kind of 'advantage'. Sen nevertheless seems to suggest a commodified notion of literacy as an aspect of well-being that has impacts that somehow function independently from the social context. This seems to go against the grain of his argument against commodity fetishism in *Commodities and Capabilities* that: 'In judging the well-being of the person, it would be premature to limit the analysis to the characteristics of goods possessed. We have to consider the "functionings" of persons' (1999: 6). Sen's work commodifies literacy through statistically oriented arguments on how literacy correlates with other aspects of well-being, particularly those indices of health, morbidity and mortality (Sen 1999), and through the claims that he makes about the benefit of literacy for individuals. His approach does not explicitly frame illiteracy in pathological terms, but it does project the idea that well-being is impossible for illiterate communities and individuals. His argument seems to suggest a universal impact that somehow operates independently ('autonomously' to use Street's [1993] term) from social context. In contrast, one of the strengths of recent anthropological writing on literacy has been the significance that it attributes to aspects of social context and, in particular, power relations and ideology, in shaping literacy practices and their outcomes (Collins and Blot 2003; Street 1993). Such a view constructs literacy as a plural social practice whose impacts are contingent upon the social context in which they are embedded.

Is it possible, then, to imagine any alternatives to this construction of illiteracy as the impossibility of well-being? Or a state that would take illiteracy and multilingualism seriously enough to ensure that non-literate people, and those speaking a language other than Nepali (in this case around a half of Nepal's adult population), were not discriminated against in their interactions with government and non-government institutions? Civil society activists in Nepal are already imagining such a scenario (Chitrakar 2003; Ghimire and Sitikhu 2003). This alternative perspective on well-being however, seems to be at odds with the individualising and depoliticising view from the clinic.

CONCLUSION

As philosophers have argued, at some deep-seated phenomenological level the well body and subsequently well-being, is absent to us, and only realised through its *dys*-appearance (Leder 1990). In other words, we are reminded of the absence of a healthy functioning body only when it malfunctions. To expand this phenomenological truism metaphorically to the body social and politic, we are led to refract the health of the social and political (for example, illiteracy) through their absence. But this symptomatic reading of the malfunctioning body is then too easily and unthinkingly medically mapped onto an entity that comes to stand outside social relations; that is, it becomes a fetish, an object, or, in the view from the clinic, *a disease*. In this chapter we have attempted to think through the implications of this discursive pathologisation in the context of Nepal. The attempt has led us to think outside the usual boxes (of health development and literacy programmes) and examine the tropes of pathologisation more broadly in practice as they cut across fields of intervention and practice. Before we can even begin to think about well-being without framing it through its opposite, ill-being, we have had to excavate the extent of the uses and implications of the trope. And they run deep, and generally unexamined.

One difficulty we have had is that, in trying to distance ourselves from this metaphor and its implications, we need to be wary, as anthropologists, of adopting rather simplistic relativist positions. Appropriating discourses of pathologisation, Paul Farmer – as a physician and activist – is able to manipulate them to frequently striking political effect. This is where he is best situated as he strives towards what he sees as a more equitable world. While he has been criticised for this appropriation of the moral high ground, it is not surprising that he is highly critical of anthropological relativism (Farmer 1999). For him, and those activists like him, it is efficacious to run with, and start with, the pathological. But there are limits. While the view from the clinic is politically efficacious, this position is premised on an extraordinary positional bias. The view from the clinic does not reflect all the potential relations we develop with society.

When we first presented this chapter, we were challenged on the grounds that this was only language and what relation did it have with Nepal's realities? Such a disjuncture between language and reality reflects our deep-seated metaphysical inheritance: between nature and culture; body and mind; the reality of disease and the cultural manifestations of its presentations, etc. Medicine draws its nourishment and power from these distinctions; it is precisely its capacity to delineate the contours of disease and the efficacy of its interventions that grant it such metaphorical valence and political authority. We don't deny medicine its efficacy, but we do argue, as does Haraway (2000) that 'disease is a relationship'. It is precisely the apparent incongruity of this statement that we have to deal with as we struggle to rethink well-being. Disease is a relationship, and not an entity. Pathology doesn't exist outside of broader human relations. Using the trope in other discursive sites obfuscates as much as it illuminates, depoliticises as it entifies, and covers over the very political relations of its emergence and uses as such. Well-being is not the absence of pathology, nor is politics entirely defined by its elimination. The challenge is both to be attentive to the 'metaphors we live by' (Lakoff and Johnson 2003) and to attempt to think otherwise.

NOTES

1. In a similar exercise Harper and Tarnowski (2003) attempted to articulate what was similar between forestry and health programmes in Nepal. In that work we noted that around discourses of decentralisation, many of the practices – recording and reporting, the holding of meetings, etc. – indeed a whole architecture of practices and modalities, seemed to result in greater centralisation.
2. This ethnographic snippet is from Ian Harper's fieldwork for his PhD, done between 1998 and 2000, and funded by the ESRC. The ethnographic present here refers to this period.
3. There is another slippage here, around discourses of 'economic well-being' and the 'health' of the economy. (Thanks to Neil Thin for pointing this out.)
4. The Declaration of Alma Ata (1978) defined health as a 'state of complete physical, mental and social wellbeing, and not merely the absence of infirmity' and linked its attainment to human rights as a social goal requiring the action of other economic and social sectors as well as that of the health sector (see http://www.who.int/hpr/NPH/docs/declaration_almaata.pdf).
5. See http://www.qcsr.uq.edu.au/template/Context/Societal%20Organisation/Social%20Pathology_Intro.htm
6. See http://www.qcsr.uq.edu.au/template/Introduction.htm
7. This is the case in areas of the 'state' control. In areas of Maoist government the situation may well be different.

REFERENCES

Bimala, G. and S. Ganesh (eds). 2003. Campaign for Life-related Education and Literacy. In *Kathmandu: Education Network Nepal*, Special Issue on Literacy for Social Justice [in Nepali] 14(6).

Burghart, R. 1996. The Formation of the Concept of the Nation-state in Nepal. In C.J. Fuller and J. Spencer (eds) *The Conditions of Listening*. Delhi: Oxford University Press.

Canguilhem, G. 1991. *The Normal and the Pathological*. New York: Zone Books.

Chitrakar, R. 2003. Community Literacy Scribes: Context, Rationale and Strategies (in Nepali). *Kantipur Daily*, 9 September.

Chowdhury, K. 1996. Literacy and Primary Education. *HCO Working Paper*. Washington, DC: World Bank.

Collins, J. and R. Blot. 2003. *Literacy and Literacies: Texts, Power and Identity*. Cambridge: Cambridge University Press.

Davis, C. 2000. *Death in Abeyance: Illness and Therapy among the Tabwa of Central Africa*. Edinburgh: Edinburgh University Press.

Desjarlais, R., L. Eisenburg, B. Good and A. Kleinman. 1995. *World Mental Health: Problems and Priorities in Low-income Countries*. New York: Oxford University Press.

Douglas, M. 1966. *Purity and Danger: An Analysis of the Concepts of Pollution and Taboo*. New York: Praeger.

—— 1970. *Natural Symbols*. New York: Vintage.

Dreze, J. and A. Sen. 1995. *India: Economic Development and Social Opportunity*. Oxford: Clarendon Press.

Farmer, P. 1999. *Infections and Inequalities: The Modern Plagues*. Berkeley: University of California Press.

—— 2003. *Pathologies of Power: Health, Human Rights and the New War on the Poor*. Berkeley: University of California Press.

Fasheh, M. 2002. How to Eradicate Illiteracy without Eradicating Illiterates? In *Literacy as Freedom*. UNESCO Round Table, September, Paris.

Finkielkraut, A. 2001. *In the Name of Humanity: Reflections on the Twentieth Century*. London: Pimlico.

Foucault, M. 1973. *The Birth of the Clinic: An Archaeology of Medical Perception*, trans. A. Sheridan. London: Tavistock Publications.

—— 1988. *Madness and Civilisation: A History of Insanity in the Age of Reason*. New York: Vintage Books.

Freire, P. 1972. *Pedagogy of the Oppressed*. Harmondsworth: Penguin.

Gupta, A. 1998. *Postcolonial Developments: Agriculture in the Making of Modern India*. Durham, NC: Duke University Press.

Gurung, H. 2002. Language, Literacy and Equality. Paper presented at the conference on Literacy, Language and Social Inclusion, 5 September, Kathmandu.

Gywali, D. 2004. Governance, Corruption and Foreign Aid. In S. Sharma, J. Kopoonen, D. Gyawali and A. Dixit (eds) *Aid Under Stress: Water, Forests and Finnish Support in Nepal*. Kathmandu: Himal Books.

Hacking, I. 1990. *The Taming of Chance*. Cambridge: Cambridge University Press.

Haraway, D. 2000. *How Like a Leaf: An Interview with Thyrza Nichols Goodeve*. New York: Routledge.

Harper, I. 2002. Capsular Promise as Public Health: A Critique of the Nepal National Vitamin A Programme. *Studies in Nepali History and Society* 71, 137–73.

—— 2003. Mission, Magic and Medicalisation: An Anthropological Study into Public Health in Contemporary Nepal. PhD in Social Anthropology, University of London.

—— 2005. Interconnected and Interinfected: DOTS and the Stabilisation of the Tuberculosis Control Programme in Nepal. In D. Mosse and D. Lewis (eds) *The Aid Effect: Giving and Governing in International Development*. London: Pluto Press.

Harper, I. and C. Tarnowski. 2003. A Heterotopia of Resistance: Health, Community Forestry and Challenges to State Centralization in Nepal. In D. Gellner (ed.) *Resistance and the State: Nepalese Experiences*. New Delhi: Social Science Press.

Healy, D. 1999. *The Anti-Depressant Era*. Cambridge, MA: Harvard University Press.

Horwitz, A. 2003. *Creating Mental Illness*. Chicago: University of Chicago Press.

Illich, I. 1971. *Deschooling Society*. London: Calder & Boyars.

Inda, J. 2005. Analytics of the Modern: An Introduction. In J. Inda (ed.) *Anthropologies of Modernity: Foucault, Governmentality, and Life Politics*. Malden, MA: Blackwell Publishing.

Lakoff, G. and M. Johnson. 2003. *Metaphors We Live*, revised edn. London and Chicago: University of Chicago Press.

Leder, D. 1990. *The Absent Body*. Chicago: University of Chicago Press.

Lock, M. and N. Scheper-Hughes. 1996. A Critical-interpretive Approach in Medical Anthropology: Rituals and Routines of Discipline and Dissent. In C. Sargent and T. Johnson (eds) *Medical Anthropology: Contemporary Theory and Method*. Westport, CT: Praeger.

Luhrmann, T. 2001. *Of Two Minds: An Anthropologist Looks at American Psychiatry*. New York: Vintage.

Maddox, B. 2003. Language Policy, Modernist Ambivalence, and Social Exclusion: A Case Study of Rupendehi District in Nepal's Tarai. *Studies in Nepali History and Society* 8(2), 205–24.

Martin, E. 1994. *Flexible Bodies: The Role of Immunity in American Culture from the Days of Polio to the Age of AIDS*. Boston, MA: Beacon Press.

Mosse, D. 2005. Global Governance and the Enthnograpy of International Aid. In D. Mosse and D. Lewis (eds) *The Aid Effect: Giving and Governing in International Development*. London: Pluto Press, pp. 1–36.

NFEC (Non-Formal Education Centre). 2003. *Literacy Situation in Nepal: A Thematic Presentation*, edited by G. Shrestha, S. Sigdel, H. Regmi. Lathmandu, Nepal: Ministry of Education, Non-Formal Education Centre.

Nussbaum, M. 1993. Non-relative Virtues: An Aristotelian Approach. In M.C. Nussbaum and A. Sen (eds) *The Quality of Life*. Oxford: Clarendon Press.

—— 2006. *Frontiers of Justice: Disability, Nationality, Species Membership*. The Tanner Lectures on Human Values. Cambridge, MA: The Belknap Press of Harvard University Press.

Paalman, M., H. Bekedam, L. Hawken and D. Nyheim. 1998. A Critical Review of Priority Setting in the Health Sector: The Methodology of the 1993 World Development Report. *Health Policy and Planning* 13(1), 13–31.

Pigg, S. 1997. 'Found in Most Traditional Societies': Traditional Medical Practitioners between Culture and Development. In F. Cooper and R. Packard (eds) *International Development and the Social Sciences: Essays on the History and Politics of Knowledge*. Berkeley: University of California Press.

Ritzen, J. 2000. *Education and the Poor: Eradicating the Plague of Illiteracy*. Washington, DC: World Bank.

Samson, C. 1999. Biomedicine and the Body. In C. Samson (ed.) *Health Studies*. Oxford: Blackwell.

Sapkota, S. 2004. *Health Management*. Kathmandu.

Scott, J. 1998. *Seeing Like a State*. New Haven, CT: Yale University Press.

Sen, A. 1990. Gender and Cooperative Conflict. In I. Tinker (ed.) *Persistent Inequalities*. New York: Oxford University Press.

—— 1999. *Commodities and Capabilities*. New Delhi: Oxford India Paperbacks.

—— 2002. *Literacy as Freedom*. UNESCO Round Table, September, Paris, URL (consulted May 2007): http://portal.unesco.org/education/en/ev.php-URL_ID=4848&URL_DO=DO_TOPIC&URL_SECTION=201.html

—— 2004. Why Should We Preserve the Spotted Owl? *London Review of Books* 26(3), 5 February.

Street, B. 1993. *Cross-cultural Approaches to Literacy*. Cambridge: Cambridge University Press.

Thapa, H.B. 2002. *The Anatomy of Corruption*. Kathmandu: ESP.

Thin, N. 2005. Happiness and the Sad Topics of Anthropology. WeD (Well-being in Developing Countries) Working Paper 10, URL (consulted May 2007): http://www.bath.ac.uk/econ-dev/wellbeing/research/workingpaperpdf/wed10.pdf

UNESCO. 2000. *Education for All, Year 2000 Assessment, Nepal Country Report*. EFA Assessment Committee, Ministry of Education, Kathmandu, Nepal.

—— 2002. *Education for All: Global Monitoring Report*, URL (consulted May 2007): http://portal.unesco.org/education/en/ev.php-URL_ID=11283&URL_DO=DO_TOPIC&URL_SECTION=201.html

World Bank. 1993. *World Development Report 1993: Investing in Health*. New York: Oxford University Press.

Young, A. 1995. *The Harmony of Illusions: Inventing Post-traumatic Stress Disorder*. Princeton, NJ: Princeton University Press

Zwi, A. 2000. Introduction – Policy Forum: The World Bank and International Health. *Social Science and Medicine*, 50, 167–68.

2 GOOD WAYS AND BAD WAYS: TRANSFORMATIONS OF LAW AND MINING IN PAPUA NEW GUINEA

Eric Hirsch

I

When I returned to the Udabe Valley in 1999, I arrived at the Ononge Mission airstrip and had intended to travel back to Visi, the place further down the valley where my initial research during the mid-1980s had been based.[1] However, a *gab* ritual (see Hirsch 2004) was being performed nearby Ononge and most people from Visi were present there. I decided to stay with my friend and fieldwork associate Alphonse Hega at Yuvenise, near the *gab*, and to observe the ritual until its completion. I then wanted to travel back to Visi and spend time there before departing the field. As it turned out, the completion of the *gab* only allowed me one night's stay in Visi. Before I left Visi with Alphonse, a pig was killed and betelnut, rice and money I brought was distributed to the Visi people assembled. Before the food was divided, a speech was made by Bodi, son of Kol Usi (see p. 55). In his speech Bodi indicated that I had been away a long time and that people thought I was dead. He also said that the people at Ononge 'wasted' my time, due to the duration of their *gab*. He then went on to say:

Your time is already up. White man's time. The time that you marked has come. You came down here and are going back. So we cannot sit together and eat properly. If you go back and think of coming back again, when you come back we will eat good food together. This is because you came. Afi and Dube died,[2] I killed this small pig. The rice and betelnut you brought we will cook it, eat together and then you and Alphonse can go. OK.[3]

Although he did not say as much, this way of conducting myself was, from the local perspective, not good. It did not exhibit 'good ways' (*mad ife*). Eating and then just leaving meant that I was not recognising the people I was eating with, by engaging in talk, chewing of betelnut, telling of stories and so on. I was living according to the 'clock' alone. Because I was a 'white man', and such people have different ways, it was deemed acceptable on this occasion.

What Bodi was saying to me and those assembled there was that the next time I came I had to exhibit good ways and stay, eat and talk properly.[4]

My attitude to time-keeping ('white man's time') was similar to other (negative) manners rhetorically attributed to white people by Melanesians, such as living according to money (that is, being dependent upon money for what one eats or where one lives), or living far from or separately from relations. However, one convention brought by white people is often singled out as contributing to the good ways of Melanesian peoples. This is expressed by Merlan and Rumsey (1991: 28–29) writing about the denizens of the Nebilyer Valley:

> People ... strongly assert the significance of 'government law' (*gavman lo* [as expressed in Tok Pisin]) relating it to the European advent and the resulting imposition of centralized administration. On many public occasions orators allude to the harsh times of warfare before *gavman lo* and declare that times have changed, and they too are different people now.

Merlan and Rumsey (1991: 29) then go on to observe:

> People recall with special interest the methods of the *kiaps* (patrol officers), the arm of the Australian Administration with which they were most familiar before Independence ... they talk of the suppression of tribal fighting, and the jailing of offenders.... In all of this talk, there is a certain admiration of perceived strength, and even of violence successfully used to accomplish ends.... Certain institutions developed under the Australian Administration are seen by local people as continuing mechanisms of *gavman lo*, foremost among these perhaps the village *kot* (court) system, local offices decided by election (Magistrate, councillor), the system of regional and national elections, and the maze of provincial bodies ... with which some local people at least come to develop a certain familiarity.

These observations have direct parallels with the Fuyuge people and their own colonial and postcolonial experiences. Among the latter, law became an element of good ways because of the manner in which it encouraged particular kinds of sociality while discouraging other, bad, kinds. Everyone, in principle, can participate in law, as in access to village courts. It is a concept and value that contributes to what an outside analyst might refer to as 'freedom'. Law enables locally perceived reciprocal relations of a good manner, such as using courts instead of violence (or courts after violence, instead of more violence). The notion of good ways is defined by recourse to its inverse, 'bad ways' (*mad ko*) – such as killing or stealing. And yet, bad ways can also be seen as 'good', as the case of the Australian patrol officers mentioned above indicates: their use of force and violence could be seen to generate good outcomes.

It is apparent, then, that colonial projects in Papua and later New Guinea were informed by conceptions of welfare or well-being to be implemented on the native societies. Hubert Murray's long period as Lieutenant Governor (1908–40) has been characterised as a paternalistic, humanitarian form of rule: he 'was an ardent defender of Papuan rights and well-being' (Kadiba

1989: 279). Murray sought to avoid the errors of exploitation in colonial regimes such as Australia and elsewhere. Papuan lands were not expropriated and villagers were largely maintained as villagers. He sought to change the villager by altering the conditions of village life, bringing 'civilisation' in the form of law and an ordered village existence. Similar conceptions of externally imposed well-being also informed missionary projects of conversions. French Catholic missionaries operating in colonial Papua, for instance, saw their work as allied with, but also distinct from, that of the government. They had to recognise that the law of the colonial state was dominant in civil matters but that the law of God reigned supreme with regard to moral and religious matters.

II

Among the Fuyuge people with whom I worked, this legacy is implicated in their own conceptions of 'well-being'. There is no Fuyuge word that translates as well-being *per se*. The closest Fuyuge notion is that of *mad ife* (good ways). There is also the related idea of *an ataeg* (true person; see Fastre' n.d.; cf. Leenhardt 1979 [1947]). The Fuyuge see themselves as true persons in comparison to white people. True persons live according to the ways of *tidibe*. *Tidibe* is a creator force that 'laid down' the ways or customs and landscape of the Fuyuge, and ultimately all derives from *tidibe*. Thus, true people eat certain kinds of foods, have distinctive living and social arrangements, transact with one another in particular ways and speak a unique language. To steal and to kill, for example, is not conducive to good ways of living. At the same time, though, these are things that true people did in the past and continue, to a degree, still to do. It is for this reason that the Fuyuge say they need the person of the *amede* in order to perform their important ritual, *gab*. *Amede* are persons said to have good ways, in that they do not steal or kill and have the capacity to both look after others and to unify the minds of men and women in the performance of ritual.[5] Only certain men with distinct origins become *amede*; Kol Usi (see p. 53) and his elder brother Yavu Inoge are *amede* in Visi. The *amede* is what enables the Fuyuge to magnify a core feature of their social relations: that is, the capacity to act reciprocally as both agents and patients, most vividly in their ritual. Thus each creates a perspective in which the other can be seen – as agents who take action and patients as objects in the regard of others (Gell 1998; Strathern 1999: 263 n.6).

In the past there were men among the Fuyuge who were renowned for their fighting and killing capacity (*ha u bab*). They would be sent off by their *amede* like hunting dogs to kill an opponent. In this case, others were only treated as objects or patients. People were terrified by these men but also respected their powers and capacities. Until the arrival of the colonial government and missionaries, there was an intrinsic relationship between *amede* and *ha u bab*. The *gab* ritual could not be performed under conditions of fighting and killing, but the killing capacities of the *ha u bab* were vividly displayed in the headdress adornments these men worn. Their power was visible, but it was also contained by the good ways of the *amede*, who made the ritual performance possible. However, by the time I began to conduct research among the Fuyuge, the ways of the *ha u bab* were only a recollection from the past. This is because, as the Fuyuge asserted to me, the government and missionaries had come and put the law into their heads. By this they meant that these persons had made the Fuyuge think and see differently, and that fighting and killing as it was conventionally practised had become ways of the past. Putting law into the head implies that one can think and talk properly, think and talk good. Law becomes like (good) talk – that is, it can be the basis of relations (persons) and persons can be the basis of law (talk). Like money, law is seen as a form through which capacities can be demonstrated. But money also leads to 'bad ways': violence, jealousy, sorcery and killing. That is why *amede* are not meant to handle money (that is, be involved in *bisnis* [business, money-making activities]). Fuyuge now demonstrate their knowledge of law as both agent and patient in the reciprocal conduct of social relations – on either a 'small' everyday scale or the magnified scale of ritual.

The assertion that the Fuyuge had the law put into their heads is one that encapsulates a complex history, one highlighted above in the quotations from Merlan and Rumsey (1991). It is a history of patrol officers and missionaries intervening in the conventional conduct of the Fuyuge and introducing notions – such as law – that had no place in Fuyuge thinking previously. This was also associated with forces of coercion that were unprecedented in previous Fuyuge experience – firearms, handcuffs, prisons and incarceration, courts and trial, etc. In short, an administrative machinery where government and missionaries often worked in conjunction to eliminate practices that were contrary to their conceptions of civilised conduct and thus their sense of what constituted well-being.

The Fuyuge actively transformed themselves in relation to this often violent colonial past. What the government and missionaries brought in the form of law was subsequently appropriated by the Fuyuge as a positive innovation in their modes of conduct. Fuyuge men and women told me they could now walk and move without constant fear of attack. By getting the law into their heads people knew that those involved in fighting and killing would be punished by the government. In short, law has been converted into what the Fuyuge perceive as good ways and in many respects is emblematic of what we might call Fuyuge well-being. By law the Fuyuge mean two related things: they mean the legal conventions that regulate conduct and they mean conventions of the present that must be followed. So, the pervasive use of money is said to be law; money is law in that its use must be followed or obeyed. The conversion of law in this manner by the Fuyuge is a demonstration of power. The Fuyuge conjure up an imagery of patrol officers and missionaries breaking the spears of warriors over their heads and thus imparting the law this way. What this imagery highlights is the capacity of the Fuyuge to convert or transform the law of the colonists to the purposes of Fuyuge sociality. It is through this capacity to effect such conversions that Fuyuge demonstrate their effectiveness. This efficacy is analogous to converting live pigs into killed and divided pigs that flow into exchange relations.

What I have just described as the conversion of law for the Fuyuge is far from unique and has been described elsewhere in Papua New Guinea (PNG) in parallel terms (see Demian 2003; Lipset 2005; Merlan and Rumsey 1991; Strathern 1985). What particularly interests me about this example is its difference from the state regime of resource extraction that has occurred since the mid to late 1980s in various parts of PNG, including that of the Fuyuge. In both cases there is a conversion of Western-derived notions into local forms, but the consequences and effects are significantly different. This difference is of interest as it highlights how people are able or unable (as the case might be) to transform externally imposed ideas and institutions into forms that sustain their sense of good ways.

III

There are two features of these cases that I want to draw attention to in what follows. The first feature is that of scale. The second feature is that of distribution. I suggest that there is a significant scale difference in terms of the implementation of law and that of resource extraction that has implications for their respective incorporation. The scale of Western-derived law and its associated organisation, although more powerful than previous Fuyuge experience, was of a size comparable to other Fuyuge entities. In the case of resource extraction – mining in the Fuyuge instance – the scale is largely difficult to comprehend: the relative size of the operation itself, the amounts of money it depends on and creates in turn, the kinds of people the operation needs to interact with, etc. In a related manner, the way in which law and associated colonial projects were and are distributed throughout PNG is very different from the distribution of resource extraction. Where the first was evenly distributed as an outgrowth of the colonial state, the second is distributed only where abundant, exploitable resources are found. The conceptions of well-being that inform these colonial and postcolonial projects are, it seems, radically different. Whereas one was meant to promote a colonial version of local 'freedom' – freeing the natives from what were perceived as 'uncivilised' practices – the other draws on the discourse of 'living standards': an outgrowth of the global paradigm of sustainable development, where 'needs' are to the fore (see Sen 2004 and p. 63 below).

Government in colonial Papua, as noted above, was administered through a system of patrolling and the establishment of administrative centres. Previously uncontacted or little-contacted areas were patrolled so that they could be mapped and their cultural and linguistic boundaries established. The first patrol officers to work in an area often provided vivid descriptions of the native situation and attempted to identify 'problems' – such as warfare between collectivities – that required further attention and resolution. Many of the early patrol reports from the turn of the twentieth century concerned with the Fuyuge that I have consulted are detailed accounts of attempts to apprehend 'murderers' and bring them to justice (see Hirsch 2001a). What is clear from these accounts is that Fuyuge men and women do not understand the intentions of the pursuing patrol officers and their native police; notions such as 'murderer' or 'law' or being taken to prison, for example, do not make sense in local conceptions.

In conjunction with these early patrols, officers would recommend to their superiors where they thought police camps should be established. These were camps based in the local area, where one or two patrol officers and a contingent of native police were stationed for extended periods of time. They were placed in areas of endemic fighting and warfare. For example, in the Udabe Valley a police camp was established at Kambisi during the mid-1920s because of a series of payback killings between Kambisi and their neighbours. The government was also prompted to place the camp there by the missionaries, who were stationed directly across the valley at Ononge and had been there since the previous decade.[6] Although the camp was formally in operation until the 1930s, two years after it was started it was empty most of time as patrols focused on new 'problem' areas among neighbouring language groups, such as the Tauade (see Hallpike 1977).

Once villagers understood that patrols would become a periodic feature of native life, patrol officers began to select men as village constables, who were responsible for reporting breaches of government law to the patrol officers and/or resident missionaries and for maintaining orderliness in village life. Subsequently, when government – and particularly the missionaries – began constructing a local engineered trail network, these men were responsible for maintaining its upkeep. Among the Fuyuge, village constables were not terribly effective in government or missionary eyes. From the Fuyuge perspective these were the men that patrol officers sought out during their periodic patrols, even if they were absent at a *gab* ritual, to be harangued for their ineffectiveness. As village constables they were aligned with these powerful figures and they and their relations partook in this power. It is through these complex relations, organised and maintained over several decades, that people like the Fuyuge came to view themselves as people who knew the law, unlike their ancestors who did not (cf. Kituai 1998).

The point I want to stress here is that the process I have briefly described for the Fuyuge is one that was replicated in similar fashion in other areas either prior to or after it occurred among the Fuyuge. Each village, each valley, each cultural and linguistic region was submitted to this administrative logic. The processes of incorporation varied (see Merlan and Rumsey 1991: 242) but there was general recognition that everyone had to assent to government (and mission) law, whether as a resource in which one could participate or as a way of distinguishing between a wild past and a tame present and future. There was no sense in which one valley, for instance, had the law and another did

Good Ways and Bad Ways

not. People might say that the other valley did not follow the law properly; that people did not have 'good ways' and stole from and killed each other. This might be because their *amede* were not strong and effective, or because there were too many of them and they were unable to properly assert their power. But it was not because their ancestors had not been submitted to the law; they just might not have gotten it correctly. So there is a distributional logic at work in the past and present of the law that means access to it is a general possibility: one can, so to speak, transform the quality of social relations – as good ways – through getting the law into one's head.

Law also has a specific scale. The patrolling process I succinctly described above for the Fuyuge entailed the perception of a new landscape of places. Men and women were now part of a district and had to know its name and headquarters (such as Kairuku, or later Goilala and Tapini). The power and effectiveness of patrol officers were presented by the size of their patrols (police, carriers, etc.) but also by the size of the area and the places – such as prisons or courts – that they and others like them encompassed. One of my older Fuyuge hosts, Kol Usi, mentioned above, recently (1999) told me a story which included how his father had been asked by a patrol officer to give the name of his district, i.e. did this Fuyuge man know where he was now located in terms of government law and administration? Peoples such as the Fuyuge have converted or transformed this scale of law into their own imaginings; into the conduct of their sociality and what they imagine constitutes 'good ways'. And again, the scale of law was analogous wherever it was distributed, so that the landscape of places that the implementation law entailed was potentially incorporated into local conceptions and conduct.

It needs to be stressed here that my Fuyuge hosts directed my attention to the virtues of law and the way they actively appropriated it from the government and missionaries, as constitutive of 'good ways'. It is not my intention to romanticise or glorify this historical process. There is plenty of evidence to show that, on occasion, patrol officers acted inappropriately with the Fuyuge and others (see Kituai 1998; Sinclair 1981). Equally, it is not the case that the Fuyuge now live without violence and always follow the law. Their capacities and thus what we can gloss as their 'well-being' flow from this conversion of an imposed system into their own form. What I want to suggest is that this is an outcome of the generalised distribution and scale of law. The intention of the coloniser was to uniformly distribute this virtue of 'civilisation'. Peoples like the Fuyuge, among others in PNG, were able to perceive an analogy between law and their 'good ways', and the limits of their 'bad ways' as conventionally practised. Today, in fact, Fuyuge contrast their lives in the villages with life in Port Moresby, the national capital, where they say there is no law. As Reed notes more generally:

Across the country, Mosbi, as it is known in Tok Pisin, is linked with wild dangerous and noncustomary behaviours.... Stories circulate of the outrages committed there, of sexual promiscuity, rape, intoxication, theft and casual violence. Popular songs played on the radio portray the capital as a city out of control, where almost anything can happen. (2003: 61; cf. Goddard 2005)

IV

I now want to contrast what I have said above about the colonial implementation of law and its incorporation into local notions of good ways with local incorporations of the postcolonial state's relation to local environments and the use of natural resources. Here we find a very different distributional logic and scale, and I am interested in comparing the capacity for local conversions. Again, this issue was brought to my attention by my Fuyuge hosts and the recent introduction of a copper and gold mine in their area. Although the mine is operating in an adjacent Fuyuge valley to the one in which I have worked, it has begun to influence my hosts in a number of ways. Most significantly, the mine possesses a number of exploration licences for areas of land surrounding the mine. This has led to local discussions about who 'owns' the land on which potential mining may commence. This is ownership of a Western sort, with precise boundaries and precise owning individuals (whether individual 'clans' or persons). It is not the way the Fuyuge conventionally think about land or their relations with it. What these Fuyuge discussions entailed was who owned what land and how one established these boundaries of ownership. These discussions were initiated because of the way that royalties from mining are distributed, and they are only distributed to landowners. So, in order to access any potential money that would flow from the mine if the operations were enlarged, people need to convert themselves into landowners. This conversion process is problematic because it means conceptualising the land in a way that lacks local parallels. In other words, unlike knowing the law, becoming a landowner is potentially contrary to the constitution of good ways. It is potentially contrary to good ways because it means creating a separate and permanent relation to the land that excludes the possibilities of conversions with respect to the land.

The distributional logic of resource extraction is very different from that of law or other colonial and postcolonial projects, such as the introduction of cash cropping. Resource extraction only occurs in environments rich in valuable, potential commodities such as minerals, timber or fish. Over the last two decades, resource extraction in PNG has expanded and intensified as the state has attempted to balance its increasingly precarious budget. A complex set of arrangements between the state and commercial resource extractors, such as mining companies, has led to the establishment of large and medium-sized operations, often in areas not easily accessible by foot or road. These so-called 'lucky strike' communities benefit from resource rents, in compensation for the use and degradation of the land and local environment. In conjunction with these operations, mining operators are nowadays compelled to provide modern housing, schools and other facilities to demonstrate that they are raising the standard of living of the people in exchange for using and altering their environment. The overriding rhetoric of these operations is about how living standards are being raised.[7] This is visibly manifested in brochures and websites produced by these commercial concerns, which repeatedly draw attention to these community enhancements.

The distributional logic of resource extractive projects has distinctive local implications. As I have indicated, the mining companies require the precise ownership of the exploitable land to be specified and quantified. For people like the Fuyuge, as elsewhere in PNG, their relation with the land is analogous to their relations with persons – that is, it is multiple and extends or contracts depending on the particular event (e.g. the planting of new gardens or cultivation in a neighbouring area via an affinal relation). The precise specification of boundaries and quantification of persons 'owning' the land means that there will always be those who are excluded, but who see themselves as 'owners' as well. Of course exclusion of persons for various reasons occurs, for example, when pigs are *not* contributed to another person's life-cycle rite performed in *gab* (e.g. lack of suitable pigs, bad feelings between the persons concerned, etc.).

The case of resource extraction and land ownership is different and this has to do with the scale of the enterprise itself. To illustrate: in Fuyuge *gab* ritual, men and women reciprocally coerce others to perform as dancers and as pig killers. It is never certain whether their performances will be true to their claims until the event is actually revealed and witnessed. Even then there will be different assessments, but the expectation is that men and women will seek to perform well in order to appear capable and powerful, as this is a demonstration of good ways in making *gab*. I raise this example of *gab* because an analogous relation is constructed with the mining operation, and especially with respect to land ownership and resource rents. Where the mining operation coerces the local people to disclose themselves as the appropriate landowners, the people expect, in return, that they will be appropriately compensated for the use of their land and environment. Are the mining companies, though, actually revealing an appropriate exchange or are they concealing more than they should? This uncertainty is an intrinsic feature of social relations among the Fuyuge and other Melanesians. The scale of the mining operations, the numbers of personnel involved, the size of the equipment and resources extracted all indicate a huge store of wealth, much larger than that actually revealed and distributed to landowners. This perception, or misperception, as the case may be, has significant implications for the dynamics of relations at local and national level.

In PNG historically resource rents were a form of economic surplus that was divided between the postcolonial state and private capital 'according to a rationally calculable and mutually advantageous formula' (Filer 1996: 1). The state share was then to be invested into long-term economic growth and a move away from such resource dependency. However, this post-independence vision and policy has increasingly contended with a second. In this conception, resource rents 'belong by right to customary "resource owners", whose ultimate ownership of national natural resource' (Filer 1996: 1) has been obscured by the legacy of colonial law – where all land and resources below it are inalienable and belong to the state. If resource rents are appropriated by the state and private capital, this means a serious deduction from the so-called natural rights owners, and this has to be justified and accepted by the customary landlords.

Over the nearly three decades of independence, there has been a general reversal of policy from the first to the second. Instead of the monies being invested in a national fund for the creation of physical and social infrastructure, it has made some PNG elites very rich, many others increasingly poor, and has led to the increased demands by local landowners – through numerous legal and political contests with national and foreign 'stakeholders' – to get their fair share. At a national level this has meant the funds available for the development and maintenance of infrastructure – roads, schools, health facilities, etc. – are not readily available and the deterioration of this infrastructure has been profound, as noted by anthropologists, among others (see Gewertz and Errington 1999; Knauft 2002).

V

At a local level this has meant that men and women excluded as landowners, but who feel they have a rightful claim to compensation, can agitate either formally or informally against the mine and government. As a consequence, these people often move to the vicinity of the mine and live with relations in the anticipation that their claims will be met and the monies concealed by the mine will flow to them. This has occurred at the Tolukuma mine, located in the Auga Valley of the Fuyuge. In addition, because the mine is the only source of employment in often relatively isolated areas (such as Tolukuma), numerous other Fuyuge, and others from neighbouring cultural groups with connections to local people, camp around the mine in the hope that some form of employment will be secured. This concentration of people in a small area, some of whom have been provided with modern houses and facilities by the mine and many who are excluded from these living arrangements but seek to access them through the morality of kin and affinal relations[8] is not conducive to the making of good ways. This is the source of continual local conflict. And because the national and provincial governments have insufficient funds to provide adequate roads, schools and health facilities, among other infrastructure, these are now provided by resource extractors, such as mining companies, as part of their contractual arrangements, and form a visible and potent feature of their campaigns to show how they are improving local 'living standards'.[9]

Tolukuma mine, for instance, started production in 1995 with Dome Resources, an Australian mining company. In 2000 it was sold to the South African company Durban Roodeport Deep Limited. Since February 2003 this company has published a small newsheet, four pages long, called *The Tolukuma*

Times (*TTT*). Each issue features modest items about local development projects sponsored by the mine. The following is an extract from one story:

> Tolukuma's commitment to the local community included sponsoring the new Court House and the local Police Station. The mine also provided numerous benefits to locals including medical evacuations and transportation of building and other materials to using its helicopter. (*TTT* February 2003: 2)

The point I want to highlight here is not to suggest that these facilities are useless and not needed; very much to the contrary. Rather, that their distribution is dependent on the agency of the mine management and is not a general resource that is available, in principle, equitably. This is the predicament created by the distribution and scale of resource extraction in PNG. As Colin Filer says:

> The question then is whether the recipients gain more from the opportunity to invest, squander, or squabble over their own pile of [resource rent] than the nation as a whole loses from the deterioration of 'government services' which are funded from the same source? (1996: 27)

Two of my hosts in the Udabe Valley articulated contrasting views about this matter when I spoke to them in 1999 about the possibility of the mine expanding its operations into their valley. Alphonse Hega was very concerned about the environmental consequences. He could see the effect the mine tailings were having on the Auga River and destruction of forest land for mining operations would seriously affect people's capacity to garden. He had already written to the NGO Conservation Melanesia requesting information and assistance. But Alphonse's educated and more cosmopolitan outlook was fairly unique among the Fuyuge.[10] By contrast, his uncle Kol Usi articulated a more conventional view. Kol was primarily concerned that he was properly recognised as a landowner. Due to a dispute about the boundaries of land that had arisen since the mine started exploring in the Udabe Valley, Kol did not want others to 'eat' his money, as he put it (see Hirsch 2001b). He wanted the money that would flow from the mine so that 'he could buy some sugar, eat it, and then die'.[11] This is not 'greed', so to speak, but an outlook comparable to what was done with the law: the money is converted into a form that sustains the 'good ways' of living together. Money/sugar has this capacity as it can flow between people and sustain the moral obligations they invest in one another. Unlike law, however, it is only available to a limited number of people.

VI

My comparison of the conversion possibilities of colonial imposed law and postcolonial resource extraction draws attention to a medieval distinction, recently noted by Sen (2004) between *patients* and *agents*, and referred to in a different context at the start of this chapter. Sen argues that 'we are not only patients, whose needs demand attention, but also agents, whose freedom to decide what to value and how to pursue it can extend far beyond the fulfilment of our needs' (2004: 10). The specific question he addresses is whether environmental issues and priorities are simply about fulfilling our needs or also about sustaining our freedoms? Do we maintain and enhance well-being by satisfying our needs or also by preserving and expanding our freedoms?

In the PNG example of resource extraction, the land and surrounding rivers are degraded by mining to satisfy the needs of both the state elite and local landowners for much desired and difficult to obtain money, housing and associated facilities. From the Fuyuge perspective, they seek to convert the form of the mine in a way analogous to the conversions performed in their *gab* ritual. Each side coerces the other to reveal their concealed capacities: there is the mutual coercion between the Fuyuge as potential landowners and the mine as potential store of wealth. However, there is no reciprocity in the sense of one side acting first as agents and then as the objects of regard as patients. Rather the conversion, it seems, entails the loss of the capacity to live in good ways – with respect to the land and surrounding environment as much as in one's social relations, although the standard of living of many landowners now includes desired modern houses as emblems of living like white people and mine-provided facilities. The Fuyuge are only patients in this arrangement.

By contrast, and perhaps ironically, the imposition of colonial law by government and mission alike has been appropriated as a profound and powerfully beneficial innovation. 'Getting the law into one's head' means that social life and social relations could be conducted in ways not conceived before. Law has been converted to the mutual relationship of agents and patients. Although the Fuyuge do not use the notion of freedom to describe their experiences, something like it in native concepts is clearly implied by their evaluations.

What I have suggested is that the scale and distributional logic of these different forms – law and resource extraction, specifically mining – have distinctive implications for the way they have been converted into valued capacities. I am proposing that the Fuyuge notion of 'good ways' (*mad ife*) involves people having the ability be both agents and patients with respect to one another. Law historically among the Fuyuge and other PNG peoples has been appropriated as a way of enlarging this range of capacities. This is, perhaps, because law came to be akin to Fuyuge notions like *tidibe* – creator force – a form that is everywhere and inheres in everything. It is from this basis that one is able to assume mutually different perspectives and to do so is to have the capacity to be powerful. By contrast, resource extraction does not facilitate such mutually related perspectives for people like the Fuyuge and others. There is no form that can be appropriated to this effect. Rather, as Sen's analysis suggests, one is simply a patient and it is very questionable indeed for peoples like the Fuyuge whether their standard of living, and in this sense a distinctive form of well-being, is actually augmented in the process.

NOTES

1. I warmly thank both the editor for inviting me to take part in such a stimulating conference and the conference participants for their insightful comments and questions. For any errors that remain I can only thank myself. The chapter draws on different periods of fieldwork, most recently supported by the Cambridge and Brunel Universities joint research project, 'Property, Transactions and Creations: New Economic Relations in the Pacific', funded by the UK Economic and Social Research Council (grant no. R000237838). I am very grateful to Alphonse Hega, Kol Usi and my other recent hosts in Yuvenise and Visi.
2. Afi was an older man who had recently died. Dube, who acted as an informal field assistant during my initial fieldwork, had died some years before.
3. The speech was translated into English with the assistance of Alphonse Hega.
4. Phrased differently it might be said that Bodi was drawing attention to what has been called 'the fractality of the Melanesian person: the talk formed through the person that is the person formed through the talk' (Wagner 1991: 166). Persons (talk) are enchained in other persons (talk) and this must be acknowledged and negotiated in any context.
5. The *amede* is meant to be figure of good ways but this can never be known for certain and there are always competing perspectives on whether this is true or not. *Amede* are seen as enabling the consolidation and holding together of paths upon which people and things flow. To make and hold the flow is to have strength and power. In the literature, *amede* has been translated as 'chief' (see Hallpike 1977).
6. The missionaries were also concerned about the 'English' influence that might result from the police camp and sought to obviate this by increasing their own presence in the area.
7. This should be the case for the country as a whole but, as Filer (1997) has documented, this has proved very difficult to implement.
8. Or waiting to be recognised as a landowner by the mine.
9. During August 2005, *The National* (PNG) newspaper reported that '[d]isgruntled over royalty payments, landowners torched a building and other facilities at the Tolukuma gold mine in Central Province'. The article goes on to report that:

    [l]ast month, disgruntled landowners shut down the hydro plant at the Auga River to disrupt work at the mine site. They were unhappy over compensation they got from the use of their river used for the plant. The villagers living along that river tampered with the power lines that supplied electricity to the mine to express their disappointment over compensation payment for the use of their river. (30 August 2005)

10. Shared also by the environmental campaigner Matilda Koma, a Fuyuge, who comes from the neighbouring Hele [Kodige] Valley.
11. Compare a similar sentiment expressed by one of Stuart Kirsch's (personal communication) Yonggom associates with regard to the compensation payments from the Ok Tedi mine: 'I am an old woman. I don't have the strength to garden or make sago anymore. I want them to distribute the money quickly, so that I can taste some sugar before I die.'

REFERENCES

Demian, M. 2003. Custom in the Courtroom, Law in the Village: Legal Transformations in Papua New Guinea. *Journal of the Royal Anthropological Institute* 9, 97–116.

Fastre', P. n.d. Manners and Customs of the Fuyuges, trans. M. Flower and E. Chariot, unpublished manuscript.

Filer, C. 1997. Resource Rents: Distribution and Sustainability. In I. Temu (ed.) *Papua New Guinea: A 20/20 Vision*, Pacific Policy Paper 20. Canberra: ANU, National Centre for Development Studies, pp. 222–60.

Gell, A. 1998. *Art and Agency: An Anthropological Theory*. Oxford: Clarendon Press.

Gewertz, D. and F. Errington. 1999. *Emerging Class in Papua New Guinea: The Telling of Difference*. Cambridge: Cambridge University Press.

Goddard, M. 2005. *The Unseen City: Anthropological Perspectives on Port Moresby, Papua New Guinea*. Canberra: Pandanus Books.

Hallpike, C. 1977. *Bloodshed and Vengeance in the Papuan Mountains: The Generation of Conflict in Tauade Society*. Oxford: Clarendon Press.

Hirsch, E. 2001a. Making Up People in Papua. *Journal of the Royal Anthropological Institute* 7, 241–56.

—— 2001b. Mining Boundaries and Local Land Narratives (*Tidibe*) in the Udabe Valley, Central Province. In L. Kalinoe and J. Leach (eds) *Rationales of Ownership*. New Delhi: UBS Publishers.

Hirsch, E. 2004. Techniques of Vision: Photography, Disco and Renderings of Present Perceptions in Highland Papua. *Journal of the Royal Anthropological Institute* 10, 19–40.

Kadiba, J. 1989. Murray and Education: Some Observations on the Ambivalence of Colonial Education Policy in Papua before World War II. In S. Latukefu (ed.) *Papua New Guinea: A Century of Colonial Impact 1884–1984*. Port Moresby: National Research Institute and the University of Papua New Guinea in association with the PNG Centennial Committee.

Kituai, A. 1998. *My Gun, My Brother: The World of the Papua New Guinea Colonial Police, 1920–1960*. Honolulu: University of Hawai'i Press.

Knauft, B. 2002. *Exchanging the Past: A Rainforest World of Before and After*. Chicago: University of Chicago Press.

Leenhardt, M. 1979 [1947]. *Do Kamo: Person and Myth in the Melanesian World*, trans. B.M. Gulati. Chicago: University of Chicago Press.

Lipset, D. 2005. 'The Trial': A Parody of the Law Amid the Mockery of Men in Post-colonial Papua New Guinea. *Journal of the Royal Anthropological Institute* 10, 63–90.

Merlan, F. and A. Rumsey. 1991. *Ku Waru: Language and Segmentary Politics in the Western Nebilyer Valley, Papua New Guinea*. Cambridge: Cambridge University Press.

Reed, A. 2003. *Papua New Guinea's Last Place: Experiences of Constraint in a Postcolonial Prison*. Oxford: Berghahn Books.

Sen, A. 2004. Why We Should Preserve the Spotted Owl. *London Review of Books*, 5 February, 10–11.

Sinclair, J. 1981. *Kiap: Australia's Patrol Officers in Papua New Guinea*. Sydney: Pacific Publications.

Strathern, M. 1985. Discovering 'Social Control'. *Journal of Law and Society* 12, 111–34.

—— 1999. *Property, Substance and Effect: Anthropological Essays on Persons and Things*. London: Athlone.

Wagner, R. 1991. The Fractal Person. In M. Godelier and M. Strathern (eds) *Big Men and Great Men: Personifications of Power in Melanesia*. Cambridge: Cambridge University Press.

Part II

Persons

3 WELL-BEING: IN WHOSE OPINION, AND WHO PAYS?

Wendy James

As the chapters in this book illustrate, there is something doubly elusive about the concept of well-being: to what *other terms* can it be reduced, if any; and how can it be related to social theory or a rationale for social practice? Corsín Jiménez raises questions of the location and size of well-being, as part of the search for an approach to social theory which takes proportionality as its touchstone. Lambek points to the way that any social phenomenon – let me add as examples a family, a city, an enclave, a class or a movement or a revolution – cannot adequately be studied in isolation but must be related to its context at other levels in a hierarchy of social phenomena. Other studies here provide plenty of justification for this emphasis on the inescapable conditions of social life – that we are always dealing with relations between parts and wholes, variously defined. One way of clarifying our present discussions is to recall that some concepts relating to the social sphere, and some modes of social theorising, do aim directly at understanding better what might be the nature of the 'whole' in a given instance, before trying to account for its parts. All the classic modes of social and political theory in fact do this: utilitarianism, Marxism and Durkheimian sociology for a start. However, the question of how current soft liberal theory posits a 'social whole', as against the persons who happen to populate the immediate vicinity of an ongoing project, is a very slippery one.

It is instructive to set current notions of 'well-being' alongside related concepts with a longer lineage, for example the concept of 'welfare', which has an honoured place in classic social theory, in the history of nations and, arguably, in the key world religions (see Laidlaw, ch. 8 this volume). 'Welfare' can only be imagined, and put into practice, in the context of a very clear social whole, where responsibility can be located for the ongoing lives of persons to whom some obligation is publicly acknowledged. Decisions about funding the welfare of soldiers, of prisoners, of the unemployed, are made by those more fortunate or powerful, on behalf of society 'as a whole'. Even religious alms are provided for the needy with a view to a benefit in more valuable moral currency accruing to the donor and the religious institution as a whole. The provision of welfare is always recognisably a political matter, entailing the redistribution of resources between the 'parts' of a wider social world, on more or less consensual principles relating to need. On the other hand, 'well-being' as a concept is not geared to the needy. In contemporary usage, in practice, it is part of a gloss on the promotion of consumer interests in the enhancement of 'self'. While the rich do not 'need' welfare payouts, they are certainly spearheading the drive to promote 'well-being' – the evidence is around one all the time, through the media (editorial as well as advertising) and commerce. Walking through stores such as Sainsbury's, you will find several well-stocked shelves of luxury items displayed under the sign 'Well-Being' – supplementary foods, natural alternatives, herbal remedies and all manner of aids to the good life. Those who, over recent years, have been obliged to use special food stamps or welfare coupons to do their shopping in the UK will probably not have been able to afford this style of well-being. The difference between the concepts is particularly clear if we apply them to pets: we know what is meant by the welfare of cats and dogs, and both public projects and private charities have been set up to cater to the needs of strays. But the 'well-being' of pets is a concept appealing essentially to personal owners who can afford special individual care for their pets. 'Well-being' in this sense is difficult to regard as an obligation on the part of the wider society. A handy test is to ask how the benefits of welfare or well-being are actually funded; who pays? By and large, I think a crucial difference will be found between the public funding and the private purchase of these 'goods' or benefits.

If we look up 'well-being' on the internet, there are hundreds of entries – mostly seeking paying customers – promoting the well-being of children, cats, the psychological well-being of non-human primates, deep meditation using ancient sounds, from welfare to well-being, luxury vacation wellness spa, beauty products, well-being in pregnancy, or the elimination of stress and worry. There is an interesting entry on the US Army home page too. Well-being has strong consumer appeal; it sells products; it is big business. Welfare is not such a glossy concept; it is not big business in the consumer world, though big business is obviously interested in big contracts with the welfare providers. Welfare is not sold to consumers, but is something to be provided for others through the framework of public decision, via governments or large organisations. Its cost is set against increased productivity or some other usefulness of the investment, such as voters' support; in regular professional armies it is supposed to make for good discipline, not to fuel any burgeoning sense of private contentment with life among the soldiers. This care for the welfare of large populations *in order that they may be effective* in an economic sense, or a military sense, or useful in a political sense, runs through into our modern-day concerns for world-wide and national health programmes. The spread of AIDS in Africa is too often represented as likely to produce damaging results for the world economy, and that therefore major funding should be found for research and action to alleviate the plague. Whatever generalised action by states or organisations can be taken in this context, or in other situations of mass human tragedy and terrible loss, such as in Africa's refugee camps, falls squarely into the category of welfare. Welfare here is constituted as provision made for abstract others *by the social whole* and in its own long-term interests. However, in my view it is linguistic and moral sleight of hand to call such anonymous mass provision, with its ultimately interested rationale, the promotion of 'well-being'. The official may compose guidelines to implement aid for the urban poor, or the living conditions of students, but these are part of bureaucratic policy-making for these specific categories – the officials themselves would almost certainly not accept the same basic conditions for their own 'well-being'. The current sense of this phrase is a subjective state over and above the basic satisfaction of needs as these are perceived even by the subject him or herself. You should aim to be positively brimming with physical health, self-confidence and maximum happiness (cf. Neil Thin, ch. 7 this volume). Is this really what the authorities can provide?

There is plenty of evidence that the older sense of *welfare* is being obscured by the widespread adoption of today's user-friendly terminology of 'well-being' in administrative, charitable and humanitarian contexts. This is tending to obscure the difference between the way these terms relate to social context. A person never does (or did) speak much of their own welfare, but of the welfare of others for whom they are supposedly responsible – and these are mainly categories of people, bunches of folks within the population, whose health and fitness is measured against what they are able to contribute to the needs of society as a whole: the miners, the soldiers, the unemployed, the schoolchildren, the prisoners, the refugees, etc. There is an instrumental interest behind the provision of resources to make possible this collective kind of welfare: although today and even in the past the moral rhetoric can be laid on thickly, there is a point to giving prisoners exercise or schoolchildren proper meals. The essentially political-administrative project of ensuring the welfare of the people fits well with the utilitarian tradition, with socialism and with all political theories relation to the modern nation-state, democratic or not. It has always seemed reasonable to try to assess the standard of welfare of a population, and devise ways of measuring it; though I hate in practice to see the way that tiny starving children have to be shoved into harnesses for weighing, and stretched out on boards for measuring, before the humanitarian agencies can provide a percentage figure of the famished under-fives, along with death statistics, in their applications for emergency funding.

However, I think it is misleading for the administrative authorities to conceal the pragmatic modern, even modernist, project of welfare behind the language of the essentially subjective moral domain from which the current, possibly postmodern, usage of the idea of 'well-being' has emerged. This is a domain we can scarcely separate from spiritual and religious values (see Harper and Maddox, ch. 1 this volume, for a relevant study in Nepal). But whereas, in the old days, the church and community life might have offered that extra comfort to one's life, it has become normal in the rich world for people now to pursue independently ways of enhancing their day-to-day existence – we could very appropriately say their workaday existence, because 'well-being' is more than the level of health and fitness required by, and possibly even paid for by, your employer. It belongs to the modern sphere of leisure. Here are the spiritual retreats, the vitamin supplements, the special yoga or music classes. Mainstream social theory has never found it easy to deal with the sphere of leisure, let alone the sense of individual fulfilment which seems to be the other side of the modern demands of paid labour. As the modern industrial world has grown in its demands upon human beings, so has its counter: the elaboration of individual autonomy and the idea even of rights to emotional fulfilment, from the Romantic period onwards. In this context, we can see more clearly the importance of recognising the invasion of the territory of welfare by the desirable imagery of well-being.

There can be no doubt of the sources behind much of the desirability of current ways of enhancing one's personal 'being' very much in the phenomenological sense of 'being-in-the-world', one's stage presence almost, one's felt agency. Some of the techniques are explicitly add-on supplements to boost one's capacity; others are protective, in the manner of amulets, a sort of private insurance taken out against future hazard or even the ill disposition of others. There is a competitive aspect to it as well; you find yourself up against others in the social arena, and, with your positive feeling about yourself, and the security of full protection, you are more likely to succeed. 'Success' follows on from the attainment of well-being, in the subtexts of the consumer ads. No wonder athletes are tempted by performance-enhancing substances. And yet the satisfaction of the achievement of an outstanding Marathon depends on more than that fact itself; there is a social dimension too, one needs to gain the approbation of one's peers before a sense of well-being kicks in. Here is an aspect of *well-being in the world* which the philosophers, utilitarian or phenomenological, do not always grasp: one does not exist alone, but rather in structured 'game-like' patterns of interaction with others (see Rapport, ch. 5 this volume; and cf. James 2003). Modern well-being, no less than welfare, though in a rather different way, in this sense has a very social aspect. Well-being may today be an ideal sought by individuals, for themselves or for others they are deeply committed to, but individuals today are a distinctive phenomenon in themselves; the way they imagine their personal goals, and act upon them, has to be seen in its socio-cultural context. The way that individuals pursue their sense of well-being can even end up in direct conflict with the ideas of the state, or some organisation, about the welfare of the population as a whole: for example, in the case of vaccinations, where modern states find it difficult to impose blanket legislation because some individuals see vaccination as damaging to them personally. People in refugee camps, or armies for that matter, are not allowed to opt out of vaccination programmes, whatever their variant views on personal well-being. Clashes of this kind make it difficult to elide 'welfare' and 'well-being' as though they were the same thing; the refugee authorities, or army officials, know best, and can impose their prescriptions for the general welfare as they see fit. I shall return to the scenario of the refugee camp later.

The points I have been making so far relate to the modern world of industrial nation-states. It is in this context that we find the emergence of the twin ideas of mass welfare, and of individual well-being, a notion which I have suggested above can be linked with the Western Romantic tradition. These ideas are quite different ones, and can actually clash with each other in specific situations where the individual resists what the state considers advisable for the general good. However, while keeping the distinction clear in our minds on an analytical level, we can see that in practice the rhetoric of state health authorities and other large organisations has increasingly come to co-opt what we have to call the consumer-appeal of the idea of well-being, as if the interests of all individuals could be merged with those of the whole. This paradoxical principle is of course at the heart of the utilitarian tradition, and, perhaps because of its ambivalence, the utilitarians have great difficulty with the very notion of well-being. We can see this from our perspective in anthropology, especially since we have come to see the lives of individuals and their qualitative experiences at the heart of our studies, but always have to place our intimate portraits against the backcloth of a wider stage and the more powerful characters who walk it. Another problem with the utilitarians for us in anthropology is, of course, that they take so much for granted about the social world: their arguments presuppose broadly egalitarian social relations against the background of the modern nation-state equipped with welfare provision of some kind, broadly in circumstances of peace and prosperity, and the recognition of a degree of basic personal rights. These presuppositions are the frame, for example, within which James Griffin's elegant arguments are worked out (1986). The Third World is mentioned by Griffin only in passing, as a potential recipient of our charitable aid. Amartya Sen devotes a great deal of discussion to the developing world in general terms (for example 1999), but the political and human realities of the world beyond our shores and our own complicity in what is happening there rarely become central to his arguments.

In thinking more generally, and globally, about individual and local social well-being, we have to distance ourselves from moral philosophy's assumptions about the broadly peaceful and 'uniform' nature of social relations (and the a-historical imagining of first principles, as with Rawls on fairness and justice, 1999 [1971]). Social theory's 'limitations', to pick up part of Corsín Jiménez's discussions in the introduction, too often include a failure to recognise the conditions of opposition and conflict from which social life is inseparable. Even publicly endorsed violence has tended to be treated from on high as the implementation of reasonable punishment or the 'just war'. I have always had an interest in moral philosophy, but have found it difficult to make connections with empirical social research. In my own research in north-east Africa, whether in relation to my own or others' fieldwork, or in the investigation of documents relating to nineteenth-century history, I have had to regard the 'normal' background of people's lives as a theatre of conflict. What difference does this make to thinking about 'well-being' or 'the good life'? How would one work out some of the arguments of the moral philosophers in the context, for example, of America's Wild West in the old days? Here there was, as yet, no general peace, no state-guaranteed security over the whole region. There were locally negotiated zones where the peace of the government sheriffs held, and here we could possibly start to discuss what might constitute 'well-being'. There were also locally controlled areas where the writ of the outlaws held, but the question is a difficult one as to whether the kind of individual well-being enjoyed there, linked to the success of proud armed escapades, could be treated in the same way. This scenario helps us recognise the difficulty of identifying well-being in some politically, and therefore philosophically, neutral way. It is however much easier to point to situations in which it does not exist. The real world is by no means normally in a state of sufficient peace and stability; there may be ongoing conflicts which rule out even the possibility of a reasonable level of welfare, by 'modern' standards, let alone the individual fulfilment we associate with well-being. Many of these scenarios are partly the outcome of the spread of modern political and economic interests, and can scarcely be disentangled from their effects. It is in such contexts that the contradictions in applying ideas of well-being anywhere and everywhere become most obvious.

Before I give some examples of this, we should consider an important and very anthropological question: what can we say about welfare and well-being in socio-cultural worlds other than the modern nation-state? There is of course provision by 'traditional' authorities for the needy; there is charity; there is the network of family and neighbourhood reciprocities on which people can draw in time of difficulty. But the 'welfare' sector, if we wish to call it that, is not so easily separated from those more personal ideals and practices to which we might apply the term 'well-being'. In fact there is not the same tension between them. In the ethnographic literature on 'pre-modern' societies we can find plenty of examples of the use of techniques and substances to enhance the potency of the person, or provide protection – they are usually called 'magic'. It is very clear from the ethnographic record that in such examples the enhancement or protection of personal capacity is directed towards quite specific forms of social relations. Among the Azande, essentially a rather egalitarian social world held together by a remote political elite, you need protection against your social equals (Evans-Pritchard 1937), whereas in contexts where assumptions of human hierarchy run deep, protection may be needed against the occult powers of inferiors (Lewis 1971). In social worlds oriented to self-defence and fighting readiness, the powers of persons may be positively cultivated to meet danger and combat, as with the cult of masculine prowess among the Gisu of Uganda (Heald 1989). An important argument remains to be worked out as to how far we can equate the Western ideal of 'well-being', which is supposed to lie in the person as such, with the wider social arena in which that person is seeking agency and effectiveness.

When that wider arena is one not just of individual competition against a morally neutral (or fairly conducted) set of measures such as business or sports success, but of competition as a very specifically placed agent in a world where the background is one of actual or potential insecurity, 'well-being' as personal effectiveness becomes a highly political notion.

The crisis in Darfur in western Sudan, since the escalation of civil war there in 2003, has hit the headlines in an extraordinary way (see De Waal and Flint 2005), and like others with a Sudan connection I have been approached by the analysts and the media to make comments. What is happening in Darfur is to be understood as a fast-forward version of the decades of civil war that have plagued the south of the country. The scale of death, suffering and displacement, mainly the result of government-sponsored counter-insurgency, has led to an unprecedented outpouring of global concern for the welfare of hundreds of thousands of strangers. And yet, the closer the media and the cameras get to conditions on the ground, the more difficult it becomes to administer welfare in a fair and neutral way. In trying to get across what it is like there, I have found the Wild West analogy very helpful. The UN wants the pro-government militias disarmed; the government is not in a position to do this because it needs them to keep down the rebel groups; but the militias are likely to defend themselves if necessary, as 'outlaws' typically do. They have been recruited to lead a massive counter-insurgency in Darfur in the way that similar, or even elements of the same militias have led counter-insurgency in the south of the Sudan over two decades. In a scenario of this kind, how can authorities tell the difference between the needs of one deserving group of displaced and another, or even the civilians and the armed groups? The displaced 'civilians' are visibly in need of welfare provision; it would be a distortion of the English language for the aid agencies to speak of providing conditions for their well-being. Perhaps the 'well-being' lies elsewhere, at least temporarily, with the successful guerrilla projects, and militia leaders.

However: compare Darfur a generation ago (see Barth 1966). Farmers and herders were not permanent and separate categories, crops were grown and animals herded by everybody; there were interactions and intermarriages of Fur and Baggara; there were no hard and fast 'ethnic' lines; anthropologists could write of 'nomadism as an economic career' for all, and agriculture as a safety net for herders (Haaland 1969). As for 'well-being': here we could tease out perhaps a more anthropological way of seeing things, viewing human beings not in isolation but as deeply engaged in managing their own social relations, having schemes, projects, memories, self-reflection and so forth. The utilitarian tradition cannot really stretch to accommodate the specific forms of historical positioning of the individual in such a context: here we could look to other kinds of philosophical writing, and my own guide here has to be R.G. Collingwood (1939, 1993 [1946], 2005). Self-knowledge in the context of an awareness of the world of others, of the past and one's relation to it, and of the impetus behind one's own actions, comes into focus as a part of all our consciousness, and must surely be a part of any wider consideration of well-being.

I have argued that 'welfare' and 'well-being' are separate in their basic connotations, and in particular that it is very awkward to try and apply the latter to interests outside the immediate life of individual persons and their close circle. However, in current practice, in the common discourse of liberal politics and economics, and perhaps especially in the work of charities and overseas development agencies, the currency of 'well-being' has come to occupy the space that formerly would have been seen as welfare work. There is an element of sleight of hand here: by employing the language of *individual well-being* over and above what would be otherwise recognised as basic needs, the lack of provision for the *truly fundamental social needs*, which a political historian or social scientist would recognise, can become almost invisible. But the projects of the aid agencies have to be politically blind in order to be allowed to operate at all: and here the language of well-being, oriented to individual or specific household needs, rather than the wider whole, finds a useful niche. Funded of course by governments or charities, the practical work of the aid agencies is in fact closer to the older models of 'welfare', and of course is deeply political in its relations to donors, many of whom, in good old-fashioned ways, are keen to keep the anger of the hungry at bay. I will illustrate this briefly with reference to the Bonga refugee scheme in Ethiopia for Sudanese who fled their homes in 1987, and for whom repatriation arrangements were only just getting under way by 2006 (James 2007).

When crises first occur, with military incidents as with earthquakes, the aid agencies use the relatively straightforward terms of emergency need on the 'welfare' model. However, as happens too often, inertia sets in after emergency displacement to the point where the aid agencies turn to the more extended projects of long-term 'development', and here the language of 'well-being' does come in. I had the experience, in the year 2000, of acting as consultant on an anticipated new programme of Community Services in the western refugee camps in Ethiopia. Most of the surviving Uduk-speaking people, among whom I originally worked in the 1960s, were displaced by civil war in the late 1980s and since 1993 have been in Bonga. The UN had been designing Community Services schemes to ensure that refugees had the chance of more in life than just calories and shelter. In his foreword to the 1996 version of the manual *Community Services in UNHCR: An Introduction*, the director of the Division of Programmes and Operational Support noted that it had become recognised that emergency response in refugee situations must go beyond material relief. Whether for large groups or for individual victims of persecution, the response 'must also address their social, human and emotional needs, and help to heal psychological wounds'. The manual advocated an approach which helps people to help themselves and to help others in need, reaching and giving priority to those who need it most. Community Services activities were said to rest on certain fundamental principles about human beings, which are:

1. The dignity and worth of individual human beings.
2. The capacity of persons to change no matter how desperate their situation.
3. The inherent desire of all human beings to belong to and contribute to a larger supportive community.
4. Every person has a right to live a fully human life, and to improve his/her circumstances.
5. Persons are entitled to help when they are unable to help themselves.
6. Others have a duty to help those who are unable to help themselves.
7. The ultimate goal of Community Services is self-help. (quoted in James 2001: 29–47)

The manual outlined many ways in which these ideal goals of the 'community approach' could be pursued, in particular with respect to assisting communities to meet the needs of the vulnerable and to supporting their own initiatives for self-development.

I wrote a full report for the Dutch non-governmental organisation (NGO) ZOA Refugee Care, who expected to get the new UN budget for this work in the western refugee camps of Ethiopia (James 2000). But my own role was full of ambiguity, as the Ethiopian government opposed the UN's plan to give the budget to this small and foreign-led NGO. They already had community service projects in place and argued that they should have the new funding also. My fieldwork was hampered by the time taken up in these arguments, and I had to put up with an official government minder for the first few days (James 2001).

My report does, however, dwell at length on some of the differences between the aspirations of the refugees and the rhetoric of the UN ideals. Here, let me just mention two topics which I did not cover at the time because they were, and are, so sensitive. First, there was a consensus among all branches of the UN and NGOs, together with the Ethiopian government refugee agency, that the refugees should be persuaded to practise family limitation, that is, birth control. The refugees were totally of a different mind, arguing that as they had lost so many people in the long and repeated flights from persecution and war, they were entitled to have as many children as they pleased. A year or so after I was there, I heard that one foreign volunteer who was working with the family planning project was treated in an extraordinary way by the refugees; they simply refused to speak to her (whereas they normally have a friendly and cooperative attitude to visitors). Here was clearly a deep gulf between the welfare of the community as a whole, as seen by the authorities, and the 'well-being' of the body of the people as they saw it themselves. The second topic, which was even more sensitive, is that of the official distinction between the morally deserving and those others of whom almost nothing is said officially: the morally culpable, the men who carry arms. As everybody knows, at least in principle, the existence of refugee movements and camps implies the continuing conduct of war or preparations for war in the medium distance. In Bonga, as would have happened in any other such community in the world, the morale (and sense of well-being?) of the refugees markedly improved between my visits of 1994 and 2000: and I am quite sure that the basic reason for this was that, on the first occasion, their homeland across the frontier was in the hands of the Sudanese government soldiers, whereas it had been taken by the SPLA in 1997 and was still in their hands in 2000 (and indeed up to peace agreement of 2005). That year, there were lads singing about recent victories and bringing down planes; they hedged when I asked if they had been there themselves, but clearly they knew people who had.

How can we properly speak about 'well-being', of a community or individuals in it, when those people have had their lands, livelihood and many of their relatives lost to war and flight? At the same time, there is great uncertainty after 17 years whether the return from Bonga, which started in 2006, will secure rights to land and resources, let alone the relative personal freedoms of the 'traditional' way of life within the Blue Nile State, newly set up as a regional unit to handle complex issues of citizenship within this marginal part of the Sudan. I have already argued in print that the language of 'empowerment' in such circumstances, for example by putting women on committees in refugee camps, is false coinage (James 1998). Here I have made some similar comments with respect to 'well-being'. The displacements caused by Sudan's civil wars were once compared to me (in 1988) by Mark Duffield, then in charge of Oxfam's programme in the Sudan, with the Scottish clearances. He did not see that things could ever return to the previous state; the only chance would be one day for the displaced to return as labour on large agricultural schemes. At the time I could not believe this would be true, but now I see that he was probably justified in what he said (Duffield 2001). Those people who may return one day, and this category now includes the hundreds of thousands, possibly more than a million, displaced from their homes in Darfur, will be in desperate need of welfare provision, in the modern sense, and funded by modern means. Whether a time will return for talk about 'well-being' is very problematic. The discourse of 'human rights' is more obviously applicable and relevant in stark situations of this kind, and of course is more transparently political and connected to a version of social theory. Indeed, without 'rights', which by definition have to be guaranteed by some kind of 'social whole', is it reasonable to speak at all of the possibility of well-being?

REFERENCES

Barth, F. 1966. Economic Spheres in Darfur. In R. Firth (ed.) *Themes in Economic Anthropology*. London: Tavistock.
Collingwood, R.G. 1939. *An Autobiography*. Oxford: Clarendon Press.
―― 1993 [1946]. *The Idea of History*, rev. edn. Oxford: Clarendon Press.
―― 2005. *The Philosophy of Enchantment: Studies in Folktale, Cultural Criticism, and Anthropology*. Eds D. Boucher, W. James and P. Smallwood. Oxford: Clarendon Press.

De Waal, A. and J. Flint. 2005. *Darfur: A Short History of a Long War*. London/New York: Zed Books.

Duffield, M. 2001. *Global Governance and the New Wars: The Merging of Development and Security*. London/New York: Zed Books.

Evans-Pritchard, E.E. 1937. *Witchcraft, Oracles and Magic among the Azande*. Oxford: Clarendon Press.

Griffin, J. 1986. *Well-being: Its Meaning, Measurement and Moral Importance*. Oxford: Clarendon Press.

Haaland, G. 1969. Fur and Baggara. In F. Barth (ed.) *Ethnic Groups and Boundaries: The Social Organization of Culture Difference*. London: Allen & Unwin.

Heald, S. 1989. *Controlling Anger: The Anthropology of Violence among the Gisu*. Oxford: James Currey.

James, W. 1998. Empowering Ambiguities. In A. Cheater (ed.) *The Anthropology of Power: Empowerment and Disempowerment in Changing Structures*, ASA Monographs 36. London: Routledge.

—— 2000. 'Community Services for Sudanese Refugees in Western Ethiopia: Working Proposals for Bonga and Sherkole'. Unpublished report. Netherlands/Addis Ababa: ZOA Refugee Care.

—— 2001. 'People-friendly' Projects and Practical Realities: Some Contradictions on the Sudan–Ethiopian border. In M.-B. Johannsen and N. Kastfelt (eds) *Sudanese Society in the Context of Civil War*. Copenhagen: University of Copenhagen North/South Priority Research Area, Centre of African Studies.

—— 2003. *The Ceremonial Animal: A New Portrait of Anthropology*. Oxford: Oxford University Press.

—— 2007. *War and Survival in Sudan's Frontierlands: Voices from the Blue Nile*. Oxford: Oxford University Press.

Lewis, I.M. 1971. *Ecstatic Religion: An Anthropological Study of Spirit-possession and Shamanism*. Harmondsworth: Penguin.

Rawls, J. 1999 [1971]. *A Theory of Justice*, rev. edn. Cambridge, MA: The Belknap Press of Harvard University Press.

Sen, A.K. 1999. *Development as Freedom*. Oxford: Clarendon Press.

UNHCR. 1996. Community Services in UNHCR: An Introduction. Unpublished report. Geneva: UNHCR.

4 PRIMED FOR WELL-BEING? YOUNG PEOPLE, DIABETES AND INSULIN PUMPS

Griet Scheldeman

Diabetes is, to use the phrase with which young people describe it, 'when your pancreas does not work'. 'Not working' here is not producing insulin to take up sugar in the blood stream. This means you have to administer insulin to your body. The standard way do this is through injections, with syringes or pens. At set moments of the day (two to five times or more) you inject a certain amount of insulin to cover the food and activity up till the next injection. Concretely this means that before breakfast you need to know what you will be eating and doing until lunch. A fairly new method to administer insulin is the insulin pump. This technological device, continuously worn on the body, injects every three minutes a small amount of insulin. By pushing buttons you can add extra insulin on the spot, every time you eat. The difference from injections is twofold: first, the continuous insulin flow imitates closely the workings of a pancreas: keeping the blood sugar levels stable has significant health benefits. By freeing the user from injections of set doses at set times, and thus allowing flexibility and spontaneity, the pump also improves quality of life.

This chapter is about young people with diabetes. The scope of their well-being is vast: it includes medicine, physiology, biology, chemistry, psychology. Since the discovery of insulin, almost 100 years ago, a plethora of biophysical and human sciences have been working towards improving their well-being, their health. Thus here I will not talk about that. I will not talk about what science and clinical and psychological research have discovered about how to improve the well-being of people with diabetes. Instead I will talk about the youngsters themselves. How do they aim to improve their well-being?

The young people in question are teenagers (age 11–17) with diabetes who are treated at an outpatient paediatric diabetes centre at a large state-funded teaching hospital in Millness city, Scotland.[1] For one year I conducted fieldwork at this centre, observing clinic consultations, interviewing health carers and following some patients to their homes and families. Throughout, my main research question was: how do young people in Millness live (life with) diabetes? Not only how *do* they do it but, probing at the diverse shaping – both limiting and enabling – factors, how *can* they do it? In other words, how is diabetes in Millness made into a certain illness by specific social, cultural and relational circumstances (Scheldeman 2006)?

Ten young patients participated in a pilot insulin pump project. In this chapter I introduce you to three of them, each with their own 'existential dynamics' of life with diabetes and an insulin pump. These young people live for today, their focus is on quality of life (today) rather than health (present and future). As they do not have a ready reflexive narrative on their chronic illness, I will start from their embodied experience and focus on how they 'do' diabetes and the pump. Consequently, throughout what follows I will take well-being as 'what it means for life to go well' (Parfit 1984; Weale 1998), with life as a 'bundle of doings and beings' (Sen 1993: 31).[2] Specifically, I will look at how teenagers Callum, John and Sara aim to 'better' their being through a technological device, the insulin pump.

'DOING' DIABETES: YOUNG PEOPLE

However ... finding out about young people's experiences with diabetes and the pump is not easy. Familiar with the pump, they find that 'there's nothing to say', as Callum puts it: 'I have a pump, it works.' Hence my focus on 'doing' diabetes: what happens, how does the pump work? A focus which in turn shaped my methodology. Both out of appropriateness – no point in standing outside with reflective analysis, as this is not what the people involved do – but also out of necessity. How to get (in)to this action? I resolve to observe everyday life and interactions, and for a few days I wear a pump – merely to get to the mechanics and practicalities, a possible topic of conversation and shared experience.[3]

In order to understand the experience of young people on a pump, I resolve to start from their embodiment. Anthropologist Thomas Csordas defines embodiment as 'an existential condition in which the body is the subjective source or intersubjective ground of experience' (2000: 181). I combine Csordas's interpretation of embodiment as a methodological attitude demanding attention to bodiliness, with the notion of 'bodily subjectivity' put forward by another phenomenological anthropologist, Michael Jackson.[4] For with embodiment I also mean the fact that we live in and through a body. We engage with the world by grace of our body.

For young people with diabetes, this embodiment can be problematic, as they are twice confronted with their body: by puberty and by diabetes. While puberty changes the way their body looks and works, diabetes means that one organ, the pancreas, goes its own way. In other words, their body, as they knew it, falls apart. Their diabetic body not only makes them *feel* hyper or lethargic, it also *demands action* from them: they have to do what so far happened automatically: administer insulin. Moments when our body confronts us are not usual. Usually, when all goes well, we can take our body for granted. Our body recedes in the background. I borrow here philosopher-cum-medical doctor Drew Leder's concept of *the tacit body*. He posits that our body necessarily operates in a tacit fashion. When all goes well, the body disappears. 'As I gaze upon the world, I cannot see my own eyes' (Leder 1990: 113). In moments of illness, the body forcefully appears (in Leder's terms, it 'dys-appears': appears in a negative, interrupting way) and cannot be ignored. It demands attention. It demands the interpretation, control, intervention of a conscious I. At those moments we wrestle with our embodiment.

How does this wrestling with embodiment translate concretely? As I approach life as a 'bundle of doings and beings', I also look at embodiment through an action lens: what does living with (a body that has) diabetes mean young people have to do and cannot do and be? During my research it soon became apparent that in Millness being an adolescent and having diabetes were seen – and actively portrayed – as incommensurable. I was often told by adults, both diabetes health carers and parents, that adolescents 'wanted to be adolescents'. This meant they wanted to be free to do what they wanted, be spontaneous, act on the spur of the moment, do as their friends did, and they certainly did not want to be told what to do. Unfortunately, as the diabetes nurses phrased it, 'diabetes is all about being told what to do'. There are management routines to be followed: insulin injections (three or more a day), blood tests (four a day), a diet and schedule to be adhered to, activities and food to be planned ahead. Diabetes interferes with the adolescents' lives. The best thing would be not to have it – they are often reminded of that by the health carers saying to them: 'I wish I could wave my magic wand and make it go away' – as this is, so far, impossible – the next best thing is not to have to think about it and not having to act on it.

And here comes the insulin pump. It is used to achieve exactly this. The pump gives back to young people what diabetes took away. It gives back their freedom, by taking their minds off diabetes and by putting them in control again. In control not necessarily of diabetes, but of their lives. With a pump, adolescents can be adolescents again.

How does it work? The young people in Millness enact the pump in such a way that it stops diabetes interfering with their lives. They are in a situation to do this. Unlike young people in other centres, where the new treatment comes with guidelines and strict conditions of usage imposed by the health carers, in Millness, as it was a pilot project, the young people were introduced to the pump in a three-hour session, and then left to explore and use it on their own, with help from a pump nurse in case of questions or problems. As diabetes interferes in people's lives in different ways, how to stop this interference also differs. Three scenarios show different enactment by different actors, bodies, diabeteses, pumps and contexts in play. The stories of Callum, John and Sara.

Callum

So I told him, I said 'We have to make economies', and I said 'Callum we're going to get rid of ...' and I was going to say his separate phone line, but his face was stricken and [she pulls her hand down over her face] he went quiet and pale and he said: 'The pump?' And I said, 'No, kid, I would never take away the pump.'

Callum's mum is telling me how her son is so much happier with the pump. 'He has said to me it has made such a difference to his life, that he doesn't have to be regimented about his life, he just does beep-beep-beep.' Callum is 15, was diagnosed with diabetes when he was nine. He lives with his mum, his dad left when he was one. Callum is into technology. He loves gadgets. His room looks like an office, it is very connected and filled with beeping noises; from his swivel chair he operates several remote controls, the stereo, the TV – now he is considering a remote to operate his pump. He spends his days surfing the web and hanging around with his few good friends. When I ask Callum what diabetes means to him, both practically and as to who he is, his answers quickly switch to: 'but now with the pump ...', dividing his life with diabetes (six years) into 'before' (five years) and 'with' the pump (one year). For example, when I ask what diabetes means he has to do, he replies: 'I have to remember to inject, do blood sugars, remember to eat something, but now with the pump ...' He tells me his 'goody two shoes' friend Ben takes care of him. 'We go back a long way. He tells me when to eat sugar, goes and gets it for me, "Have some sugar" – "Naaaahhhh" – "Come on, have sugar." But now with the pump ...' I ask if diabetes is a big part of his identity:

No, not really. Especially now with the pump, sometimes I've known people for weeks and then I'd say 'I just have to give my insulin', and they'd go, 'Oh, you have diabetes, I didn't know.' Like before the pump, I went out with friends in Millness and at night I had to go home because I had forgotten my pens.

The insulin pump has changed what diabetes means to Callum. Both what diabetes implied in the type of medical routines he had to follow, and the restrictions it put on his everyday life. Food and being relaxed matter significantly to Callum. 'Now, with the pump', he says, he can eat and do what he wants. This new treatment has changed not only his diabetes management but his life. When asked whether the pump means more work he states that actually with the pump it is a lot easier. 'You don't have to do nearly as much once you got the canula in, you don't need to do anything.... I really don't understand why some people say the pump is much work, the pump does it all for you.' Yet, his casualness may be misleading. While he says he doesn't need to do anything with the pump, he does a lot. The difference is that what he does, he doesn't see as a chore, or even as doing something, because he does it automatically, it has become second nature to him. What he does not find worth telling, but does several times every day is: count the carbohydrates in what he eats, guess an appropriate insulin dose to cover this carbohydrate intake, administer the insulin to his body. He does this every time he has a meal or even a snack, which must be often, knowing how much he likes food and likes to eat when he is bored, which is all the time. Let's say this is around eight times a day or more. Compare this with the three injections he took each day. The dose was fixed by the health carer, the time was fixed, he only needed to twist the end of his insulin pen to get the correct dose, put the pen in his body, let the insulin get through, and that's it. This would take three short moments of his day, at fixed times. Merely fulfilling the procedure, no thinking, no calculating. With the pump, every time he eats something, he has to think to count the carbohydrates involved, has to think how many units of insulin are needed to cover this and has to 'bleep' to give the correct dose. Remembering, counting and converting, all this happens quickly in his head and he doesn't even think about it. The 'bleeping' he does by pushing the buttons on the pump in his pocket, he doesn't take it out, he just counts the bleeps. The pump is an extremely low-impact means of delivering insulin. The pump puts Callum in charge. He decides what and when (insulin to give, to eat, to do other things). He doesn't have to stick to routines any more. He doesn't have to remember to inject, to test blood sugars, to eat something. He does not have to remember, but he performs the same routines, yet he does them automatically, reacting to one of his actions and cravings (eating, feeling not well). For Callum, then, these are not routines. What he minds about routines is the fixedness in time and the additional schedule to fit into lifestyle which traditional fixed injections imply. The pump makes things easier, he does not have to remember and think any more to take his insulin pens with him. Callum does not like to have to remember. He is good at forgetting. Callum also does not like to have to take things. He forgets and loses them. He does not want to have to take a bag. He carries everything in his trouser pockets, which are heavy with keys, personal stereo, mobile and now also the pump. Callum's quality of life has improved greatly. His experience with the pump is a success story. Diabetes does not keep him from doing anything.

And his health? From a health perspective, things look different. Before the pump Callum was a strict and conscientious manager of his diabetes. He would test his blood sugars five times a day, note the results in his diary, take injections on time and stick to fixed meal times. He had strict blood sugar control. On the pump all this changed. Callum noticed the pump did a lot for him, and he decided to use the pump to his advantage. He started to eat all day, he blew up like a balloon, he quit doing blood tests, kept no diary. His blood sugars rose, his control was less tight. Had he continued to manage his diabetes with the pump as conscientiously as he did before the pump, his blood sugars would be almost non-diabetes-like, and he would have a good chance of avoiding complications later in life. But he lives for today. Today the pump allows him to eat ten donuts if he wants to. He feels in charge of his life, does what he wants and is happy.

John

Like Callum, John was a strict manager before the pump: four blood tests a day, keeping a diary, excellent control. Like Callum, once on the pump, John discovered the freedom of life before diabetes, and quit management:

Primed for Well-Being?

no more testing, no diet. Unlike Callum, this did not work for John, for several reasons. One was his mum, another was his body, another was the pump; in fact, they were all linked together. John is 15, has had diabetes since he was six. He lives with his mum, a biomedical researcher, and her partner. Mum is very involved in John's diabetes. John was a model patient: good tester, strict control. When he started to use a pump things changed. John gave up his diabetes management routines. He savoured the 'freedom' offered by the pump. He describes his pump thus:

> It's part of me. It helped me a lot. It made me feel more free about diabetes. I could do what I wanted when I wanted. On injections I felt stuck. I felt stuck for having to eat a massive breakfast, a full-size lunch and a big dinner.

With the pump John could finally eat a little, or even nothing, according to what he felt like, hungry or not. 'The pump makes me forget more about diabetes. Like I still remembered I had diabetes but it helped.' The freedom John talks about is to have to think less about diabetes. It is also having to do less. He stops doing blood tests: 'I wanted to test less 'cause the whole thing about the pump is freedom, it's a big change.' This freedom eventually became a poisoned gift.

> My blood sugars were getting higher. I wasn't testing as much, which I now know was a large mistake. I was feeling iffy, had more peaks ... it was my fault 'cause I wasn't testing as much. Then it started to bother me. I got sent home from school often for having problems with the pump, like infusion sets were coming out, insulin would run out. ... It was lack of maintenance, it was just there, I neglected it. ... Then it was getting too much with infusion sets, I got scars. I had pain where they were, I didn't have enough place to change around. I also left the set in for too long, four to five days. By that time all had become too much.

His dad said: 'It was the only thing we were talking about here. It was dominating everything.' And his mum added:

> John started to look like he had this big weight on his shoulders, a big responsibility. He would sit there on the sofa, head down and just like waiting to get it, the criticisms, and then he just said, 'That's it mum', and we phoned the nurse and told her John wanted to go back to injections.

Since John has been back on injections his blood sugars have gone down. He is testing again.

While the pump made strict managers Callum and John want to do less diabetes management, with Sara the opposite happened. Having given up on diabetes management before the pump, through the pump she started to take diabetes seriously.

Sara

'Before the pump, diabetes was a negative thing, all bad, something I was lumbered with. Now, it is something that must be overcome.'

Sara is 15 and lives with her elder brother and mum and dad. Her passion is music; she plays the piano and cello and sings folk songs. A clever and headstrong girl, she'll often say she does not believe in doing things she's not convinced of, so she'll just not do them unless she sees the point. She lives her life by her own rules. Consequently life is not always easy. She struggles to live life according to her convictions, at school with her teachers, at home with her parents, in the clinic with the health carers, who would often call her 'difficult'. Sara was diagnosed with diabetes when she was 12. Unlike Callum and John, she was not a good manager of her diabetes. She had given up, did not test and even did not take insulin anymore. She says injections did not work for her, she felt bad and consequently got discouraged. 'I probably made it worse, 'cause I wasn't bothered. I was eating the wrong things, forgetting to take my insulin. Nothing was working so why bother? ... I had given up; I didn't want anything to do with diabetes.' Since things could not get worse, Sara was offered the chance of trying a pump. As Sara was not interested at all, her mum had to take control of the pump for the first weeks. Sara refused to do anything with it. Today Sara has forgotten this start, because the pump made a sea change in her diabetes. She noticed the effect of getting insulin in her body, she started to feel better and, consequently, after three years of ignoring diabetes, she took up diabetes management. I ask her how the pump was for her:

At first I was reading all food packets religiously, the nutrition information on the back, but I got the hang of it quite quickly. I look at what I'm eating and I guess how much I need to add and I usually get it close. Now my blood sugars have come down and I feel better.

Sara's main aim is to feel better.

When my blood sugars are high, I can't move, my vision is blurred, I couldn't read books, which I do a lot, I couldn't sight-read the music, when playing the piano. I just wanted to be able to play with my neighbour's children without being exhausted and see what the teachers wrote on the blackboard. ... I concentrate on doing the right thing, before I was bingeing on the wrong food, now I eat more sensibly. I've looked at alternatives, at healthy things, so I eat fruit and sandwiches. I still eat chocolate but less.

How come this change? 'I think the change ... the insulin made the start, then I felt I was better and I began to eat more sensibly.' She had a reason not to binge any more, she felt the difference. From then on, once she noticed how good she could feel, she took up diabetes management: mainly by bolusing and by eating fewer sugary things and chocolates than before. It meant a sea change in her 'doing' diabetes. The pump is her friend; she puts it on the piano when she is playing. In case the cartridge runs out at night, she has a full one on her bedside table, so when the pump alarm goes off (meaning empty cartridge) she puts in another one and it's fine. 'I sleep through everything else, but this wakes me up.'

On injections, Sara felt she had no control over her diabetes or life; she had given up, nothing worked, why bother. The pump gave her agency in her diabetes and thus in her life. It made her feel better and finally she could see the effects of her own actions.

Well-being: A matter of control?

John's mum sums up the pump as follows:

> The main issue with the pump is that we felt we had no control any more. Before the pump, John had good control, we knew what was going on; on the pump, after a while his blood sugars started going up and things happened and we had no control.

An appropriate way to analyse these different scenarios is to use Michael Jackson's (2002) suggestions for a phenomenology of the relation human–machine, in which he sees the intersubjective dynamics between human and machine (like our other intersubjective relations) as pivoting on a balance of control. We seesaw between what we can control of our own fate through technology and what not. Jackson states that our sense of being similar to or different from a machine is a function of how we interact with it, concretely: when our sense of control (our sense of self, our identity) diminishes, our need for boundaries between us and the machine increases. At the base of this lies Jackson's existential thesis that 'all human beings need to have a hand in choosing their lives and to be recognized as having an active part to play in the shaping of their social worlds' (2002: 333). Already in the stories of Callum, John and Sara I have made clear how this aspect of control works, and not control over diabetes but control over the place of diabetes in life.

Though Sara took up diabetes management through the pump, so she could do more of what she wants (read, focus), she is an exception. Most young people in Millness stop working on diabetes with the pump. While never very dedicated to elaborate management routines – and here Callum and John were exceptions – for the young patients the pump was an opportunity to do even less. This is puzzling, since the pump offered the opportunity to achieve good blood sugar control (and thus better health later in life). How come the young people did not take this chance? Because they did not see it as one, health not being their major goal. What matters to them is that they can do as they want now, their quality of life today. Thus with the pump they manage less, as they see that this is what the pump is for. In their words: 'Since the pump is there to take your mind off diabetes' and 'I wanted to test less, 'cause the whole point about the pump is freedom.'

A sense of control, more precisely control over identity and self, is paramount to their well-being. This has become apparent in how young people aim for better-being through the pump. The youngsters use the pump to do more what they want to do, to be themselves and not ruled by diabetes management. With the pump they can put diabetes in a box: tangible, visible, confined to a small place. It stops interfering with life.

Well-being: A matter of relations?

There is more. I would like to approach well-being from a wider angle and shift the emphasis from 'control' to 'relations' other than those of control. Can I say (paraphrasing Jackson) that well-being is, amongst other things, a function of relations? I would be tempted to say a function of the relations of self with other, with 'other' understood as body, parents, a piece of technology, friends, etc., but this holds the risk of seeing self as standing on its own, while it is self only by grace of and in continuous relations with other. My reason for stressing relations is two-fold.

One is to draw attention to other relations constitutive of our identity and sense of well-being, like sharing, caring, giving and respecting, which might be lost sight of when focusing on control. Concretely, Callum's well-being as his feeling of control over his identity (he does what he wants) is not worth much if he does not have a caring mother or doctor who keep in mind his well-being of the future, and thus remind him to do certain things now so as to be healthy later. While this is an essential aspect of well-being, especially when talking about young people and a long life ahead, in the limited space of this chapter I will merely briefly touch upon this towards the end, when I discuss the broader social and health care context in which the young people enact their pump. For the moment I expand on the second reason. Merely looking at Callum's interaction with the pump there are more relations at play than Callum's control over his identity. I like to draw attention to the rich gamut of 'actors' at play in any given event or moment, which again may be overlooked by focusing on the sense of control of (and by) oneself. The pump is enacted, not only by its users but by a combination of actors and contexts. This performance changes continuously, as all actors change. Here I take inspiration from the technology-in-action approach of those science and technology scholars who stress 'performativity' and 'enactment'.[5] These authors stress the plethora of aspects involved in any action and remind us to refocus our lenses to see what is at play. While an analysis of the scenarios in these terms would be overambitious, let me attempt a quick taster to offer a different, more multidimensional story.

The stories of Callum, John and Sara show how technology is enacted in different ways. Though their goal was similar: better-being, namely, less interference of diabetes in daily life, the way this was achieved – or not, in John's case – differs. Because the entities involved differ. Callum, John and Sara are different people, with different bodies, different diabetes, different parents, different friends, different ways of life, different histories and different aims.

Callum has always managed his diabetes himself and his mum accepts this and says it is Callum's diabetes. Callum has himself, his body, his pump and his friends to deal with. His friends think his pump is cool, that's easy. His body is not allergic to the plasters, does not bruise at the insertion site. The pump works well, does not play up and is happy being ignored by Callum for

Primed for Well-Being? 89

most of the time. Callum himself is comfortable with technology, both with operating and wearing it, no issues there.

John has always managed his diabetes together with his mum. The pump, John's body and his mum do not combine well. John's body does not agree with the pump, the insertion sites become infected and bruised. The pump does not behave well: there is always a technical hitch. Mum and the pump do not agree: mum feels she has lost control; before the pump she knew exactly what was happening, now she continuously fears the next hitch. The pump has taken John's diabetes out of her hands.

Sara did not manage her diabetes. She did not let her mum tell her what to do. Sara hated her body as it did not do what it should. While headstrong Sara wanted to rely solely on herself, she could not rely on her body. The pump changed this. It connected Sara to her body. The pump functioned well, the body reacted well; Sara could act on her body, manage her diabetes and could be independent from her mum.

We have seen how John quit the pump because 'things were out of control' (his body, the pump, his management, his mum). It is easy to show what goes wrong to explain why something did not work out. However, locating what went wrong will never give us the full picture of all that needs to go right for something to work. Like the tacit body that recedes in the background when all works well, when things work, they are taken for granted.

But how come the pump works? What does it take for the pump to work well, which in this context means, to improve the young people's well-being, concretely to have diabetes interfere less? I suggest that the pump works by changing the way the young people embody diabetes. I could say that the pump can make a different diabetes.

I return to Jackson's intersubjective dynamics of the human relation with technology. He distinguishes between complementary relations – when a machine works well, we can identify with it – and antagonistic relations – when a machine starts to malfunction, we feel the need to stress the difference, the fact that it is a machine. I look at the complementary relations of, for example, Callum and Sara with the pump, to find out what actually happens.

The young people on a pump make a distinction between their life before the pump and with the pump. Life with the pump is almost like life before diabetes. The difference comes down to being free again.

How does it work? Diabetes in a box

How can they forget about diabetes, what freedom do they mean, with this machine that is always there, as a visible and tangible reminder? The answer is simple: exactly because it is always there you can forget about it. I explain.

I check with Sara. What's this freedom with a pump, it's always there? 'Exactly, it's always there. It helps you with your diabetes.' I ask Callum the same question and he replies: 'Indeed, so you don't have to think to take insulin and pens with you.' Concretely, life on injections: dreading the moment you know you will hurt yourself, then slowly pushing in the needle, inflicting lumps and bruises in the process, feeling like a pincushion, and repeating the whole process in three hours' time. Also, always remembering to take your extra bag with pens and insulin with you, a matter of life and death. Life on the pump: inserting the canula once and you can forget about it for the next three days; any time you need some insulin, you put your hand in your trouser pocket and push the buttons: an unobtrusive gesture, no pain, no fear, like adjusting the volume on your minidisc player.

Compared to the continuous physical reminder of painful injections, the pump is merely there, on you, doing things in a non-invasive way. It does things (gives insulin every three minutes) so you don't have to do them, you can forget. It operates in a non-invasive way (no pain, no interruption of activities) so you can forget. It is on you, so you don't have to remember to take insulin or pens with you: you can forget. The pump becomes a companion, is not 'a machine' any more; the young people have a personal bond with it, something they did not have with injections. Sara calls the pump her friend: 'It helps me. The pump is me too, it's my soulmate.' William, another 15-year-old also happy on the pump, says: 'My friend says I'm a robot, he's full of poo. I find it annoying, I don't like the idea of being attached to a machine 24 hours a day.' How would William describe it then? 'It's like it's there, but it isn't. It's just a circuit board with some plastic case. It's more a gadget that helps me with my diabetes.'

When the pump works, it recedes and with it the diabetes can momentarily blend into the background; if the machine works in a tacit mode, diabetes is present too in a tacit mode. Diabetes on injections means a continuous confrontation with the body: both the body and diabetes demanded attention, the intervention of a conscious I. Thus on a pump the young people embody diabetes in a different way. From a physical, since painful illness, diabetes, as it is lived, has become a more mental thing: forgetting, remembering, thinking. Diabetes is no longer all over the body/place. It is confined to a box.

'DOING' DIABETES (BIS): HEALTH CARERS

So far I have described how young people with diabetes wrestle with their embodiment and how they enact an external technological device to ease this wrestling and to achieve better-being. This is only half the story. Half the story about how this enactment takes place and half the story of well-being. For this enactment as it happens in Millness is unique and differs significantly from the enactment of insulin pumps in other diabetes centres and other countries. In what follows I briefly sketch the local context of this enactment: how the Millness health carers approach adolescents and diabetes treatment. I also mention health, a major part of well-being, especially in a medical setting – so far as absent from this chapter as it seems to be from the young people's minds.

Primed for Well-Being?

The centre where the present research took place featured at the bottom of the league in an international comparative study: the blood sugar levels of their young patients were significantly higher than in other centres. When health carers from centres with 'good' results (that is tight blood sugar control) confronted their Millness colleagues with their centre's 'bad' results – both in the US and Europe this fact was 'famous' – their standard reply was: 'But our quality of life results are the best.' To which, more than once, I heard the critical colleagues respond along the lines of: 'What quality of life? When they go blind and lose a leg when they're 20?'

The health carers in the paediatric diabetes centre in Millness claim to know what adolescents are like and what they want. From this platform they enact the adolescents' well-being.

So what are young people like? The professional discourse on adolescents in Scottish society today aims to 'empower' adolescents at an early age (at the age of 12) by emphasising their autonomy and rights, instead of subjecting them to authority and stressing their duties. Add to this the social situation of the city of Millness, characterised by financial hardship, third-generation unemployment, teenage pregnancies, violence, broken families, unhealthy diets, and the picture becomes rather grim and complex. It means that the well-being of adolescents in Millness is an issue. It also means that often there are no loving parents around who have the time to care for and guide their child in its quest towards adulthood. The young people are indeed 'independent', but without a safe place in which to experiment through trial and error, without a safe time zone in which to grow towards being an autonomous person, able to make informed choices and decisions. No time or place to practise, it is for real. They live and act in the here-and-now, with full consequences for the rest of their lives. For example, having a baby at the age of 14, taking drugs at 15, dropping out of school at 16. The problem is not that they live in the here-and-now, the problem is that there is no one around to keep in mind their future. For example, when they have diabetes.

The paediatric diabetes team in Millness understands that adolescents want to be free and do as their peers do. Diabetes, both the illness and its treatment, puts a spanner in the works. Being an adolescent clashes with (having and managing) diabetes. Diabetes is a chronic illness and what you do (or omit to do) now has implications for later. Since adolescents live now – as is often stressed by the adults – the adults take care of their future (concretely by making the adolescents act now in a way that safeguards the future). Or do they? Not really. How come?

Life in Millness is such that, for many young patients, diabetes 'is a mere detail' in their lives, the least of their worries. Growing up in Millness is such that parents often have no time or interest to give advice and support. If life for young people is difficult, diabetes makes it even harder. The diabetes team in Millness has made a conscious choice in its care approach to adolescent patients. This choice was based on experience, a strict approach scared adolescents away and they were lost to diabetes care all together. So it was judged a better option merely to keep them on board and hope they would get through adolescence without too much damage. The choice was also based on a specific philosophy of care, it was called a 'holistic' approach: a concern with the whole person, not just the biophysical body. Thus the health carers, with the emphasis on 'carer', provided support, a listening ear and understanding. The physical body was put on the back-burner.

In consultations and interviews with health carers, patients and their parents, 'health' is barely mentioned – quite puzzling in a medical context – all talk centring on the new buzz word: quality of life.[6] Both patients and parents appreciated the health carers' concern with quality of life: these doctors and nurses understood *what it was like* to live with diabetes, they would not present them with any difficult or unreasonable demands with regard to managing it. While patients and parents took on the concept, they did not adopt the term (cf. Rapport, ch. 5 this volume). Instead they spoke about 'being happy', 'living their lives' and 'being kids'. Concretely, the concern with the young people's quality of life focused on their 'doings and beings'. Could they do what they wanted? Could they be spontaneous adolescents? A standard question the head diabetologist asked his young patients in clinic was: 'Does diabetes keep you from doing anything?' If answered affirmatively, several solutions would be suggested, the motto being (an often-heard slogan in the diabetes world): 'It's about fitting diabetes into your life, not your life around diabetes.' Intensive management, which meant doing four blood tests a day, carrying a test kit with you at all times, keeping a diary with the results and deciding on which insulin dose was needed on the base of the test curves, was not an option. Young people would not do it and it would make diabetes more of a burden. Hence the high blood sugar results in the international comparative study. Hence the standard and proud reply: 'But our quality of life results are the best.'

TO CONCLUDE

Michael Lambek starts his chapter in this volume with the question of whether well-being is not always 'at least the implicit subject of our work'. I would answer with an unqualified yes. The well-being of the young people in Millness was the leading thread running through my PhD research. As mentioned before, their well-being is shaped by physical and mental health, family, relationships, health care and the wider social and cultural situation they live in, and is thus vastly more complex than described here. Nevertheless in this chapter I chose to talk about one aspect of it: how young people actively pursue their own – what they perceive it to be – well-being. (Not unlike Rapport, this volume, who describes how the hospital porters moved in and around the hospital in their own ways, 'in ways they had determined to be the best for themselves'.) In the introduction to this volume Corsín Jiménez reminds us how every theory of well-being (and I may add every morality) carries a social theory within. Indeed, I opted for this approach as it accommodated the concept of the person I wished to celebrate. Writing as an anthropologist on the topic of well-being, I feel it is crucial to see and portray people as creative and sense-making beings, as produced in and through their acts and practices (see Lambek, ch. 6 this volume; Corsín Jiménez, ch. 9 this volume), in short, as both embodied (with active bodies, skills, desires, emotions) and embedded (in practices, in concrete social and cultural situations) selves. By showing people as creative beings always already in context (Rapport's 'elucidating well-being for particular individuals in particular moments and moods' [this volume]), ethnographers can perhaps alert political, economic or philosophical discussants of well-being of the dangers of abstraction.

So much for how I feel anthropologists can write *about* well-being.

But can (or should) we also write *for* well-being? Can we advocate well-being, or should our writing be limited to describing and interpreting life as we observe it? I illustrate with the young people in Millness. My choice to focus on their own creative pursuing of well-being was a difficult one, as it meant leaving the broader picture (their health, their future lives) out of the equation. Though a surprising route when talking about life with a chronic illness I explained my reasons for doing so above. Had I not chosen to foreground the active, creative person, I may have dismissed the young people's relaxed attitude to the insulin pump merely as them 'misusing' the pump. While I admired the young people for their creative engagement, I was also worried. I knew that here they had a technical device that could greatly help them to significantly improve their health (as well as their temporary quality of life) yet they did not use it for that. In his first claim for an anthropological perspective on well-being, Michael Lambek (this volume) rightly reminds us how 'quality of life cannot be simply open freedom of choice. Well-being must include guides in the making of choices.' While freedom is important, good health definitely is too. Is it wrong for me to make a value judgement, or, on the contrary, can we, as anthropologists, write about well-being without being engaged? Would neutrality not be masked negligence? In practice, could we take (writing about) well-being – I refer back to the start of this chapter – not only as (writing about) 'what it means for life to go well', but rather as 'what it would mean for life to go better'? This brings us back to Lambek's warning (this volume) of the possible hubris associated with the subject of well-being.

ACKNOWLEDGEMENTS

The PhD research on which this chapter draws was made possible by a research grant from Disetronic Medical Systems, the insulin pump manufacturer which also funded the pilot pump project at the paediatric diabetes centre in Millness. I am grateful to the young people who shared their pump stories with me, and to the welcoming diabetes team at Millness Hospital. I also wish to thank Alberto Corsín Jiménez for inviting me to take part in the well-being symposium at the University of Manchester.

NOTES

1. Throughout this chapter I use pseudonyms, both for place names and people, to safeguard anonymity of the young people involved.
2. As Parfit phrases it: 'what makes a life go best' (Parfit 1984, quoted in Brock 1993: 96).
3. I acknowledge that my wearing of an insulin pump was merely a tenth of what it really is. No strings attached for me, just a tube I could detach whenever I became tired of the experiment. I am not a young person nor do I have diabetes.
4. Jackson expounds the phenomenology of Merleau-Ponty, for whom 'human "being-in-the-world" *is* bodily being' (Jackson 1996: 31).
5. See sociologist John Law and colleagues (Law and Hassard 1999; Law and Singleton 2000) and philosopher-ethnographer Annemarie Mol (2002).
6. This is in sharp contrast to my experience from comparative fieldwork visits to other paediatric diabetes centres (in Europe and the US), where health was the ultimate goal and measure of all treatment.

REFERENCES

Brock, D. 1993. Quality of Life Measures in Health Care and Medical Ethics. In M. Nussbaum and A. Sen (eds) *The Quality of Life*. Oxford: Clarendon Press.

Csordas, T. 2000. The Body's Career in Anthropology. In H. Moore (ed.) *Anthropological Theory Today*. Cambridge: Polity Press.

Jackson, M. 1996. Introduction. In M. Jackson (ed.) *Things As They Are: New Directions in Phenomenological Anthropology*. Bloomington: Indiana University Press.

—— 2002. Familiar and Foreign Bodies: A Phenomenological Exploration of the Human–Technology Interface. *Journal of the Royal Anthropological Institute* 8(2), 333–45.

Law, J. and J. Hassard (eds). 1999. *Actor Network Theory and After*. Oxford: Blackwell.

Law, J. and V. Singleton. 2000. Performing Technology's Stories. *Technology and Culture* 41, 765–75.

Leder, D. 1990. *The Absent Body*. Chicago: University of Chicago Press.

Mol, A. 2002. *The Body Multiple: Ontology in Medical Practice*. Durham, NC: Duke University Press.

Parfit, D. 1984. *Reasons and Persons*. Oxford: Clarendon Press.

Scheldeman, G. 2006. 'Performing Diabetes: Balancing Between "Patients" and "Carers", Bodies and Pumps, Scotland and Beyond'. Unpublished PhD thesis, St Andrews University.

Sen, A. 1993. Capability and Well-being. In M. Nussbaum and A. Sen (eds) *The Quality of Life*. Oxford: Clarendon.

Weale, A. 1998. Welfare. In *Routledge Encyclopedia of Philosophy*. London: Routledge, pp. 702–06.

5 ON WELL-BEING, BEING WELL AND WELL-BECOMING: ON THE MOVE WITH HOSPITAL PORTERS

Nigel Rapport

PREAMBLE

Well-being, I shall say, is an aesthetic notion, a matter of feeling. This is from Virginia Woolf:

Life is pleasant. Life is good. The mere process of life is satisfactory. Take the ordinary man in good health. He likes eating and sleeping. He likes the snuff of fresh air and walking at a brisk pace down the Strand. ... Something always has to be done next. Tuesday follows Monday; Wednesday Tuesday. Each spreads the same ripple of wellbeing, repeats the same curve of rhythm.... So the being grows rings; identity becomes robust. What was fiery and furtive like a fling of grain cast into the air and blown hither and thither by wild gusts of life from every quarter is now methodical and orderly and flung with a purpose – so it seems. (1983: 177)

The way Woolf invokes the feeling of well-being – as *the achieving of a purposeful, methodical rhythm* – suits my purpose.

In her memoir of her father, Mary Bateson describes Gregory Bateson as searching, up to the time of his death, for a moral system based in aesthetics (1984: 83). Appreciating 'patterns which connect' mind and nature, order and perception, calls for an aesthetic sense, Bateson himself explained (1980: 16) – a recognising of shapes and forms rather than quantities – and to do so was also to appreciate the coming together of information and value in human life; yet, 'consciousness and aesthetics' remain 'the great untouched questions' (1980: 226). Well-being, in Bateson's estimation – I might suppose – is *conjuring a perceived connection between the rhythms of selfhood and the shapes and forms of its environments.*

Drawing on recent field research among porters in a Scottish hospital, this chapter considers notions of well-being in the workplace and for individuals in a particular occupational group: 'professional well-being'. It will draw on Woolf's and on Bateson's insights, appreciating *well-being as a moral system based on what are perceived to be appropriate rhythms and movement.*

INTRODUCTION

Constance Hospital is a large, state-funded teaching hospital in Easterneuk, east-central Scotland, catering to a wide range of medical need. Among its thousands of employees, patients, students and visitors are some 135 porters (all but two being men). Their job is to traverse the miles of hospital corridor (30 miles, purportedly) ferrying people and *matériel* from place to place. For almost a year I too worked as a porter;[1] this chapter offers an interpretation of 'well-being' as I feel it was understood and lived by a number of porters who became my workmates.

The chapter offers an 'interpretation' of well-being because the notion is an unvoiced one among these people. Porters speak about 'being well', and ill and sick, about feeling happy and unsatisfied, also about things 'going well' and people 'doing well'; 'Well!' is, too, a common conversational interjection and conjunction. From this common discursive practice – the porters' habitual, routine, everyday ways of behaving and conversing with one another in Constance Hospital – I shall extrapolate, nonetheless, and *give voice to an understanding of what gave porters a sense of well-being, and how they accrued that sense*.

The chapter is interpretive, too, insofar as it raises the question of whether a genuine sense of well-being is always implicit: something of which people refrain from making themselves routinely conscious for the way this may alter its nature or duration. At best, well-being may represent a retrospective awareness.

The chapter revolves around a number of other paradoxes besides. My informants' well-being as 'hospital porters' is situated in a milieu of the sick: in a place where family and friends, as well as strangers, come to be cured or die; here is a place where 'the perks of the job' are a service from which employees only benefit through being themselves unwell. But then there may be a more general tension between 'well-being' and 'being well', since there would appear no necessity for the two phenomena, or the two conceptualisations, to overlap.

Finally, there is a tension between well-being and becoming. An argument may be made that human experience is a trajectory: a continuous movement between moments of being, an experience of betweenness, of transition and becoming. The chapter therefore tracks porters 'on the move': between parts of the hospital plant, between jobs, between relations, exchanges, satisfactions and identities, their well-being felt to be a matter of satisfactory process (Woolf) through certain perceived environments (Bateson).

MOVING AS PORTERS

'I'm just back from six weeks off', Dave tells me shortly after I have begun working as a porter and we have together fetched two patients in wheelchairs from Medical Physics. 'I had two weeks' holiday and then four weeks' sickness', he elaborates. 'It's good to get back here for a rest! [We laugh] And I'm pleased to get that first job under my belt: I'm back in the swing now.'

Dave's commentary contains a number of informative themes: concerning how a balance is to be sought between the worksite and elsewhere for retaining an even-tempered life; also, how sickness combines with vacations, together affording an appropriate and necessary time away from the worksite; lastly, how there is a rhythm to time spent at the worksite which provides an overall sense of security, but which can be lost or forgotten if not practised regularly. In the larger ethnography that follows we shall return to these themes. They will condense into a portrayal of well-being among porters in Constance Hospital as concerning *the routine ways in which they made an accommodation between, on the one hand, certain life-rhythms they felt happy with, and, on the other, the regimen, the rules and the site of the hospital.*

While my conclusions concerning well-being are an interpretation of what is not said, I shall hope to present my ethnography in such a way that the worldviews of individual porters are manifest, and their voices sound authentic.[2] The ethnography distinguishes between four aspects of porter movement: movement around the hospital site; movement between the hospital and the outside world; movement between being a porter and being a patient; and the fragility of the experience of movement.

Moving around the hospital site

Wilbur and I are in the Artificial Kidney Unit (AKU), where patients come weekly or fortnightly, for a number of hours, to be hooked up to kidney dialysis machines:

Wilbur: It's awful watching them deteriorate over time: from AKU to ward 1 to 13. One woman, I remember, began coming in all smart and done-up [he signs coiffeured hair]: 'Where's my chair?' [in a perky voice]. Now she is shrivelled and sick, in bed in 1, and doesn't care about anything.

Henry explains to Bill, a new porter, that the Coronary Care Unit (CCU) is:

... where you go if you're not ill enough for ICU [Intensive Care Unit]. They do tests and check you, over a few days. Say you had a car accident and they wanted to keep an eye on you, then you'd go there.... Mind you, you can go in with nothing, and come out with everything! ... You know, I'd never come in here to be cured; I'd be better telling the wife to get a knife and operate on me on the kitchen table.

These extracts are interesting for the contrast they set up between 'patient' careers and porters'. Patients are moved around the hospital site on wheelchairs, beds and trolleys, under the volition of doctors, nurses and, primarily, porters; patients do not decide, and often they remain ignorant of, timings and routes. Furthermore, they traverse an itinerary which reflects their condition, often a deteriorating one. There is even a sense that, once caught under hospital surveillance, the patient might never escape, however healthy their original condition.

It was commonly repeated among the porters that the hospital administrators and doctors were incompetent and uncaring, that the MRSA virus then spreading throughout Constance Hospital and temporarily closing wards was due to the laziness of nurses in not washing their hands, and that, in general, the hospital was responsible for causing much of the ill-health it claimed to be curing. When it came to dealings with the porters in particular, the common discourse was that the porters had to look out for their own health and take precautionary measures because the hospital did not care – was even remiss in passing on the information porters might use to acquire security for themselves (cf. Rapport 2004). As Roger explained to me:

I had a hepatitis shot, Nigel. I'm fed up with the jobs I've been given: cleaning blood and who-knows-what off the floors. I'm fed up playing by the rules, you know? I feel there's one set of rules for some and another set for the likes of me and you.

In stark contrast to patients, then – and also to doctors and nurses – *porters ensured that they moved in and around the hospital in their own ways: in ways they had determined to be the best for themselves.* In contrast to the demarcated careers of the patients, and in contrast to the narrow specialisms, the particular knowledges and businesses and confinements of the medical specialists, porters were generalists of the hospital site: traversing it all, connecting up all the specialisms, having favourite, idiosyncratic, possibly secret routes and shortcuts (and long-winded diversions), proud to know the best places to 'get lost', hide, smoke, waste time.

Let me give a sense of these movements.

Alastair is often reading the newspaper or listening to the radio or chatting over a cup of tea in the inner room of the porters' lodge ('buckie') when the charge-hand in the outer office will receive notice of a job from one of the wards and look round to see who is available to take it on. 'When you've finished that tea/reading that article/with that radio quiz, Alastair', the charge-hand might say, 'would you go to [Ward] 26 to take a patient Woody to the front door, please?' And even if the charge-hand is not so explicitly patient, Alastair will receive the order without any recognition and go on doing what he has been doing for some further minutes – even a quarter of an hour. Then he will slowly get to his feet and with some concluding witticism or remark wander out of the buckie as if embarked on a purpose of his own.

Alastair is a senior, experienced and respected porter; Oliver is young – his small physique making him seem younger even than his years – and often the butt of others' humour. But Oliver has a bubbly personality and mien, and is not snubbed or sheepish for long (even when part of his left ear was bitten off one Friday night in an Easterneuk pub, and he found himself occupying a hospital bed for some days). He has asserted a place, a public personality, for himself in the extroverted, teasing, *macho* environment of the buckie, and he holds his own. When out weekend-clubbing, he will sometimes return to the hospital and the buckie to show off his fashionable togs to those still working their shift. And when at work he is equally careful with his appearance: the mousse in his hair, the crease in his canvas trousers. I notice that whenever he gets up to go on a job, and whenever he gets the urge in a corridor, he will make sure that his porter's yellow or blue polo shirt is tucked into his trousers but with enough slack to then be folded over the top of his trouser belt, to the length of about two inches.

Being a charge-hand, Sean finds himself more or less confined to the buckie during the working day. He is a respected sub-manager, but being a fit and energetic man – in his forties but still the mainstay of the porters' football team – he also has a lot of nervous energy to use up. He will rarely, therefore, sit at his desk, facing the row of telephones and awaiting jobs to parcel out, for long. Normally he will stand in the corridor, hands on his hips, within reach of the phones but more able to assess the events of the hospital through the passing traffic, and always ready for action. Often he will swing on the door jamb of the buckie. He fidgets a lot, and also scratches his bottom, keenly and unselfconsciously. If he has a drinking, footballing or fighting story to tell he is quick to do so, and others looked on guardedly as the large circular scar on his throat (from a street fight with a bottle in earlier years) begins to throb red with his narrational exertions.

If the above behaviours represent individual habitualities, then collectively, too, there was a 'porterly' way of moving around the hospital. Near the beginning of my fieldwork, Dwayne had informed me, with irony in his voice and some bitterness, but also with humour, that: 'We porters are always "cheeky chappies", Nigel. Cheery, with a smile on our faces to cheer up the patients. Don't you know?' He was referring to porters' institutional position in between the expertise and professionalism of medical staff and the ignorance and discomfort of hospital patients and visitors; there was a liminality to porters, being normatively and instrumentally hospital functionaries with a trained and responsible job, and at the same time tricksterish figures, jesters and jokers, more belonging to the everyday, healthy but uninformed world outwith the hospital. Through their 'cheeky', 'cheery' clowning, porters were to make the gap between hospital and the everyday seem bridgeable and less vertically (hierarchically) oriented.

Acknowledgement of this institutional-tricksterish role took a number of forms among the porters. It was satirised (Kevin [as he pushes a patient in a bed with a nurse in attendance]: 'Some porters are cheeky, some are just truthful – like *moi*!'). It was lived up to, with porters making light-hearted and jocular conversation with patients, even going into mime and slapstick, as they escorted them round the site. It was also used as licence, to exaggerate porters' distance from, and disrespect of, the norms of hospitalisation. The line between laughing with and laughing at patients, for instance, could be a fine one, and porters passing each other in corridors while in the midst of jocular exchanges with their respective patients (who were often seated below the porters and facing away from them) would make it known to each other – by hand movements or rolled eyes or other physical signs, or by stopping their pushing and their conversing with the patients and suddenly taking up a more important exchange with their fellow-porter – that their sharing anything light-hearted with this patient was a sham.

Finally, the tricksterish liminality was made manifest in the porters' physical embodiment: in their postures and their gestures, in how they would comport themselves as a group in the hospital's public spaces. There was a bored and uninterested slouch, often, to porters' posture while awaiting work, and there was a casualness while undertaking it; there was an irreverence to the boisterous japing, pushing and shoving that might accompany a group of porters traversing a corridor. Porters, it was collectively made known, had their real place successfully negotiating the masculine streets, pubs and football pitches of larger Easterneuk, and their time in the confines of Constance Hospital was on sufferance only. In contradistinction to the Constance mission of care, they would continue to comport themselves as men.

Moving between the hospital site and outside

A significant part of the induction talk on being a porter which I (and five other new employees) received from a portering sub-manager, Pat, concerned the proprieties of attending the worksite. Time cards were a vital part of our duties and we were informed that if we clocked in or clocked out three minutes too early or too late then we would be docked 15 minutes' pay. If we were sick then we were to phone in 'sick', or have someone phone for us, and inform the charge-hand, 'within one hour of the start time', or else be docked a day's pay; if we were sick for longer than three consecutive days then, 'by the seventh day from the start of sickness', we had to bring in a Self Certification Form ('SC2') which we had signed; if we were sick for longer than seven consecutive days then we had to produce a Medical Certificate ('MED3') signed by a doctor, 'by the seventh day from the effective date on the certificate' (and as soon as that sick note was out of date, another was due, the same day). Lastly, if we were absent from work for more than a number of days over a certain period we could expect to be assessed on our return – a 'back-to-work interview' – and may be sent to Occupational Health for a lifestyle check. It was our responsibility, similarly, to learn how to push wheelchairs so that we did not hurt our backs or overtire our muscles (Pat: 'It's no good being a porter and then injuring yourself, and being on the sick').

Beginning working as a porter I was to find that attendance at the site formed a significant part of porters' discussion: managing attendance to their own satisfaction was important for portering well-being. It became apparent that attendance at the hospital site, as with movement within and around it – was geared to a certain rhythm that the porter aspired to control. A sense of well-being did not accrue from always being at work or often being off sick so much as from *a movement between worksite and home (or worksite and vacation) of which the porter felt in control* – at least adding significant input of his own. Getting the overtime one wanted or felt one needed or was due was a constant item of deliberation, then, and also source of friction between porters if one was seen to be being favoured by the managers (who dealt with overtime requests). Likewise, not receiving the holiday dates one requested, if one was due days, was seen as managerial 'cheek' and a source of grievance.

On Well-Being, Being Well and Well-Becoming

But let me concentrate on the way that sickness was used to engineer absence from the worksite, and in accruing a proper rhythm of attendance:

Arthur: I was ill last week, Nigel, that's why you didn't see me. Well, I was ill Monday and Tuesday, and then I stayed off; 'cos you get the same shit [from management on your return] whether you're off for two days or the whole week. I did some stuff round the house with a hammer that needed doing – keep my wife quiet for three or four weeks anyway!

Tom: I know three people who have phoned in sick this morning at least! It's what you call 'the Friday illness': a long weekend!

Discussion among the porters concerning sickness was a commonplace in the hospital. Charge-hands voiced their fears or complained when a day's workforce threatened to become too depleted; they wondered whether so-and-so was genuinely sick or not, and whether so-and-so had phoned in sick once too often and would now be paid off by management. Other porters exchanged views on how they liked it when they were covering for sick colleagues and might be asked to work in parts of the hospital they did not normally frequent. Occasionally the effect of employees' sick pay on the hospital's large financial debt was mentioned, though this, too, became a topic of comedy (Frank: '5000 people may be employed here but 2500 are on the sick at any one time!'). What exercised people more in this connection was the right to sick pay, and the proper demand that this be at a rate equal among all porters, all ancillary staff, irrespective of any other terms of their hospital contracts: whatever their differences in duties and conditions of work, as sick individuals they were the same.

What was striking about all this discussion, moreover, as in the above extracts, was the absence of any explicitly moral accenting – certainly one of blame. It was expected that porters would take days off work due to sickness, and that they might combine this with a holiday, or use the time for particular purposes, or otherwise manage it to their satisfaction. It was annoying and demeaning that management even went through the motions of testing the authenticity of porters' sick claims, as in the following extended extract from Martin:

I changed my home phone number so Peggy Cox [the portering manager] can't phone me any more. Last year when I was in the US [visiting a brother-in-law] I planned to file an insurance line [send in a sick note] when I came back, and get an extra week. But my brother found the letter lying in the flat and handed it in for me – thinking I'd forgotten! [We laugh.] So Peggy rang my house, and asked to speak to me urgently or to get me to phone; it was about my insurance line: how come I knew ahead of time I was gonna be sick?! ... I didn't know it had been sent! Eventually I had to phone Peggy from the States, tell her the truth and say I knew I'd need a week off 'cos of jet lag and that. Mark [Peggy's deputy] accused me of fraud and said I was lucky to be still employed; he said I'd have to work the week off my holidays. And I think they're still holding me to that.... But at least they're giving me some of the time off I requested. I just got back from a break, but then I took Thursday and Friday off, sick, 'cos I just couldn't face coming in. Now I've got my back-to-work interview: gotta go and face the music. 12.30. (Which is my lunch time, so I'll have to make sure I gets my half-an-hour some other time.) I've got my story ready – and it is a formality. Just so long as you remember what you said you were off with (or they can catch you out)! ... But I'm still pissed off at having to go. Why do you need to tell them it all again!? ... 'I had "sickness and diarrhoea".... No, I don't know where I got it from.... (The beer!) ... No I didn't see a doctor.... Because you don't need to till seven days: just fill in a certificate yourself.' ... What a waste of time!

[I could see Martin was nervous, despite the bravado, and I was interested to meet him again after his back-to-work interview.]

Mark said: 'So what was wrong?' ... 'Sickness and diarrhoea' ... 'Did you go to a doctor?' ... 'No' ... 'Why not?' ... "Cos I didn't need to!' ... 'But you signed off for four days.' ... 'No! Two days.' ... 'Four days: you didn't phone in again for work till Sunday night.' ... "Cos I don't work Saturday and Sunday anyway!' ... 'That doesn't matter. You must report for work as soon as you can. Do you know about Occupational Health?' ... 'Yes.' ... 'Do you know that if you signed yourself off sick for three days on three occasions I can send you to Occupational Health and you have to go?' ... 'Yes.'... Oh, 'Just Fuck Off Mark', you wanna say! What a waste of time, Nigel.

What was being asserted here, by Martin and others, was the right of porters to institute a regimen of being physically on-site and being elsewhere that they found viable. It was not the case, they would say, that this translated into being absent as often as possible. They actively sought overtime possibilities; they would come to work early on occasion, and in their civilian clothes during their holidays, just to chat with and lend support to their colleagues and keep up to date with hospital and Easterneuk gossip. Indeed, if they were away from work for too long a stretch, often they would claim boredom:

Desmond: I thought I'd come in 'cos I'm just sitting bored at home. Not that I got out of bed till 2 p.m.! [He has his baby son with him, and a septic finger in a large bandage.] But the finger's more annoying than painful.

It was not that they avoided the worksite, then; it was that porters sought to incorporate the hospital into their spatial life-worlds in such a way that there was a balance between the time spent in Constance and that spent elsewhere, and that movement between the two – between work and recreation, health and sickness, excitement and boredom – and also the meaning of the two – whether Constance Hospital was exciting or boring, a site of work or recreation – was to some extent at least a matter of negotiation (cf. Rapport 2007). Their sense of well-being derived from feeling in control of this balance.

Moving between 'hospital porter' and 'hospital patient'

We have heard Wilbur describe the depressing way in which patients 'deteriorate' as they stay for longer periods on the hospital site. Colin informed me, furthermore, that being around so many ill people 'rubs off on you' and made you feel like you needed a change, a long holiday: 'It's not exactly a

On Well-Being, Being Well and Well-Becoming

cheerful place!' For Fred, their being ill even made the naked woman you encountered in an operating theatre unattractive: 'You don't think of them like that.' And Jim told me of his luck, never having been ill himself or having had to see a doctor. Alongside these comments, however, was a commonness, even a kind of keenness among porters to discuss, even welcome, their own illnesses and ailments. Alongside their *machismo* was a readiness to admit to accidents, ailments and feeling unwell, and for this to be a regular part of daily exchange in the buckie. There might be a number of reasons for this. As with Martin, above, sickness is a route to time away from work, to sick notes and sick pay, and, so long as other porters were not unreasonably inconvenienced, it was an appropriate claim, an expectable strategy. Also, certain kinds of ailment would point to the stresses and strains of working hard and playing hard: stress fractures from the pounding of hospital corridors; strained ankles and wrists from five-a-side football collisions. But more important for my purposes here was claiming illness as a kind of right – a demand for equal treatment, even favouritism, in the hospital setting – and thus effecting another kind of movement around the hospital whose timing the porters themselves determined: from working in the buckie to being treated in clinic or ward; from porter to patient.

Working in a hospital, surrounded by people who can expect to be cared for with kindness and skill, and catered to with patience and generosity – and for free – on account of being 'ill', the porters determined to be 'ill' themselves on a certain regular basis; it was only fair that, being employees – not to mention tax-payers – they were granted equal if not special access to the services that their place of employment provided. This, too, was part of their sense of professional well-being. (After all, if they worked in an Easterneuk factory or shop they would expect similarly to have access to its produce – at the very least, its 'seconds' – at favourable rates.)

When they felt ill, then, or had an accident at work, porters used their special knowledge of the hospital site and its medical staff to move themselves quickly to the point of delivery of care. And if, for some reason, this was not forthcoming, as in the extract below, porters took umbrage: felt outraged, mistreated, and had recourse to their own methods of redress:

Josh: Lee went down to Ward 26 yesterday 'cos he had a sore throat and wanted to know if he was contagious to others but they wouldn't even look at him! They said he had to be referred there by a doctor! And their Senior House Officer wouldn't look either. So Lee just said 'Fuck it! All he wanted was to see if he was contagious' ... [Sean tuts, and others in the buckie make sympathetic noises.]
Arthur: He should've gone to A and E [Accident and Emergency].... Fuck 'em in 26!
Josh: So Lee is off today, and didn't get his golf game in yesterday either ...

There was often a wry humour in their tone as porters recounted to one another the ailments and mishaps of those among them who had ended up in Accident and Emergency or a hospital ward – Oliver, with his ear partly bitten off; Albert, a charge-hand, come up with red blotches all over his face. Getting into an accident or getting sick was a kind of foolishness, but it was also sometimes inevitable and hardly a matter for disapproval. On the contrary: being ill on a routine basis, and putting oneself in a position to receive due care and attention from the medical facilities in the hospital when this was the case, was only taking what one was due. *Moving in a routine way, and on a possibly regular basis, between the roles of porter and patient was, too, an important means by which the porters at Constance maintained a kind of professional well-being.*

The fragility of movement

Before completing my ethnographic account, it should be emphasised that the 'achievement' of well-being I have interpreted above, through various kinds of routine movement, was not without its difficulties, hazards and stress. Porters' general claims – to properly moving about the hospital on their own itineraries, to sickness and sick pay, to hospital treatment and care – could be challenged by administrative and medical staff, and needed vigilance and solidarity – shop-stewards, union membership and threats to take industrial action – to maintain them. On an individual level, porters would compare their successes at staking claims, while those who 'failed' – being found smoking or skiving when the workforce was small, being refused sick pay, being kept in a long queue to see medical staff or not seen at all, being kept too long as a patient in a hospital bed – could become objects of ridicule. *Just as well-being called for a balance or proportion to be achieved between work and play, health and sickness, and so on, so there was a proper proportion to the way the claims one staked should be recognised* – by other porters and by hospital staff in general. Here was the aesthetic quality to the sense of well-being, and to the conditions that had to be satisfied for its accrual. 'Too long' a wait to be seen by a doctor when claiming illness, 'too sluggish' a return to the buckie to receive another job after completing a first, 'too often' away sick ... and the porter could feel – and other porters could try to make him feel – that he had lost face, and lost the sense of well-being too.

This kind of fragility to one's individual well-being – its contingency and temporariness, its possible dependence on how others made one feel – connects with another, even more threatening kind, however, which must also be addressed: a fragility which is useful for reminding us that well-being in the workplace of a 'professional' kind is not finally separated off from other kinds, or from a general sense of well-being that individual porters might espouse. I am referring to the dangers of being seriously unwell, and dying.

On coming to work one Monday morning and entering the buckie to clock in, Wilbur, the charge-hand on duty, asked me:

Have you heard about Ben? Ben Goodie? [I shake my head and look apprehensive.] He died of a heart attack. [Wilbur half grins, from embarrassment, and I do not know if

On Well-Being, Being Well and Well-Becoming

he is serious. I say nothing.] You know Ben Goodie? Wee Ben? [I nod.] Well, he died yesterday. Yeah, really. He collapsed and was brought in here, but was already dead.
Nigel: God! When is the funeral?
Wilbur: It's not in *The Gazette* [local newspaper] yet, but the funeral will probably be Wednesday. We'll have a collection, when it's announced in *The Gazette*.
Nigel: I can't believe it! I saw Ben on Friday. He seemed full of energy!
Wilbur: Aye! He was always jumping around: full of energy.
Nigel: Was he known to have been ill?
Wilbur: He used to go to the blood clinic, Area 6, once a month to have his cholesterol checked, but I dunno if he was ill besides that.

Throughout the day, and those following, Ben's death, post mortem and funeral were common topics of conversation among the porters. And the nature of the commentary was revealing. Shock was registered, concerning the fatefulness of life and the fragility of its routines in the face of death: 'Awful tragedy about wee Ben. It's not real!' 'You work all your life and you expect some time at the end.' 'Just shows you, like. Here today and gone tomorrow.' 'When the Man calls you, you gotta go.' 'You dunno when your time comes. You could be away any time.' 'Look! Ben's name on the Tote List.... He'll not be winning there again.' 'What a shock about Ben! Imagine dying when you're just standing ordering a pint.'

Also, recollections were enunciated – as from me, above – concerning Ben's personality and the last time it was encountered: 'I saw him on Friday and he seemed fine: didn't complain of anything.' 'I spoke to him Friday, too. "Rog!" he called.' 'I went on a few jobs with Ben: I liked the way he explained things: "Some boys will do it like this, but I don't...." ' 'Such a nice man: kept to himself; did his work.' 'A nice wee man. Yes, always bouncing round the place ... seemed full of energy. Actually I thought he was older than he was 'cos we were recently discussing someone who was 63, and nearing retirement, and Ben said he'd be there soon and wondered what he'd do then.' 'No, Ben was a real gent, and will be missed. One of the few to be (not like you, Wilbur, you cunt!)'

Connections were made, too, between the speaker and Ben's life, and warnings drawn from his death:

Donald: Like Luke said, at his age Ben shouldn't have been pushing it. He should've retired. He was 62 or 63, aye? Just a few years off retirement anyway. But he was still always on his feet, bouncing around.

Tom: My father-in-law is like Ben. Can't rest at home; he goes crazy – climbs the wall – even though he's retired.

Luke: I know that Ben had high cholesterol but besides that.... Maybe he died 'cos of the stress of portering! [I laugh: Luke is serious.] No: all that pushing of beds was too much.
Nigel: But Ben used to be in the Navy!
Luke: But he wasn't pushing boats there!! [We laugh.] Ben used to drink in the Central.

Nigel: Is that your local?
Luke: I've been there. But it's for older people, like. Well, people in their fifties and more. It's up the road from my Club – where the singing is also better!... But I'll probably end up there, at the Central!

However, the fullest commentary from porters surrounding Ben's death endeavoured to retrieve the routine features of the situation: to link the death to those everyday processes, choices, decisions and acts of movement which porters felt had some predictability in their lives and over which they had some control (and with which I have associated porters' general senses of well-being).[3] This is begun, of course, by having stock, formulaic phrases – as above – with which to construe the event in the first place: 'Just shows you!' 'Here today and gone tomorrow!' 'A real gent!' Formulaic language, as Fillmore elaborates (1979: 94–5) – cliches, bromides, proverbs, greetings, leave-takings and politenesses – can itself lend fluency and consolation in marginal occurrences such as bereavement, where the bereaved and their interlocutors alike may feel inadequate to the situation.

Routinisation then continued by the porters detailing as far as possible the circumstances surrounding Ben's last moments, and what had occurred and had been occurring since. By focusing attention on these details, they could hope to convince themselves of the seeming inexorability – and the security – of everyday life and its ongoing, known and owned regularities. Fred, for instance, described to me how:

I drink in the Club next to Ben's. So someone came in to tell us. He died at 12.10 p.m. – just keeled over at the bar when he went to get drinks. The club only opens at 12, so he was probably just on his first drink, or maybe not even had one yet!

When I asked Wilbur what age Ben was, he retrieved for me the Hospital Mortuary Slip from the charge-hand's desk. These are forms that accompany every body that porters deliver to the mortuary and deposit there, recording the person's name ('Benjamin Goodie'), age ('60'), height ('5 feet 4 inches'), width at the shoulders ('N[ormal]'), time of death, and those porters responsible for escorting the body: 'Alastair Dent' and 'Desmond Hagley'. Having shown me Ben's form, Wilbur carefully clipped it back on the pile of other 'Recent Deaths', which he filed in the desk drawer (until other porters wanted to inspect it).

Later, on a job together, Alastair Dent gave me his own account:

Arthur Miles [the charge-hand] told me on Sunday they were bringing in Ben, who'd just collapsed. But they reckon he was 'away' before he reached here.... My old man used to drink in the Central like Ben, and they'd sometimes have a chat. But my dad was sitting in the back room when Ben collapsed in the front. At the time they just thought it was a bad turn ...

Nigel: And then you and Desmond dealt with the body. Wilbur showed me the form.
Alastair: Aye. Well, what we do is to send people for the body who knew the person well. It's the best we can do when there's a body to collect that is known. To show some respect.

Nigel: Right. That's nice. Where was the body?
Alastair: In a body bag in A and E.... So now we're collecting money for his widow. Either for flowers or, if they say 'None', then just to give her the money to do with as she likes: 'Here, we collected this: do what you like with it', like. You know £10 has been collected already from Ward 4! And we didn't know he even knew anyone from there! ICU [Intensive Care Unit] maybe, but not 4.... We'll try and get as many porters at the funeral as possible. Obviously they won't let us all go – they need some porters in the hospital still! But we should get a good showing. And there'll be a bus going from the Central. And apparently he worked for five years in 'The Cash' [Easterneuk Cash-and-Carry shop] so there should be a few from there. So, altogether, there should be a fair showing.

In the days that followed, porters gave one another updates on the state of affairs: whether *The Gazette* had yet announced the date of the funeral; how there would be a post mortem requested by the police (since the death was sudden), which would be undertaken at the Easterneuk Royal Infirmary; how Ben's son had arrived from London to identify the body, since it transpired Ben was not married to the woman he lived with and she could not legally do the identifying (whereas the whereabouts of his wife were unknown); how Desmond would take charge of the porters' collection of donations. On the day of the funeral, a large contingent of porters attended, while those unable to negotiate leaving their shifts showed some embarrassment. The day following, a bottle of whiskey arrived in the buckie for the porters' consumption, courtesy of the hospital laboratory for which Ben did the portering (and there was talk of how drunk some porters were at the funeral itself). Finally, a card from Ben's partner, Meg, was pinned to the buckie wall, with thanks for the porters' flowers and their collection: 'Ben loved coming home and telling stories about his workmates. I'm pleased you will miss him, as I will.' No one removed the card, many glanced at it, and it stayed up until it was accidentally dislodged and a cleaner swept it away.

Ben's death thus came to be woven into the ongoing fabric of the 'mere process of life' (Woolf) of portering routine. As with the death and dying of hospital patients in general, the distinctiveness and the strength of the porters' workaday routines afforded them a place – emotional and conceptual – even in this circumstance, where a sense of well-being could flourish.

'The aims of life are the best defence against death', Primo Levi could write even of Auschwitz (1996: 120) – in conditions, that is, of far less tolerant institutionalism and hierarchy than a British National Health Service hospital. Aiming to return to and maintain their everyday working routines after the shock of Ben's sudden death gave the porters a means to reassert a sense of well-being. The ripples of well-being (Woolf) spread out in concert with the routine processes of everyday life. ('We should be undone' were it not for 'the happy concatenation of one event following another in our lives'; Woolf 1983: 158.)

DISCUSSION

In their outlining of the possibility of a universal theory of human need, given the same biological potential to be harmed or flourish, Len Doyal and Ian Gough identify what they call 'objective human goals'; these include 'basic needs' such as health and autonomy, and 'intermediate needs' such as nutritional food and clean water, protective housing, a non-hazardous work environment and also physical environment, appropriate health care, security in childhood, significant primary relationships, physical security, economic security, appropriate education, safe birth control and conditions of childbearing (1991: 2–4, 157).[4] The difficulty of conjuring with abstract definitions such as these, however, and drawing up definitive lists, soon leads their discussion to notions of 'harm' and 'flourishing' tied to 'successful social participation' (1991: 50–51). Well-being comes to be understood as physical, intellectual and emotional opportunities to interact with fellow human beings, over a period of time, in ways that are valued by actors and reinforced by others. Well-being comes to turn on having the resources to participate as a full member of a social milieu in a particular form of life; while a lack of well-being comes from being deprived of those 'conditions of life ... which allow [people] to play the roles, participate in the relationships and follow the customary behaviour which is expected of them by virtue of their membership of society' (Townsend 1987: 130).

The usefulness of this kind of effort at definition and evaluation may ultimately be the way in which it turns matters of human need and harm into questions of *context*. 'Well-being' in the abstract is far harder to elucidate than well-being in particular times and places, situations and milieux, exchanges, interactions and relationships. If one further allows that 'context' is a matter of perception, that there will likely be at least as many definitions of context as there are actors (Rapport 1999), then one ultimately reaches the point of elucidating well-being for particular individuals in particular moments and moods. Likewise, 'successful social participation' (Doyal and Gough) by 'full members' in 'customary forms of life' (Townsend) does not necessitate us thinking in any essentialistic way about belonging with significant others to particular collectivities. As with 'well-being', social interaction is an aesthetic matter: deploying shared forms whose content and quality different individuals are responsible for determining distinctively for themselves. One can attest, then, to collective forms of well-being – porters moving round the hospital at times together, say – and to the role others might play in affecting an individual's momentary sense of, and claims to, well-being. while still remaining cognisant of that aesthetic quality that finally makes well-being a matter of an intrinsically individual testimony. Well-being as a function of participation in collective forms of life ultimately translates into *how successfully specific individuals feel they are interacting at particular moments with those whom they would claim as significant others at that time*. The wider point is to insist on 'quality of life' not as a generalised concept but as something which refers precisely to the indeterminate 'qualia' of life, the aesthetics of 'quality'.[5]

The additional challenge I have faced in this study is that well-being has appeared among the porters of Constance Hospital only as a result of my own acts of interpretation. For the porters, 'well-being' remained unvoiced – implicit, perhaps unnamed – while I have worked to identify a phenomenon I might paraphrase as 'that which – for particular individuals, and for particular individuals working as hospital porters, and for particular individuals working as members of a group of porters at Constance Hospital – furnishes a sense of connection, of alignment, with the circumstances and happenstances of a life' (alternatively: 'what it means for a life to go well', Scheldeman, ch. 4 this volume).[6]

It is interesting to note, moreover, how often an implicitness is reflected in other contributions to this volume. For Ian Harper and Bryan Maddox, well-being is something that only becomes visible via sickness. For Eric Hirsch, 'the good ways of the true people' (alias 'well-being' among the Fuyuge) entail the transformation of opposites: well-being accrues from the violent obviation of loss. Alberto Corsín Jiménez sums this up by identifying well-being as something always measured against its absence. He would go further, indeed, and describe the appropriate social-scientific accounting of well-being as an illumination of the implicit and invisible – *the virtue of any social-scientific account being the balance it provides between aspects of human life which are always and inevitably contrastive*: not only the implicit and explicit, invisible and visible, then, but also the existential and the moral, the analytical and the ethical. Conjuring with the phenomenon of well-being in a social-scientific text allows us to represent the 'well-being' of social science *per se* as a kind of exercise in interpretation and balance. In my encounter with the porters of Constance Hospital (as in other fieldworks), I have endeavoured to provide such a balance: between my voice and theirs, between my interpretation and their life-worlds; also between a faithfulness to what I interpret to be their understanding of *well-being* and my own version of more general notions of human *welfare* (to echo the distinction Wendy James introduces).

The anthropologist writes as an 'aesthete', according to Richard Werbner (2004: personal communication), but also as a 'citizen'. The *aesthetic* appreciation of phenomena encountered during fieldwork – the authentic representation of informants' interpretations in all their forceful, energetic and charismatic life – exists alongside a *moral* appreciation of individuals' opportunities to live in the equitable fulfilment of their capacities. (This is how I would understand Neil Thin's call for a social science which recognises the fullness which comes from juxtaposing the 'happy' against the 'sad'.) The aesthetic and the civic, the empirical and the ethical, have different potentialities and different consequences, however. In writing about well-being among hospital porters and moving between these poles, I advocate the fuller significance that derives from recognising movement per se as anthropological method (Rapport 2002).

ENVOI

The focus of this chapter has been on movement: on a close tie I have construed between senses of well-being and moving around and through Constance Hospital, and moving between roles and states. Well-being has come to appear as a kind of balance, a proportionality. This is not a kind of stasis, however; it is a balance of movements – which can be difficult to achieve and maintain, and fleeting. Moreover, while this chapter – and my research as a whole – has taken the hospital as the centre of attention, there have been glimpses of individual porters determining their lives beyond the workplace, too, in terms of routine movements: regular times at which they play golf, for instance, or drink or sing in particular rooms at particular pubs, or can expect to change their regular 'watering holes' as they age. A 'deathly' tedium and a 'deathly' demeaning of their self-esteem are overcome by porters having aims and destinations, in the hospital and beyond, whose routes and timings they would put themselves in positions to determine (Woolf): they find a balance between rhythms of selfhood and ambient shapes and forms of the self's working and leisure environments (Bateson).

When I began working as a porter, others appeared to doubt my commitment, my interest or my stamina. Was this some kind of 'between-job' for me, they asked? Was it not 'three weeks' I would be at Constance – surely 'up to a year' was a mistake? Did I really expect to be able to come to terms with the rigours – and the tedium – of the job without my feet giving out? I felt threatened by these doubts at the time, and defensive. And certainly there were elements of *rites de passage* in the probing, and the testing of the likely loyalties of an outsider who was also from a university. But I also came to recognise how frequently porters would talk of portering as a kind of 'between-job' for themselves too; they had had, mostly, a history of employment outside Constance Hospital and the wider National Health Service – in the Navy or Army, as factory workers and managers, as painters and builders, as shop assistants – also a history of unemployment and of travel, and they could not imagine, many of them, that they would be here forever, or even for long. Moreover, they could be openly disparaging of the job and of those who could get no better – even in the buckie and surrounded by other porters. This was a 'shitty job', Jim for instance informed me, and he was at the same time a student at an Easterneuk university because he did not want to 'go on doing shitty jobs for the rest of [his] life'; Dave, the charge-hand, was to be pitied, Oliver told me, as was Desmond Hagley because they had been portering here for years and had not experienced something different (and better). This kind of irony – being a full-time porter and at the same time willing to cast aspersions on one's current status – makes sense, I suggest, if the movement we associate with the porter's well-being includes a kind of becoming: a moving to new statuses and jobs.[7] As well as the other kinds of movement around and through the hospital, *porters' sense of well-being derives from the expectation (and the history) that portering at Constance is* not necessarily to be their lot always, or even for very long. Aiming not always to be as they are now – not in the same jobs, not in the same pubs – the porters move between present and coming states. Their well-being entails a sense of well-becoming: a 'projection' (Rapport 2003) by which, however implicitly, they imagine a life of future, proportionate movement for themselves.

ACKNOWLEDGEMENTS

The research on which this chapter is based was funded by the Leverhulme Trust (grant no. XCHL48), under the aegis of their 'Nations and Regions' programme, and part of the 'Constitutional Change and Identity' project convened by David McCrone of Edinburgh University.

This chapter was drafted while a Visiting Professor at the University of Melbourne. I am very grateful to the anthropology department there, especially Andrew Dawson; also to the anthropology seminar at the University of Adelaide, including John Gray, Simone Dennis and Michael Wilmore. I thank Alberto Corsín Jiménez for the invitation to consider my data through the lens of well-being.

NOTES

1. I was not employed by the National Health Service but by the Leverhulme Trust. The Management of Constance Hospital allowed me to work as a porter, undertaking the same work and under the same conditions, while I conducted participant-observation. The research for the Leverhulme Trust focused on the nature of national identity and nationalism in a hospital setting.
2. My fieldwork practice was not to tape-record informants but still to aim at a precise memorisation of interaction by writing down as much of exchanges between porters as I could remember, as soon after the event as possible.
3. Cf. Peter Berger's account of the relationship among the following complex: everyday life, a commonsensical reality, a sense of control, death, theoretical explanation and metaphysics (1969: 30–31).
4. In a comparable exercise, Ryff and Keyes found well-being to comprise: self-acceptance, positive relations with others, autonomy, environmental mastery, purpose in life and personal growth (1995).
5. One may contrast this with attempts by psychologists to generalise upon 'quality of life', drawing up a QOL Index (Diener 1995), and seeking statistically to measure and compare 'the quality of life of cultures' (Diener and Suh 2000).
6. I would want to distinguish the implicit notion of well-being from more explicit and vocal definitions made by porters concerning 'what it is to be a porter at Constance', 'how we anticipate the hospital authorities will behave' and 'how we will uphold what we see as our rights in the face of others' deprecations'. These defining, collective self-images and working practices – of a portering sub-culture *vis-à-vis* the hospital as hierarchy – I have described elsewhere (Rapport 2004). They come down to a set of eight attitudinal propositions which operate as a rhetoric of belonging, owned and exchanged by the porters as a group. Namely:

    (1) Being a porter means coming to terms with being a nothing, at the base of a hospital hierarchy topped by doctors;

(2) Being a porter means being ignorant about what life for the doctors at the top of the hospital hierarchy actually entails, and vice versa;
(3) Being a porter means turning the distance and ignorance between them and doctors into a source of stereotypical and apocryphal otherness;
(4) Being a porter means turning the distance and ignorance between doctors and them into a kind of contractual stand-off;
(5) Being a porter means having the potential to develop the contractual stand-off with doctors into relations of a joking and casual kind;
(6) Being a porter means being used to regarding doctors as authority figures in everyday life, and bringing this regard into the hospital as a means to domesticate the work environment;
(7) Being a porter means using knowledge of everyday life to lessen the import of the hospital hierarchy and the authority of doctors as such;
(8) Being a porter means recognising doctors as fellow human beings trying, like them, to make do and get on in a world of institutions, rules, norms, and circumstances they do not control.

7. Cf. Ralph Waldo Emerson: 'If a man carefully examine his thoughts he will be surprised to find how much he lives in the future. His well being is always ahead' (1958: 35).

REFERENCES

Bateson, G. 1980. *Mind and Nature*. Glasgow: Fontana.
Bateson, M. 1984. *With a Daughter's Eye*. New York: Morrow.
Berger, P. 1969. *The Social Reality of Religion*. London: Faber.
Diener, E. 1995. A Value Based Index for Measuring National Quality of Life. *Social Indicators Research* 36, 107–27.
Diener, E. and E. Suh. 2000. Measuring Subjective Well-being to Compare the Quality of Life of Cultures. In E. Diener and E. Suh (eds) *Culture and Subjective Well-being*. Cambridge, MA: MIT Press.
Doyal, L. and I. Gough. 1991. *A Theory of Human Need*. Basingstoke: Macmillan.
Emerson, R.W. 1958. *The Heart of Emerson's Journals*. New York: Dover.
Fillmore, C. 1979. On Fluency. In C. Fillmore, D. Kempler and W. Wang (eds) *Individual Differences in Language Ability and Language Behaviour*. New York: Academic.
Levi, P. 1996. *The Drowned and The Saved*. London: Abacus.
Rapport, N. 1999. Context as an Act of Personal Externalization: Gregory Bateson and the Harvey Family in the English Village of Wanet. In R. Dilley (ed.) *The Problem of Context*. Oxford: Berghahn.
—— 2002. 'The Truth is Alive': Kierkegaard's Anthropology of Subjectivism, Dualism and Somatic Knowledge. *Anthropological Theory* 2, 165–83.
—— 2003. *I am Dynamite: An Alternative Anthropology of Power*. London and New York: Routledge.
—— 2004. From the Porter's Point of View: Participant Observation by the Interpretive Anthropologist in the Hospital. In F. Rapport (ed.) *Research Methodologies in Health and Social Care*. London: Routledge.
—— 2007. Bob, Hospital Bodybuilder: The Integrity of the Body, the Transitiveness of 'Work' and 'Leisure'. In S. Coleman and T. Kohn (eds) *The Discipline of Leisure*. Oxford: Berghahn.
Ryff, C. and C. Keyes. 1995. The Structure of Psychological Well-being Revisited. *Journal of Personality and Social Psychology* 69, 719–27.
Townsend, P. 1987. Deprivation. *Journal of Social Policy* 16(2), 125–46.
Woolf, V. 1983. *The Waves*. London: Granada.

Part III

Proportionalities

6 MEASURING – OR PRACTISING – WELL-BEING?

Michael Lambek

What could be more important for the human sciences than the subject of well-being? Is it not always at least the implicit subject of our work? And yet what could be a more problematic topic?

I confess to a double reaction to Corsín Jiménez's original call for papers. On the one hand, finally a workshop that brings the central issue of human life directly to the fore. On the other hand, what sharper sign of the hubris of modernity or the absurdity of social science than the idea that we could recognise, measure or bring about other people's well-being? Such ideas have been the goals or rationalisation of all civilising missions, from archaic empires through nineteenth-century colonial projects, to modernist social planning of twentieth-century Soviet and capitalist states and the current work of development projects of various stripes. And yet this same social science has taught us the difficulty, if not the downright folly, of well-intentioned intervention. The problems with intervention have all kinds of sources; arguments range from the reduction of social and ecological complexity to linear thinking; the inexorable logic of capital and consequences of exploitation; the scrutinising, disciplining and subjectifying powers of discursive regimes linked with new forms of knowledge and technology; to forms of cultural analysis that show it is far easier to break down other people's systems of meaning than to provide them with a rewarding pattern of life based on our own values.[1]

And yet, we are compelled to recognise and address impoverishment, inequity, injustice and other forms (or signs) of human dis-ease or trouble.

Clearly, between intervention and the refusal to acknowledge an absence of well-being some middle path, however uncertain, must be forged. How else can we criticise such enterprises as the invasion and occupation of Iraq except by means of some measure or description of human well-being? Behind politics and policies must lie ethics. The existence of ethics in human life and its significance for human practice is incontrovertible; we could hardly get out of bed without it. And yet the place of ethics in social action is largely unstudied and its philosophical or theoretical formulations vigorously contested.

One cannot talk about – let alone evaluate – well-being or quality of life without first considering the models through which we imagine such things. To standard liberal conceptions of the good life I would juxtapose an Aristotelian picture in which cultivation and practice of the virtues is central. Well-being entails the means to act with respect to the telos of human flourishing (*eudaimonia*), hence it is life in which means and ends are not fully distinguished. Ideally, it is a condition that enables people not only to act well but to cultivate positive moral character in carrying out their practices. This model sees people as produced in and through their acts and practices, rather than prefigured and standing outside them, making 'rational choices' between abstract needs or desires. Hence the meaning of 'freedom' in such a model cannot be the same as that primary value lauded in liberal conceptions of well-being as freedom of choice, whether at the ballot box or the market.

Central to virtuous practice is the exercise of judgement, a 'right', 'freedom', 'capability' or, as I will prefer, a 'capacity' which ought to be available to everyone but which cannot exist in the abstract or the open, in a cultural and social vacuum. From such a perspective the activity of bureaucratic experts measuring from the outside someone else's quality of life – generally people presumed to have a lesser quality of life than that of the experts themselves – is inconceivable.

In what follows I endeavour to write neither a manifesto for virtue ethics nor a polemic against expertise. I begin by retrieving the ideas of a political philosopher whose work ought to be better known and follow this with brief reflections on recent historical experiences of people among whom I have conducted fieldwork or simply lived, people in a number of different societies for whom participation within a relatively organic political community – a polis in the very broadest of terms – has been severely eroded or transformed yet, with some effort, partially maintained. In the final section of the chapter I will return to some general points about well-being.

I would be untrue to my own ethical insight if I were to claim for what follows the authority of science, even in its social refraction. All I can do in this chapter is provide a series of notes, observations which, for better or worse – but probably for better – do not coalesce into a unified whole. Indeed, insofar as the very subject must be caught up in the contradiction of being both inside and outside a practice, so too is this chapter.

I

If anthropologists have not paid a good deal of specific attention to well-being and the quality of life, the same can hardly be said of political philosophers and philosophers of ethics. I do not see how anthropologists can approach the topic except via their work, if only to digest their arguments and show how we might differ. In his call for papers, Alberto Corsín Jiménez drew attention to Amartya Sen, but I would like to turn to a political philosopher a generation or two earlier, and one of my predecessors at the University of Toronto, namely C.B. (Crawford Brough) Macpherson (1911–1987). Macpherson had a strong and direct influence on Marshall Sahlins, evident in their respective expositions and critiques of possessive individualism and infinite want (Macpherson 1962; Sahlins 1972, 1976, 1995; cf. Solway 2006). As will become evident, Macpherson may also have had an influence upon Sen. I restrict my discussion here to the first section of essays in Macpherson's *Democratic Theory: Essays in Retrieval* (1973).[2]

Macpherson is particularly interesting in that he provides a model that integrates insights from the Aristotelian ethical tradition with those of Marx rather than opposing ethics and political economy. In so doing he is probably closer to the spirit of Marx than those Marxist theorists who focus maximally on material factors. Conversely, his argument is more profound than those who attempt to develop models of justice that ignore Marx and take capitalism for granted.[3]

Macpherson distinguishes two kinds of maximising claims used to justify democracy – that democracy maximises individual utilities and that it maximises individual powers. He notes that 'both claims are made in the name of individual personality' (1973: 4), a point that immediately directs us to a rather large difference between the European tradition of political philosophy, on the one hand, and of social theory (Durkheim, Marx) that emphasises the collective, on the other. Macpherson lays out the alternatives brilliantly and I defer to his language:

The first claim is that the liberal-democratic society, by instituting a wider freedom of individual choice than does any non-liberal society, maximizes individual satisfactions or utilities. The claim is not only that it maximizes the aggregate of satisfactions but that it does so equitably: that it maximizes the satisfactions to which, on some concept of equity, each individual is entitled. This claim implies a particular concept of man's essence. To treat the maximization of utilities as the ultimate justification of a society, is to view man as essentially a consumer of utilities. It is only when man is seen as essentially a bundle of appetites demanding satisfaction that the good society is the one which maximizes satisfactions. This view of man, dominant in Benthamism, goes back beyond the classical political economists. It is firmly embedded in the liberal tradition and has remained a considerable part of the case for the liberal-democratic society today. [If anything, even more so now than in Macpherson's day.]

The second claim is that the liberal-democratic society maximizes men's human powers, that is, their potential for using and developing their uniquely human capacities. This claim is based on a view of man's essence not as a consumer of utilities but as a doer, a creator, an enjoyer of his human attributes. These attributes may be variously listed and assessed; they may be taken to include the capacity for rational understanding, for moral judgment and action, for aesthetic creation and contemplation, for the emotional activities of friendship and love, and, sometimes, for religious experience. Whatever the uniquely human attributes are taken to be, in this view of man their exertion and deployment are seen as ends in themselves, a satisfaction in themselves, not simply a means to consumer satisfactions. It is better to travel than to arrive. Man is not a bundle of appetites seeking satisfaction but a bundle of conscious energies seeking to be exerted. (Macpherson 1973: 4–5)[4]

Macpherson then historicises these alternatives. The pre-liberal Western tradition, whether traced back to Greek or Christian origins, is based on the idea that 'the end or purpose of man is to use and develop his uniquely human attributes or capacities' (1973: 8). In this tradition, 'A good life is one which maximizes these powers. A good society is one which maximizes (or permits and facilitates the maximization of) these powers, and thus enables men to make the best of themselves' (1973: 8–9). Thus,

From Aristotle until the seventeenth century it was more usual to see the essence of man as purposeful activity ... than as the consumption of satisfactions. It was only with the emergence of the modern market society ... that this concept of man was narrowed and turned into almost its opposite.... the essence of rational behaviour was increasingly held to lie in unlimited individual appropriation, as a means of satisfying unlimited desire for utilities. Man became an infinite appropriator and an infinite consumer ... (1973: 5)

In sum, Macpherson is suggesting that human motivations could be open rather than driven by need, and that the quality of life could be characterised by the presence of or possibility for ethical and creative *acts* rather than the consumption of material *goods*. Macpherson goes on to argue that the liberal-democratic polity is incoherent insofar as it claims to maximise both while refusing to acknowledge that capitalist appropriation of goods actually inhibits the ability of people to exercise their human attributes or power.

By its very nature [capitalist market society] compels a continual net transfer of part of the power of some men to others, thus diminishing rather than maximizing the equal individual freedom to use and develop one's natural capacities which is claimed. (1973: 10–11)

Moreover, so long as we allow the capitalist incentive of the right to appropriation, 'we cannot dispense with the concept of man as infinite desirer, nor deny the rationality of infinite desire' (1973: 33).[5]

Macpherson wants liberal democracy to drop the assumption of man as consumer and base itself more exclusively on man as a doer, thus to drop the first maximising claim and keep the second (1973: 39).

What is essential in a modern democratic theory? As soon as democracy is seen as a kind of society, not merely a mechanism of choosing and authorising governments, the egalitarian principle inherent in democracy requires not only 'one man, one vote' but also 'one man, one equal effective right to live as fully humanly as he may wish'.... This is simply the principle that everyone ought to be able to make the most of himself, or make the best of himself. (1973: 51)

Macpherson's next move is to distinguish between 'a man's *power* (understood as his *ability* to exercise [use and develop] his human capacities), and the capacities themselves' (1973: 52).[6] Human ability 'depends on present external impediments; [capacities depend on] on innate endowment and past external impediments' (1973: 52). One can measure power by examining impediments (1973: 58–59). Chief among the impediments are lack of adequate means of life, lack of access to the means of labour, and lack of protection against invasion by others (1973: 59–60). Macpherson also argues that one should measure 'down from a maximum rather than up from a previous amount' (1973: 58) since the criterion of a democratic society is the maximisation of power.

For democratic theory one adds the

... assumption, which at first sight is a staggering one ... that the exercise of his human capacities by each member of a society does not prevent other members exercising theirs: that the essentially human capacities may all be used and developed without hindering the use and development of all the rest. (1973: 54)

Macpherson recognises that this is an optimistic view (1973: 54).

Macpherson's renewal of the Aristotelian element in Marx without thereby losing Marx's critical edge is evident in his discussion of labour. Macpherson situates labour among the capacities and expands his earlier list to include capacities

... for rational understanding, for moral judgment and action, for aesthetic creation or contemplation, for the emotional activities of friendship and love, and, sometimes for religious experience ... the capacity for transforming what is given by Nature ... this is broader than, but includes, the capacity for materially productive labour.... One might add the capacity for wonder or curiosity ... one might add the capacity for laughter ... one might add the capacity for controlled physical/mental/aesthetic activity, as expressed for instance in making music and in playing games of skill. (1973: 53–54)

In other words, labour may be understood in an Aristotelian sense in which the end is not external to the means and hence understood as an ethical activity.[7] That is to say, productive labour is an end in and of itself, part of any good human life.[8]

Macpherson asserts importantly (and in some possible differentiation from Marx) that there is no hierarchical ordering among the capacities. Nevertheless, labour is critical in that it is a particular means for appropriation and inequality. In gaining access to the means of labour on the market the worker loses more than what is received by the purchaser of the labour power (that is, by the employer, the capitalist). The worker loses not only the power of his productive labour that is transferred to the capitalist. 'That leaves out of account the value that cannot be *transferred* but is nevertheless *lost* by the man who, lacking access, has to sell his labour-power, namely, the value of the satisfaction he could have got from using it himself if he had been able to use it himself' (1973: 66). This is especially the case if the manner in which workers are expected to use their capacities is different from what they would have chosen for themselves (1973: 66). This value that is simply lost rather than transferred is generally missed in the calculations of economists.

In addition, the transfer of productive power may affect workers' extra-productive power, that is, the other activities which might provide satisfaction in themselves and not just in the production of consumer goods or as a means to acquire them (1973: 67).

Macpherson asserts emphatically that both the separation of labour from other human capacities under capitalism, and the assumption that mindless production does not affect the extra-productive capacities, do violence to the human individual (1973: 68).[9] In sum:

> ... lack of access to the means of labour has been shown to diminish a man's power in three respects. First, it sets up a continuous net transfer of the material value of the productive power of the non-owner to the owner of the means of labour, the amount of which transfer, in each of the repeated transactions, is the excess of the value added by the work over the wage paid. Second, it diminishes each non-owner's productive power beyond that market-measured amount, by denying him the essentially human satisfaction of controlling the use of his own productive capacities: this value is lost, not transferred. Third, it diminishes his control over his extra-productive life. Of these three deficiencies in a man's power, the first is numerically measurable and is in fact measured by the market. The other two are not so measurable. (1973: 69–70)

Nevertheless, Macpherson observes, the latter deficiencies can be seen as greater or less by comparison between individuals or classes (1973: 70) and, presumably, gender.

I trust that this discussion has helped to put into perspective the arguments of Amartya Sen, laid out in *Development as Freedom* (1999). Sen's move to think about or measure human well-being in a framework beyond that of income analysis or utility was no doubt quite innovative for economists, and for all those planners and implementers who base their thinking on neo-classical economics. At the same time, he is much more grounded in materiality than a political philosopher like Macpherson, and more concerned with the direct effects of poverty and inequality. His attention to the real working of human relations as opposed to the ideal one of philosophers is salutary and his attempts to provide measurements of actual well-being and inequality almost uncanny.

Sen's 'capability' resembles but is not identical to Macpherson's 'capacity'. 'Capability is ... a kind of freedom: the substantive freedom to achieve alternative functioning combinations (or, less formally put, the freedom to achieve various lifestyles)' (Sen 1999: 75). It is 'the freedom to achieve actual livings' (1999: 73). Capability also refers directly to what Macpherson called impediments. It includes everything from 'being adequately nourished and being free from avoidable disease, to very complex activities or personal states, such as being able to take part in the life of the community and having self-respect' (1999: 75). It thus includes both freedom '*from*' and freedom '*to*'.

In Sen's discussion, the distinction between means and ends, or the Aristotelian recognition that means can be simultaneously ends (Macpherson's: 'it's better to travel than to arrive') is somewhat blurred. Similarly, Macpherson's primary distinction between utility and capacity is not clearly adhered to. Sen is concerned with 'the capabilities of people to do things – and the freedom to lead lives – that they have *reason to value*' (1999: 85, my emphasis). He tries explicitly to move beyond Rawls's analysis of 'primary goods', that is, those 'general-purpose means that help anyone to promote his or her ends, and include "rights, liberties and opportunities, and income and wealth" along with the social bases of self-respect' (1999: 72).[10]

At the same time, the cumulative effect of words like 'freedom', 'choice', 'achievement' and 'value' is to emphasise utility at the expense of capacity. In addressing welfare policies and development discourse perhaps Sen cannot avoid this. One might argue that it is a good thing that he mediates dualisms that are too bluntly opposed by Macpherson. But this reduces the critical edge, especially Macpherson's argument that the combination of utility and capacity arguments characteristic of liberal democracies is inherently contradictory.[11]

The emphasis on having freedom of choice implies the potential consumer standing back and reflecting on which goals might offer most satisfaction rather than the active doer, exercising her human capacities in the midst of life. That is to say, Sen appears to be missing the insights of practice theory, including the fact that humans are always already embedded in practices and engaged by social commitments.

There is also the question whether Sen's argument is inherently more provincial than Macpherson's, not questioning the spread of capitalist relations of production and more strongly grounded in an ideology of individualism. Sen is concerned with inter-individual equality or equivalence. Thus he repeatedly compares the needs or freedoms of someone who is healthy with someone who is ill or disabled. The notion of the equivalent individual stands at the root of the modern democratic state and is perhaps most strikingly in contrast with notions of persons found in hierarchical and holistic societies (Dumont 1980; Mauss 2000). Closely associated to this is the idea of the sovereign or possessive individual whose universality Macpherson challenges. Words like 'freedom', 'choice', 'capability' and 'achievement' are all certainly culturally loaded and premised on individualism rather than relationality, complementarity or hierarchy.

II

Perhaps this is a good moment to leave the political economists and return to anthropology. A critical anthropological question to pose to Sen is: *on what basis* will people 'have reason to value' the lives they can live? Here we must bring the collective – culture, society – back into the picture. What would a society that provides such reasons or enables (equitable) exercise of the capacities look like?

Reflecting on the societies in which I have lived or conducted research, I would say they have all been characterised by a significant amount of well-being. However, in none of them was well-being taken for granted; in each it was the subject of much debate, and sometimes of intervention – in sum, of politics. Perhaps this is in itself one of the chief attributes of well-being.

A utopian society is literally impossible because perfection would preclude exercise of the capacities for debate and action.

Let me say a few words about several of these places. In southern central Canada, where I have lived much of my life, collective identity is based partly on claims to enjoying a better quality of life than our neighbour to our south. Doubtless we protest our moral superiority too much – but we picture ourselves as a society with more equity and less violence, albeit higher taxes and less disposable income. Canadians prefer state-supported medicine and higher education to the open market. However, Canada certainly has its own inequities and immiseration. Ignoring regional disparities, I give but a single example from my urban milieu. Two women were taking a course of chemotherapy at the same clinic, undergoing ostensibly the same medical regime. Yet the one whose workplace was unionised had access both to six months of sick leave and to pharmaceutical insurance, while the other had been told by her employer that she would have to return to work midway through the treatment or be fired. In addition, she was extending the number of days between cycles of treatment because, being without a drug plan, she could not easily afford the expensive medicines. Canada's claims to have equitable (one tier) access to health care are not borne out in practice.

This example serves as a reminder that, in talking about well-being, we have to look not only at individuals or communities but at social wholes and the disparate positions within them. The well-being of the middle class has to be seen in conjunction with the trouble of the less privileged. And whether that malaise is recognised by the middle class, it detracts not only from the aggregate well-being of the social whole but from the more privileged class, introducing an element of repression, rationalisation, false consciousness, smugness or ethical unease. When people are oblivious to the systematic suffering of others – or rather, *because* of this very obliviousness – one cannot (from my ethical standpoint) characterise their condition as one of true well-being.

When we extend from the bounds of a single society to the global horizon, we must acknowledge that our well-being is compromised by the misery and increasing immiseration that takes place in much of the rest of the world and even to our material benefit. That is one reason, I would argue, why well-being should be characterised by moderation rather than by an excess of wealth and consumption. The very fact of my saying this from a position of material comfort is at once an index of an almost fatuous complacency – at the same time that it is meant as a critique and refusal of such complacency.

I turn next to an Israeli kibbutz, where I lived for a year in 1968 and visited for a few years thereafter. The generation of kibbutz pioneers struggled with considerable material deprivation and worked long hours at hard physical labour. Yet in other respects their quality of life was very high. They understood themselves as stretching, engaging and extending their capacities, including the capacity for manual labour previously denied them in Europe. They subscribed to what they called a 'religion of labour', in which labour was an end as well as a means. They had clear goals and saw themselves reaching them step by step. They revelled in having broken away from the constraints of the society in which they were raised. This sense of liberation was enthralling; they lived with great intensity and passion.

The kibbutz subscribed to the compelling Marxist principle 'from each according to his ability to each according to his needs' (Spiro 1963). No one went hungrier than their fellows and material conditions for all steadily improved. By the late 1960s, the gardens were lovely and members enjoyed a modern coffee house, swimming pool and overseas vacations. More importantly, there was plenty of opportunity to participate in decisions and avenues for leadership for those who sought it. Yet the kibbutz faced problems. Externally, it had to address the larger capitalist world and this led to many compromises over production. It also had to meet the needs of the state; its children entered the army and quite a number were killed. It had to come to terms with the contradiction between socialism and Zionism. Internally, too, there were problems. For some individuals the kibbutz was not a place of well-being. Demands for conformity were extreme and gave rise to the kind of jealousies, accusations and character assassinations characteristic of small, closely bounded groups. However, people did have an exit option and many of them exercised it.[12]

Well-being is no more stable than society. Any kind of model for the good life must build in the conditions for its reproduction and these will have to include motivating succeeding generations to maintain the system they inherit. Yet what is good for one generational cohort may prove problematic for the next. The chief problem faced by the kibbutz was a younger generation whose members in large number never came to fully share their parents' idealisation of the kibbutz model and never enjoyed the struggle to achieve it. The kibbutz then reproduced itself in part by shedding its young and replacing them with new recruits.

That the kibbutz failed to engage the capacities of subsequent generations with the same intensity as characterised the first suggests that a major factor too infrequently considered in evaluating quality of life is passion, that is, the passion of engagement in locally constituted practices and projects. In *Argonauts of the Western Pacific* (1964 [1922]), Malinowski described such passionate engagement in *kula* exchange and indeed this recognition is one of the most attractive features of the work. In structural analyses such concerns necessarily tended to disappear, although Evans-Pritchard (1940) famously depicted the passion of Nuer young men for their oxen.

I could go on at length about these practices. Suffice it to make three quick points without adequate discussion. First, such practices illustrate what Macpherson, after Aristotle, means by the conjoining of ends and means in leading a high-quality and virtuous life. This can be clarified by reference to MacIntyre's (1984) discussion of goods that are internal to a practice rather than external to it. Nuer youths enjoy simply gazing at their oxen; *kula* valuables cannot be hoarded and they have no meaning outside their continual circulation. Second, such practices are ethical, recognising – following Aristotle (1976), Mauss (2000) and Parry (1986) – that they balance rather than oppose self-interest and disinterest or self-sacrifice. They also provide arenas for action and the display of competence. Third, such practices are most compelling when they are intrinsically part of a total way of life rather than disembedded as, say, sport, economy or art.[13] I would add that one of the chief vices of modernity is certainly boredom.

My subsequent ethnographic cases illustrate the recognition by local communities that historical contingency and the larger context have changed the effects of valued practices. They illustrate how people respond when what were once goods internal to a given practice come to have external value (positive or negative) and when practices that were once integrated within a total way of life come to be separated as fragments from a totality. These processes challenge and undermine given ways of life, but their effects need not be fatal if people continue to be able to exert their human capacities and thereby to reflect, reinvent and recompose. Again, such acts of reflection, reinvention, recomposition, etc., do not merely enable well-being, they constitute it.

During the 1980s Muslim villagers in Mayotte deliberately closed down their complex and beautiful ceremonial system of exchange through which individuals endeavoured to exactly reciprocate the hospitality they received from others across the life-cycle and thus come to a conclusion in old age in which they achieved complete and egalitarian citizenship (that is, equal within the local community). Fulfilling these *shungu* obligations was stressful but also an opportunity to exercise one's capacities for planning, hard work, kinship, flair and enjoyment. When increasing commoditisation and inflation (including the opportunity cost of labour) undermined the practices of balanced reciprocity and the ability to feed the community from one's livestock and harvest, the system was wound down step by step (Lambek 1990, 2004).

Similarly, in Switzerland during the 1990s the male citizens of the Protestant half-canton of Appenzell Ausserrhoden voted to include women in their centuries-old annual *Landesgemeinde* – an outdoor public assembly of voters and ceremonial demonstration of the highest values of society (Bendix 1993). A few years later the entire assembly – now composed of men and women – voted itself out of existence, largely because its size seemed to overwhelm the democratic principle on which it was based.[14]

All these reforms are interventions aimed to restore some kind of balance and to maintain well-being in the long run. They respond to needs and desires but are ultimately a readjustment of the exercise of capacities. In the best of cases they redirect people from utilities to capacities. They demonstrate an active role in responding to change – engaging with and accepting it on the community's own terms, rather than simply and passively acquiescing.[15] Such active acknowledgement of change understood as an exercise and valuation of the capacities is also a central feature of my analysis of Sakalava

Measuring – or Practising – Well-Being? 125

historicity, in which ancestral spirits are called upon in the bodies of mediums to authorise change and to bless innovations, acts which they do not carry out lightly (Lambek 2002).

In sum, an aspect of the quality of life in each of these contexts is the availability of specific vehicles for reflection, communication, deliberation and decision-making. Such vehicles provide people with the practical means to engage ethically with the present and to anticipate the future by means of practices established and dispositions cultivated in the past. Another noteworthy feature is the way deployment of these vehicles combines what Turner (1982) has called the ergic and the ludic (work and play). My point here is not the functionalist one that their effects explain the presence of the institutions. The institutions are present only so long as people are motivated to continue to make use of them, and as long as such practices demonstrate 'reason to value' the lives they produce and the changes made to them. Again, a delicate balance is required.

III

These ethnographic snippets must suffice as the basis for some general claims concerning an anthropological perspective on well-being. I put these in point form.

(1) Well-being does not occur in the abstract. As human life is culturally constituted, so well-being only makes sense with respect to the contours of a particular way of life; particular structures of persons, relations, feeling, place, cosmos, work and leisure. Another way of saying this is that quality of life cannot be simply open freedom of choice. Well-being must include guides and orientations in the making of choice or the exercise of judgement, ones that affirm people's intuitions.

Well-being is constituted by means of and in respect to models of and for conduct, action and cosmos, vehicles of character formation and for collective decision-making, particular forms of relationality, kinship, friendship and intimacy, of work, politics and art, and of the production of value. The holistic structures in which anthropologists were used to articulating these dimensions of the quality of life have all been compromised or complicated by modernity and globalisation, not only by the effects of breakdown, encapsulation, commoditisation, etc., but also by varieties of pluralism, transnationalism, rationalisation and cosmopolitanism.

(2) 'No condition is permanent' – this political phrase holds for social well-being no less than for trouble (cf. Berry 1993). The well-being of individuals, families, communities and society changes continuously over time, marked by contingencies of health and illness, ageing, mortality, cycles of weather, harvests, demography, economy, conflict, warfare and so on. Think in the miniature of the dramatic plot lines of Ndembu village life (Turner 1957) and then of the way these cycles are themselves contextualised within broader regional historical movements (and ultimately transnational forces) (Pritchett

2001). Equally, then, the cultural models for well-being noted above are themselves inevitably in flux; the standards, values, practices and certainties of one generation are not necessarily those of the next. There may even be disagreement as to whether stability or novelty is a greater contributor or threat to well-being.

(3) The well-being of any given social unit, say a community, must always be contextualised with reference to the well-being of the social units at the next levels of inclusion. For us today that means that our well-being is compromised by the prevalence of suffering at the global level. Whatever the material quality of our lives, it is undermined by both the fact and the recognition of incapacity, and of the structural links between our material well-being and other people's lack. Additionally, the exercise of our human capacities is compromised by acknowledging their limits in addressing or resolving problems of larger scale, or confronting more powerful political forces.

(4) The term 'well-being' is 'studded with ... complex ethnocentrisms' (Edel and Edel 2000: 236). Debates about the good life are almost inevitably entangled with ideas about 'tradition' and 'modernity' (or 'civilisation'), and nowhere do we have to attend more closely to our colonial and missionary impulse. Generations of modernisers have had strong ideas about the good life; romantics and traditionalists have held alternate ones. Each has fantasies of greener pastures – whether behind (in the past) or ahead (in the future) and whether to the right or to the left. Presumably, exercise of the imagination is itself a central feature of human well-being. A world of well-being in which longing had been transcended would be not only literally utopian (nowhere) but sterile.

Fantasy aside, it is salutary to consider how modernity sees well-being for itself and in distinction from what preceded it. Following Habermas and, in effect, Weber, Charles Taylor observes:

... the constellation of modern beliefs and sensibility that makes the central questions of the good life turn on how we live our ordinary lives, and turns its back on supposedly higher or more heroic modes of life. It underlies the bourgeois ethic of peaceful rational productivity in its polemic against the aristocratic ethic of honor and heroism. (2004: 102–03)

Taylor argues that 'the saliency given to the private economic agent reflects the significance of the life of production in the ethic of ordinary life' (2004: 103) and notes in addition the 'ethic of self-fulfillment in relationships, which is very much part of our contemporary world' (2004: 103). Such images of bourgeois well-being, emergent in the Reformation, are beautifully portrayed in the works of the Dutch Masters, Vermeer, for example, even as they were subsequently subjected to critique in varieties of artistic modernism.[16]

(5) The attempt to develop universal standards of well-being is fraught for all the reasons just mentioned and more to follow. Moreover, the more abstract such standards, the emptier they are. Insofar as quality is distinct

from quantity, it is precisely that which is other to measurement – it implies incommensurability. This does not reduce us to a naive ethical relativism but it does suggest that the phrase 'measuring the quality of life' is an oxymoron. Moreover, such possibly well-meaning attempts at measurement inevitably dissolve quality (cf. Simmel 1978), entailing both the imposition of the discursive regimes of experts and the affirmation of a foundational model of 'the economy' which are not only themselves historically contingent but may actively contribute to decline in the quality of life.

(6) As the last sentence suggests, it is also impossible and dangerous *not* to evaluate or compare well-being and to observe that an increase in well-being (material or otherwise) for some sectors of local or global society is accompanied by a decrease for others. In many instances, then, and for reasons that may have to do as much with conflict of interest as with cultural relativism, it may be impossible to reach common agreement on whether, and to what degree or in what combination, social change has had positive or negative effects on life quality.

(7) One important issue, therefore, is how to get beyond the paradox of evaluating the immeasurable. One way round is to distinguish carefully between what can and what cannot be measured, and what can serve as an index of something else. This is part of Sen's achievement – for example, in locating the missing women. A further refinement is to distinguish what can be measured numerically from what can be understood simply as increase or decrease (cf. Macpherson 1973: 70). Macpherson also cleverly argues that while the ability to use and develop one's human capacities cannot be measured directly, it can be grasped 'by the quantity of external impediments to that ability, which is not a subjective quantity' (1973: 71). Macpherson measures constraints on ability; the fact that it is impossible to compare or measure satisfaction is irrelevant (1973: 71).

(8) It is dangerous to hold stringently and exclusively to one view of the good life and especially to assert what is best for others. A good life is constituted through living life well, not necessarily through theorising it, defending, advocating or imposing it on others.

Such a position does not presume a broad relativism. It doesn't prohibit agreement on what some of the impediments to a good life may be nor does it preclude active disagreement. Anthropologists can speak both about better and worse social arrangements and also about the incommensurability of diverse ways of life. These points are not contradictory as debates over relativism would have it. Some factors and some lines or levels of analysis enable measurement, others do not. One could argue that all societies based on a kinship mode of production offer certain things absent in capitalist societies, while admitting that distinct kin-based societies may be incommensurable with one another. How is one to choose in the abstract between Hopi and Navajo well-being or quality of life? How could we compare either of them with a tributary system like historical Bali or Buganda?[17]

Anyone who has lived in an African village knows that quality of life can be found in sociality no less than in consumption. Africans and Africanists often speak of wealth in people rather than wealth in things. Indeed, people of my generation in Mayotte found it ethically problematic that my wife and I deliberately had only two offspring. Some societies are demonstrably oppressive to women in ways that others of comparable scale or mode of production are not. The point about cultural relativism, or even ethical relativism, is not whether to embrace it or reject it unilaterally but when, and under what circumstances, to acknowledge it. This is a matter of practical judgement; in turn, the exercise of practical judgement (distinct from context-free 'choice') is perhaps a general, and possibly universal, feature of well-being.

Even when we place the exercise of the capacities over utilities, judgement is not always easy, nor is it always easy to acknowledge the judgement of others. What should we think about those Betsimisaraka of Madagascar described by Hilde Nielssen (2004), who prefer life in the bush to the agglomerated settlements on the road and who think their children don't need to go to school in order to live a life of well-being? Is sociality worth more than health? Is education in the arts of forest-living and the cultivation of the ancestors more enabling in this context than learning to read or do maths?

(9) Rather than advocate a particular form of the good life or describe its purported general or universal qualities, anthropologists show appreciation for the quality of life in various societies and for the diverse lives lived therein; we explore 'the art of living' (Lambek 2003a; Nehamas 1998). We analyse the various means societies have for maintaining or initiating passionate pursuits and practices that contain internal goods, including, most broadly, how various cultural traditions produce and encourage scenarios of life worth living and how they often find ways of making the best of things in the face of considerable impediments (including, in the most general of cases, the inevitability of death). Indeed, it is remarkable how many people have asserted that they live in the best of all possible worlds.

Additionally, anthropologists document assessments of where and when, how and why, quality of life is gradually or dramatically reduced or enhanced. We record internal debates as to whether life is getting better or worse and for whom. In other words, we examine people's ethical concerns, practices and innovations, their discussion and exercise of virtues like dignity and commitment, of principles like acknowledgement, justice and equity, and of the contrary faces of suspicion, envy and violence. We can then contribute our own theoretically and empirically informed arguments about what has happened.

It is an Aristotelian insight that well-being includes balance, for example, between security and challenge, stability and adventure (as Taylor's depiction of modernity implicitly notes). A particular balance will articulate roughly with the life-cycle and with the sort of life-stage goals proposed by Erikson (1959) (albeit possibly overly Western in their formulation), as well as with gender, class and the discursive powers of the wider society to shape, encourage or contain its members in engaging these practices.

(10) In discussing Macpherson I suggested that quality of life be ascertained by the presence of certain kinds of *acts* rather than *goods*. We can move a step further and suggest that quality of life is characterised not simply by material goods or creative acts but by kinds of *persons*, that is, by moral character. Consider the sort of hedonists whose images appear in the public media. Paris Hilton has a high quality of life by material standards – wealth, leisure, freedom of choice, etc. Yet, at the risk of being an intellectual or ethical snob, one must be dubious about the overall quality of life of a society that appears to grant such persons so much value.

Character is cultivated and such cultivation includes discipline. Durkheim's point about self-transcendence through society is relevant here. Life quality can only be produced by social means and these means include rules, taboos and obligations, not simply freedoms. If there ought to be a certain equality of opportunity for self-transcendence, so too perhaps for moral growth through confronting adversity (whether directly or through ritual, art or literature). This is recognised (or taken too far) by those forms of childhood training that require courage, endurance, etc., like a certain kind of British public school or the challenge of severe initiation rituals. There is a happy mean between indulgence and cruelty (affirmation and humiliation), but not all societies draw it in the same fashion.

(11) Taking this a step further, there is no 'no fault' good life. Well-being requires both effort and sacrifice of some kind. Value must be produced, it cannot simply be consumed. This is recognised in forms of sacrifice and asceticism as well as in the value placed on work itself. It is a critical issue for capitalist society, both for the affluent classes and for those unable to find meaningful, sustainable work.

(12) I close with a caveat. Virtuous practice, alas, does not ensure personal happiness. Not only is virtue itself consistently undermined by moral 'incontinence', but the human condition situates us with respect to contingencies that may be experienced as intractable and contradictions that may be experienced as irresolvable. An (Aristotelian) theory of happiness must be conjoined with a (Freudian) theory of unhappiness. Working from within both these traditions, Jonathan Lear speaks of 'the remainder of life' (2000), psychological disruptions that inevitably escape whatever conditions, values and practices are given or engaged upon. The result calls for a certain irony (Lambek 2003b; Lear 2003).

Biography leads to a similar conclusion. In his compelling memoir Norman Malcolm concluded that Wittgenstein's 'life was fiercely unhappy', but in the second edition (1984: 84 n. 4) he specifically changes his mind. Presumably, when Wittgenstein was deeply engaged in philosophy and so long as he was practising it well, he was not unhappy. But for some people the practice they favour is too singular; when you lose the skill or emerge from the practice, you have little to fall back on. So while Wittgenstein was a deeply ethical person and a master practitioner in the Aristotle/MacIntyre sense that should lead to – or constitute – happiness, perhaps his practice was not comprehensive enough and fell short of what he needed. Despite Aristotle's final advocation of a life of contemplation, the practice necessary for a happy life is surely broader or of a different order than contemplation alone.

I have a friend in Mayotte who was a carpenter and performer and teacher of Sufi music. While intensely engaged in these tasks his well-being was high and the same could perhaps be said for his practice as a spirit medium and as a husband and father. These practices enabled him to engage his capacities to the fullest. His well-being radically declined when he had to give up independent carpentry for work as a wage labourer and had little time or energy left for music; his power to exercise his capacities was diminished in exactly the ways Macpherson describes. But in addition, my friend's happiness was compromised from the outset by feelings of rejection and persecution rooted in his childhood. Although I have used them in quasi-synonymous fashion throughout this chapter, social well-being is not identical to personal happiness.

To conclude, anthropologists have much to learn from political philosophers. But equally, whereas political theorists often speak in hypothetical and ideal terms, anthropologists deal with the actual situations as we find them. We know that no societies are utopian, none are static, and none are without internal division and discrimination. We know further that well-being depends both on freedom from various obstacles and access to viable cultural practices and traditions through which the human capacities can be cultivated and exercised. We know that as material obstacles have declined in some places and increased in others, so too have time-tested practices been eroded or destroyed. And we know also that people need to inherit such practices or transform or invent them for themselves; they cannot simply be thrust upon them. But having so pontificated I must conclude with my original thought: what hubris the subject of well-being brings forth!

ACKNOWLEDGEMENTS

Thanks to Alberto Corsín Jiménez for inciting the paper, Jackie Solway for extremely helpful discussion and a critical reading, and Nadia Lambek for lending me some of the key sources. Fieldwork and writing have been supported by the Social Sciences and Humanities Research Council of Canada.

NOTES

1. See, among others, Boddy (2007), Li (2007), Mitchell (1988, 2002), Rappaport (1993), Scott (1998).
2. Sahlins (personal communication) drew rather from *Possessive Individualism* (Macpherson 1962).

3. See, for example, Macpherson's critique of Rawls (Macpherson 1973: ch. 4).
4. I would prefer to simply read 'humans' for Macpherson's 'man', but I think that is an open question insofar as some of the philosophers to whom he refers may distinguish the capacities of women from those of men, or may distinguish man the appropriator from woman the nurturer.
5. Macpherson recognises that we cannot go back to a society of independent producers since it wouldn't sustain the population, certainly not at the material level people expect. He admits that the absence of civil and political liberties diminishes men's powers more than the market transfer of powers, but argues that such absence or restrictions may not be necessary or intrinsic to socialist societies.
6. Macpherson offers a critique of the concept of power developed in the political science literature. From Hobbes to James Mill the concept of power is reduced to power over others (1973: 42). This is mainly extractive power, yet the empiricists mistakenly insist on distinguishing power from wealth, rejecting or ignoring 'Hobbes's definition of a man's power as his "present means to obtain some future apparent good" ' (1973: 46).
7. It may be noted that 'ethical' so defined embraces vice no less than virtue.
8. Hence Macpherson's additional expectation that technology might solve the problem of human labour is not exactly viable. It is reminiscent of Marx but also contains the sort of utopic science-fiction view characteristic of its era.
9. Of course, it is the very separation of labour from other capacities that can render certain activities 'mindless'. The distinction between fitting parts in an assembly line and shelling beans for supper lies not in the manual activity *per se* but (aside from the length of time spent at each) in the disembeddedness of the former from the social.
10. The relevant passage is drawn from Section 11 of Rawls, *A Theory of Justice* (1999: 54).
11. This is not, of course, to suggest that people do not need a minimum of utility satisfaction in order to exercise their capacities, nor desire a certain standard of material comfort, but the literature on hunter-gatherers suggests that, in certain social contexts, at least, this is less than we might imagine (Sahlins 1972; Solway 2006).
12. The cost of conformity in well-integrated, small-scale societies was a theme in the work of Benedict and Mead; jealousies and conflict were explored by authors such as Gluckman and Turner.
13. Among the most compelling if perhaps least marked of such passionate practices is the care of infants and children.
14. One common argument for discontinuing the assembly was that it had grown too large to enable a fair count of hands; it was replaced by the ballot box. The significance of the enfranchisement of women for the event is a complex issue I cannot address here.
15. The kibbutz also initiated various reforms (that some called compromises), including closing down the young children's dormitories and providing greater space for domestic life and private property.
16. Corsín Jiménez and I appear to have drawn upon Vermeer independently of one another.
17. Brody (2000) situates the key distinction between hunting and cultivating societies. He makes no bones about the ethnocentrism to which foraging peoples have been exposed by agriculturalists, nor his belief that, in the absence of external oppression, the former is a superior way of life.

REFERENCES

Aristotle. 1976. *The Ethics of Aristotle: The Nicomachean Ethics*, edited by H. Tredennick, trans. J.A.K. Thomson. Harmondsworth: Penguin.

Bendix, J. 1993. *Die Landesgemeinde in Appenzell Ausserrhoden*. Herisau: Schlüper & Co.
Berry, S. 1993. *No Condition Is Permanent: The Social Dynamics of Agrarian Change in Sub-Saharan Africa*. Madison: University of Wisconsin Press.
Boddy, J. 2007. *Civilizing Women: British Crusades in Colonial Sudan*. Princeton, NJ: Princeton University Press.
Brody, H. 2000. *The Other Side of Eden: Hunters, Farmers, and the Shaping of the World*. Vancouver: Douglas & McIntyre.
Dumont, L. 1980. *Homo Hierarchicus*. Chicago: University of Chicago Press.
Edel, A. and M. Edel. 2000 [1968]. *Anthropology and Ethics*. New York: Transaction Books.
Erikson, E. 1959. *Ego Identity and the Life Cycle*. New York: International Universities Press.
Evans-Pritchard, E.E. 1940. *The Nuer*. Oxford: Oxford University Press.
Lambek, M. 1990. Exchange, Time, and Person in Mayotte: The Structure and Destructuring of a Cultural System. *American Anthropologist* 92, 647–61.
—— 2002. *The Weight of the Past: Living with History in Mahajanga, Madagascar*. New York: Palgrave Macmillan.
—— 2003a. Rheumatic Irony: Questions of Agency and Self-deception as Refracted through the Art of Living with Spirits. In M. Lambek and P. Antze (eds) *Illness and Irony*. New York: Berghahn, pp. 40–59.
—— 2003b. Irony and Illness – Recognition and Refusal. In M. Lambek and P. Antze (eds) *Illness and Irony*. New York: Berghahn, pp. 1–19.
—— 2004. The Saint, the Sea Monster, and an Invitation to a *Dîner-dansant*: Ethnographic Reflections on the Edgy Passage – and the Double Edge – of Modernity, Mayotte 1975–2001. *Anthropologica* 46(1), 57–68.
Lear, J. 2000. *Happiness, Death and the Remainder of Life*. Cambridge, MA: Harvard University Press.
—— 2003. *Therapeutic Action: An Earnest Plea for Irony*. New York: Other Press.
Li, T. 2007. *The Will to Improve: Governmentality, Development and the Practice of Politics*. Durham, NC: Duke University Press.
Malcolm, N. 1984. *Ludwig Wittgenstein: A Memoir*, 2nd edn. Oxford: Oxford University Press.
MacIntyre, A. 1984. *After Virtue*, 2nd edn. University of Notre Dame Press.
Macpherson, C.B. 1962. *The Political Theory of Possessive Individualism: Hobbes to Locke*. Oxford: Clarendon.
—— 1973. *Democratic Theory: Essays in Retrieval*. Oxford: Clarendon.
Malinowski, B. 1964 [1922]. *Argonauts of the Western Pacific*. London: Routledge and Kegan Paul.
Mauss, M. 2000 [1925]. *The Gift*. New York: W.W. Norton.
Mitchell, T. 1988. *Colonising Egypt*. Cambridge: Cambridge University Press.
—— 2002. *The Rule of Experts: Egypt, Techno-politics, Modernity*. Berkeley: University of California Press.
Nehamas, A. 1998. *The Art of Living: Socratic Reflections from Plato to Foucault*. Berkeley: University of California Press.
Nielssen, H. 2004. Ritual Imagination: A Study of Tromba Possession among the Betsimisaraka of Eastern Madagascar. Doctoral dissertation, University of Bergen.
Parry, J. 1986. The Gift, the Indian Gift and the 'Indian Gift', *Man* 21, 453–73.
Pritchett, J. 2001. *The Lunda-Ndembu: Style, Change, and Social Transformation in South Central Africa*. Madison: University of Wisconsin Press.
Rappaport, R. 1993. The Anthropology of Trouble. *American Anthropologist* 95(2), 295–303.
Rawls, J. 1999. *A Theory of Justice*, revised edn. Cambridge, MA: Belknap Press.
Sahlins, M. 1972. The Original Affluent Society. In *Stone Age Economics*. Chicago: Aldine.
—— 1976. *Culture and Practical Reason*. Chicago: University of Chicago Press.

—— 1995. The Sadness of Sweetness: The Native Anthropology of Western Cosmology. *Current Anthropology* 37, 395–428.
Scott, J. 1998. *Seeing Like a State: How Certain Schemes to Improve the Human Condition have Failed*. New Haven, CT: Yale University Press.
Sen, A. 1999. *Development as Freedom*. Oxford: Oxford University Press.
Simmel, G. 1978 [1907]. *The Philosophy of Money*. London: Routledge and Kegan Paul.
Solway, J. 2006. 'The Original Affluent Society': Four Decades On. In J. Solway (ed.) *The Politics of Egalitarianism*. Oxford: Berghahn.
Spiro, M. 1963. *Kibbutz: Venture in Utopia*. New York: Schocken.
Taylor, C. 2004. *Modern Social Imaginaries*. Durham, NC: Duke University Press.
Turner, V. 1957. *Schism and Continuity in an African Society*. Manchester: Manchester University Press.
—— 1982. *From Ritual to Theatre: The Human Seriousness of Play*. New York: Performing Arts Journal Publications.

7 'REALISING THE SUBSTANCE OF THEIR HAPPINESS': HOW ANTHROPOLOGY FORGOT ABOUT *HOMO GAUISUS*

Neil Thin

Happiness is interesting, but awkward.

Humanity has been given various labels, the most well known of which are *Homo sapiens*, *Homo faber* and *Homo ludens*. But if we are wiser, work harder, and play more than other species, are we not also *Homo gauisus*, the species with unique capabilities for enjoying our lives and reflecting on that enjoyment? Evolutionary psychologists tend to argue that we evolved as a species capable of a remarkable range of adaptations which afford us happiness despite adversities. But they also share with many social scientists the assumption that modernity has ushered in a worrying host of new sources of suffering, making people less happy in modern civilisation than they were as hunter-gatherers (Buss 2000; Charlton 2000; Grinde 2002: 250). In contrast several social psychologists have argued, largely based on surveys, that most people in the world are happy (Diener and Diener 1996), and that humanity is becoming happier thanks to modern development (Veenhoven 2005: 61).

Regardless of beliefs about the place of happiness in characterisations of human nature, or in the evaluation of society and policy, we must surely all agree that well-being is a universal human concern and that subjective well-being, or happiness, is a core part of that concern. People everywhere want to enjoy their lives. They also want the other people that they like to enjoy their lives too. Despite the fascinating cultural variety in approaches to upbringing and in rhetoric about virtue, no sane parent in any culture hopes that their offspring will lead unhappy lives. Most of humanity is probably also concerned about whether or not an afterlife will afford us happiness, or torment, or some state in which neither of these is relevant any more. Moral codes and political systems are designed to encourage and enable people to behave so as to allow others to enjoy their lives. Happiness may not be the only ultimate good that humans have reason to value, but it is hard to think of wisdoms and virtues that can't in some way be traced to a core concern with happiness.

We should therefore expect that a century of anthropological holism ought to have developed systematic descriptions and analyses of happiness. Plausible ethnographies ought to have a lot to say about how people in diverse cultural contexts conceive of happiness, value it, display or conceal it, strive for it, anticipate it, sing and dance about it, incorporate it in moral codes and achieve it. Cross-cultural comparisons should tell us something about the ways in which beliefs, practices and institutions impinge on happiness, affecting its timing in the life-cycle and its distribution among different kinds of people. Ethnographic methods and analytical approaches should encourage and enable researchers to observe and discuss the quality of human experiences, the ways people feel about their lives in general and about specific institutions and practices in particular. Applied anthropology should include contributions to self-help and moral education literature on how best to allow people to pursue happiness without impinging on the happiness of others, and to policy guidance on how governments, businesses and social organisations might promote the responsible pursuit of happiness. I will argue that such expectations of anthropology, often explicit in its formative years, have been both frustrated and largely forgotten.

The coming year will see the publication of two collections of anthropological essays on well-being, for which there is no precedent in the history of the discipline. In the other one (Mathews and Izquierdo, forthcoming) I recommended and sketched out a set of agendas for anthropological study of the enjoyment of life. Both of these collections show that anthropologists can make important ethnographic and analytical contributions to happiness studies. Here I reflect on what we can learn about anthropology by trying to understand its failure so far to make these topics a core concern.

For much of the twentieth century, anthropologists specialised in the largely adulatory (or else descriptive-analytical and non-evaluative) study of non-civilised non-Western peoples, whereas sociologists did critical studies of the social pathologies of civilised Western peoples. As this division blurred, anthropologists increasingly emulated sociologists in focusing on pathologies, whereas sociologists in non-Western territories have avoided anthropological naivety and maintained their interest in the grimness of life and in the unfairness of social institutions. It has been left to social psychologists to assess how, and how well, social institutions and cultural systems perform at facilitating well-being.

More than other aspects of well-being, happiness has been particularly avoided by social scientists. Sociologists have done some 'objective' assessments of quality of life, but both they and anthropologists have failed to develop any systematic interest in the subjective, experiential aspects of well-being. No individual social scientist could pretend that happiness lacks interest as a topic, yet it has proved too awkward to handle. Here I explore some of the reasons for that awkwardness, and some possible ways forward.

HAPPINESS STUDIES PAST AND PRESENT

In the 1866 edition of the *Popular Magazine of Anthropology* the purpose of anthropology was said to be to 'assist all races of man to material prosperity and happiness' (Reining 1962: 595). Such thinking was normal in early social science. All the key Enlightenment and post-Enlightenment thinkers focused much of their analysis and rhetoric on happiness – its nature, its importance for policy and the effects of modernity on it. Rousseau (1754) argued that civilisation had ushered in a loss of authentic happiness. Locke, Comte, Condorcet, Montesquieu, Spencer, Marx, Weber and Durkheim were all explicitly interested in the contributions of social and philosophical analysis to the understanding of happiness, and in its relevance to social analysis and social policy. Adam Smith and Malthus both affirmed that happiness is the ultimate human goal, although economists turned their discipline into the 'dismal science' by replacing happiness with (mainly monetary) wealth and, by the start of the twentieth century, Marshall (1890: 1) was to declare that economics was no longer directly concerned with well-being but rather with material goods.

Well-being is particularly prominent in the work of Durkheim, with key terms like 'happiness', 'life-satisfaction' and 'health' cropping up repeatedly in all of his key texts. Psychologists like Wundt and Freud indulged in happiness theorising before the silencing of happiness crept in, exploring the meaning of happiness and its role in social life. William James's *Varieties of Religious Experience* (1902) is almost obsessively focused on happiness – as the ultimate good, as a personality trait of religious entrepreneurs and hence as the source of religious faith, and as a moral objective for programmes of mental self-control. It wasn't until the 1960s that a few psychologists began to follow his advice and focus on positive emotion and its manipulability.

Empirical social research flourished in the twentieth century with scarcely any attention to happiness. Happiness remained the concern of philosophers, theologians, moral crusaders, self-improvement gurus and, more recently, psychologists and economists. Major recent research compendia on happiness, even those specifically on cross-cultural perspectives, are authored almost entirely by psychologists (see, for example, Diener and Suh 2000). Anthropologists (along with sociologists) are conspicuously silent on the subject. Reference books and introductory texts on anthropology (including even key textbooks on psychological anthropology such as Bock 1988 [1980]; Harré and Parrott 1996; Schwartz et al. 1992; Segall et al. 1999) typically have no entries on happiness. Much the same is true of introductory texts on sociology, social policy and political studies. Rapport and Overing's (2000) collection of 60 essays on 'Key Concepts' in anthropology includes none on well-being, happiness, human flourishing, emotion or quality of life, finding topics like 'écriture féminine', 'the unhomely' and 'non-places' more worthy of attention.

The Anthropological Index Online, covering hundreds of thousands of articles from 1957 to the present (December 2006), has over ten times more entries for 'suffering' (239) as for 'happiness' (22), and nearly 20 times as many for 'illness' (393). Most of its 3631 articles on 'health' are actually about illness and its treatments. 'Violence' gets four times as many references (1579) as 'peace' (375). 'Development' literature focuses on failures and injustices rather than on social progress or well-being. Explicit happiness research by anthropologists has been far outstripped by research on such topics as hair (640), baskets (359), masks (721), tattooing (88), flowers (125) and alcohol (286). Interesting though these topics may be, it is unsettling that anthropological texts on such relatively minor aspects of human experience should outnumber texts on happiness by 100 to 1.

A 'Google (UK)' search on 'anthropology of happiness' (December 2006) gets 54 hits (nine in Google Scholar). 'Sociology of happiness' gets 339 (13), whereas 'economics of happiness' gets 18,500 (150) hits, 'psychology of happiness' 38,100 (488) and 'philosophy of happiness' 1280 (62). Comparisons with other anthropological topics are similarly striking: 'anthropology of religion' gets 248,000 (1190) hits, 'anthropology of gender' 29,900 (294), 'anthropology of development' 36,100 (372). Among the 5000 book titles on 'happiness' offered by Amazon (UK), the overwhelming majority are self-improvement guides, which have pitifully little reference to any kind of substantial happiness research at all, let alone to anthropology.

Veenhoven's introduction to the World Database of Happiness (1997) notes that research findings on happiness are very scattered and, for the most part, bibliographically irretrievable. Although arguing that social science research promises a breakthrough after many centuries of non-empirical philosophising, and arguing in principle for cross-cultural comparative studies of the factors influencing happiness, Veenhoven finds no anthropological inspiration worth including in his massive overview of happiness studies.

The muteness of academic anthropology on happiness is surprising, since many of us took up anthropology as part of a personal quest for happiness, with varying degrees of explicit rejection of the conventional routes to happiness into which we had been schooled. The traditional lure of anthropology for Western students includes the possibility that imagined noble and happy savages would teach us alternative routes to happiness, alongside non-Western philosophers, who would divert our attention to different life-goals such as *nirvana* and the idea of the primacy of collective rather than personal well-being. Our inattention to happiness can't be attributed to the vagueness and abstractness of the theme, since anthropologists aren't generally afraid of addressing big topics. If we can produce thousands of papers and classes devoted to abstractions such as power, alterity, hegemony, identity and culture, why have we produced virtually none on happiness? Anthropologists have been reasonably explicit in asking questions like 'What is a human being?' and 'What does it mean to be a person in culture x?' but they have been conspicuously silent on questions like 'What is a happy human being?' or 'What does it mean to be a happy person in culture x?'

This silencing of happiness is such a striking feature of the history of social science that it not only demands compensatory responses, but is also worth analysing for what it reveals about the evolution of social science. In the next four sections I will explore four sets of influences that, between them, may account in large part for the silencing of happiness in anthropology over the past hundred years. First, *anti-hedonism* (disrespect for utility as a motive, and a tendency for clumsy anthropological critiques of utilitarianism) has inhibited communication between anthropologists, moral philosophers and economists on the meaning of utility and its relation to motives. It has also inhibited recognition of the diversity of motives that are related to pleasure. Second, *moral relativism* (manifested as adaptivism or Edenic myth-making) has impeded our willingness to make evaluative comparisons of the performance of social institutions, cultural beliefs and practices in generating well-being. Third, *clinical pathologism* (the shared assumption among social scientists that pathologies are more interesting and worthy of study than the good things in life) has limited our ability to say what makes people well or have a good life, as opposed to what makes them suffer and have a bad life. And finally, *anti-psychologism* (social constructionism and, where psychology is accepted, cognitivism) has inhibited the discussion of feeling. When we do address feelings, the constructionist bias inhibits recognition of the intertwining of culture with genetic and biological factors in the generation of feeling, while (even more so than among psychologists) the pathological bias turns our gaze towards bad feelings rather than good ones.

ANTI-HEDONISM: THE FUTILITY OF SNEERING AT UTILITY

Malinowski was a passionate advocate of the appreciation of people's passions. He wanted ethnographers to represent the ways in which cultural diversity manifests itself in a diversity of sophisticated interests and pathways to the enjoyment of life. In his foundational *Argonauts* text, he warned future anthropologists that:

> ... to study the institutions, customs, and codes or to study the behavior and mentality without the subjective desire of feeling by what these people live, of realising the substance of their happiness ... is ... to miss the greatest reward which we can hope to obtain from the study of man. (1978 [1922]: 25)

Feelings, motivations and the enjoyment of life were to be given centre stage in the discipline of social anthropology.

It is surprising that neither he nor his followers managed to follow up on this declared interest in happiness, but it is also hard to reconcile his interest in happiness with his critique of 'utility' as a theory of motivation. He could hardly have been ignorant of the fact that 'utility' had generally been used by philosophers and economists as a synonym for happiness, and yet, as Frazer's

Preface to *Argonauts* makes clear, Malinowski's anti-utilitarianism is a major part of his theoretical argument. His interpretation of *kula* exchange, Frazer says, 'shows that it is not based on a simple calculation of utility, of profit and loss, but that it satisfies emotional and aesthetic needs of a "higher" order than the mere gratification of animal wants' (1978 [1922]: x).

In other words, both Frazer and Malinowski were keen that we should understand the complexity of people's motives, but in proposing this argument they made an entirely unwarranted association between the concept of 'utility' and a very restricted set of simple biological drives. In contrast to the philosophical-economic sense of 'utility', which points towards an infinite range of purposes including ultimate values, they used it in a sense closer to modern uses such as 'utility room' and – downgrading it still further – 'utility beef' (the US Government's euphemism for bad meat).

Malinowski boasts an anti-utilitarian interpretation not only of exchange but also of the purpose of 'work' (cf. Lambek's discussion of labour as an end in itself, ch. 6 this volume). Rejecting his contemporaries' common assumption 'that the native is a happy-go-lucky, lazy child of nature', he insists that Trobriand work includes 'aesthetic' rather than just 'utilitarian' motives (1978 [1922]: 58). He attacks what he calls the utilitarian myth of 'Primitive Economic Man', whose 'rationalistic conception of self-interest' was seen as the sole motivation for work. But here again the problem is not just with the confusing terminology: the implicit message is an exaggerated us:them message about the comparatively more sophisticated motives and concerns of Trobrianders when compared with civilised Westerners, whose exchanges and labours Malinowski assumed to be focused largely on basic material functionings rather than on the rich possibilities of life. Although emphatically trying to set up an alternative interpretive approach to mainstream 'utilitarian' economics, *Argonauts* fails to deliver on its implicit promises of an alternative route to studying well-being or happiness.

Oddly, Malinowski also assures us that, although gardening magic 'imposes on the tribe a good deal of extra work ... in the long run, however, there is no doubt that by its influence in ordering, systematising and regulating work, magic is economically invaluable for the natives' (1978 [1922]: 60). Without a theory of 'value' and a workable definition of 'economic', this kind of evaluative statement is not just naively optimistic but also vacuous. If the 'value' of aesthetics is defined broadly and vaguely, then of course any activity can be described as 'economically invaluable'. But this doesn't tell the reader much about the qualities being described. Does he mean that, without magic, the Trobrianders would produce less food, work less efficiently, enjoy their work less or enjoy less the fruits of their labours?

We are left to guess about this and about the larger question of whether some other cultural institutions might have performed better than garden magic at producing whatever 'values' Malinowski may be talking about. When he says later that *kula* valuables 'are of no practical use' (1978 [1922]: 86) it is fairly clear that he means they aren't directly used as tools. If the valuables contribute to health through their symbolic role in healing rituals, or to happiness through the pleasure of temporary ownership or the fun of the exchanges, they do so indirectly as part of a collective and long-term pattern of social exchange and meaning-making. Discussion of their 'economic value' (1978 [1922]: 90) is much more problematic, as this *evaluative* term depends on discussion of what people (including ethnographers and their readers as well as the people being discussed) value and why.

Malinowski was clearly trying to establish a moral anthropology, a holistic anthropology of *values, emotions* and *motives*. His critique of economics, his holistic approach to motivation and, above all, his desire to promote evidence-based and evaluative approaches to cross-cultural comparison, would have benefited enormously from a systematic approach to the analysis of motives and values. He never delivered this. Happiness should surely have featured centrally in such theorising. But it is touched on only in passing references and is never allowed to become a rubric for analysis.

More generally, to understand anthropology's reluctance to take hedonics (fun, the enjoyment of life) seriously, we must remember that, in its formative years, its exponents were fighting a battle to gain respect for non-Western lifeways. In so doing they needed to demonstrate that non-Western people had more complex motives than the mere 'happy-go-lucky' or selfish pursuit of pleasure. When David Plath first proposed research on enjoyment in Japan, he found colleagues reluctant to see enjoyment as a subject for serious discussion. He said people responded with the same kind of nervous reaction that greeted anthropological studies of sexuality. Many anthropologists were said to have 'regarded the project as preposterously amusing' (Plath 1964: 8, reviewed by Norbeck 1965: 535).

Anthropologists have had a distorted view of the Western philosophical concept of 'utility', and this partly explains why they have failed to join with other academic disciplines in developing systematic studies of the enjoyment of life. Like Malinowski, many anthropologists wanted to reveal to a civilised Western audience the complexities of people's motives in non-civilised or non-Western contexts (cf. Laidlaw's discussion of efforts to transcend the 'culture-blindness' of utilitarianism, ch. 8 this volume). A core message in many early ethnographies was: *These primitive people have much more complex motivations than you might expect.*

Malinowski's ill-informed critique of utilitarianism and of utilitarian explanation lived on in twentieth-century anthropology. Evans-Pritchard emphasised that Nuer totemism wasn't driven by 'utilitarian' motives (1956: 80). Sahlins argued that Malinowski didn't go far enough in rejecting utilitarian explanation. His book *Use and Abuse of Biology* (insincerely titled since it is only about the abuse of biology, not about its uses) notes that Malinowski's functionalism can be accused of exaggerating the role of biological need satisfaction in shaping culture (1977: 3). In criticising sociobiology as a 'new variety of sociological utilitarianism' (1977: x), Sahlins also said that it had a lot in common with Malinowski's functionalism.

But Sahlins, too, seems to lack a basic understanding of utilitarianism. An emphasis on biology and an underemphasis on culture is not a good reason to call a theory 'utilitarian'.

Throughout the twentieth century, the cold-shouldering of utilitarianism and antagonism towards it took on the character of an unseemly inter-institutional squabble of economists versus the rest, with much of the antagonism informed more by professional jealousy and boundary maintainance than by any rational or emotional objections to the core of utilitarian theory. In fact, anthropologists and economists were alike insofar as both disciplines forgot about happiness. For their part, economists were culpable not of overemphasising utility in their analysis, but of forgetting about it altogether by focusing instead on wealth and particularly on money – on the means to achieve utility, rather than on utility itself. No doubt Malinowski picked up some of his anti-utilitarian spirit from Durkheim, who passionately criticised utilitarian assumptions about self-interest being the main driving force behind social institutions. Durkheim's main argument in favour of establishing social science was to promote appreciation of the ways in which social solidarities rather than individual preferences (as economists would have it) shape our society.

This is no doubt a much fairer criticism of utilitarianism than the idea that it was a naively materialistic creed. More recently, the human rights movement, and those social scientists and philosophers who have developed theories of social justice, have added to this a further critique emphasising the moral danger that Bentham's (1948 [1776]), but not J.S. Mill's (1863), naive views on aggregate and measurable happiness might lead to policies which favoured expedient use of socially unjust means to achieve the ends of 'maximum happiness'. Many other plausible critiques of general and specific problems with variants of utilitarianism have been offered. Yet, whatever the reasons for social scientists' doubts about utilitarianism, none of them justifies a wholesale rejection of the idea at the core of utilitarian philosophy, namely that 'happiness', broadly and flexibly conceived, does and should form a central guiding principle for governance and for personal choices, and for our interpretation of moralities.

So it is quite right that we must recognise that Trobriand *kula* exchanges and Nuer cattle exchanges are (in part) about history and social connectedness, and that Trobriand gardens are about pride in aesthetics. But, in many cases, the anthropological message went further than this to make invidious us:them comparisons which went roughly like this: *These primitive people are both more sophisticated and more social in their motivations than civilised people in market economies, who have largely reduced their motives to the selfish focus on financial profit.*

A related kind of message common in early anthropology but usually less explicit, concerned the outcomes of motivations: *These primitive people are happier than people in civilised Western societies.* This 'happy savages' or 'lost Eden' message is still to be found, especially in popular use of anthropology today, and it survives in popular romantic discourse also as a 'happiness in poverty' argument which can be applied to the underclass living in 'civilised' countries: *They may live in squalor and have low life expectancy and no education, but they know how to enjoy themselves.*

Together, such messages exemplify the ambivalence of romanticism. On the one hand, romantics seek alternatives to Western civilisation as the sources of goodness, and so are disposed to portray non-Western culture in idyllic terms. On the other hand, romantics are drawn towards suffering and poverty by an aesthetic code which valorises ill-health and which finds underdogs and victims more interesting and more worthy objects of study than top dogs and people who live in comfort. It is these two faces of romantic anthropology that will be discussed in the next two sections.

MORAL RELATIVISM, ADAPTIVISM AND NON-EVALUATION

In case any readers should be under the misapprehension that anthropology has long since managed to rid itself of naive relativist adaptivism, they should take note of Bodley's entry (2007) on 'Anthropology' in the online edition of *Encarta*. Bodley assures readers that anthropologists don't believe in progress, that their relativist approach has allowed them to reveal 'that every cultural group lives in a way that *works well* for many of its people' and that 'anthropologists work from the *assumption that a culture is effective and adaptive* for the people who live in it ... [and that] a culture structures and gives meaning to the lives of its members and allows them to work and prosper' (emphasis added). Let us hope that most anthropologists today would not pretend that all cultures are equally good, and would recognise in principle that some cultures, or institutions, beliefs and practices, are better than others at allowing people to achieve well-being and to achieve meaningful lives.

Jean Liedloff, author of *The Continuum Concept: In Search of Happiness Lost* (1986), according to the cover of the book spent two and a half years 'deep in the South American jungle living with stone age Indians', and that, on the basis of what she learned there, is now in California advocating psychotherapy to help Californians recover their 'natural well-being'. Texts whose ethos is not dissimilar to that one have no doubt inspired and encouraged the typically large numbers of students taking anthropology as optional extra classes in Europe and North America. Anthropology students' quests for alternative happinesses have for many years been propelled and reinforced by reading Rousseau-esque accounts of happiness among marginal peoples. Typically, such accounts ignore all the objective indicators of suffering such as horrific rates of infant and maternal mortality, malnutrition, physical violence and homicide.

You can't study anthropology for long without becoming involved in debates about the pros and cons of 'lost Eden' myths or of 'salvage' ethnography. A few pages before declaring his interest in happiness, Malinowski more famously declared in the Preface to *Argonauts* an exasperation with the 'tragic' prospect of our subject matter 'melting away' (1978 [1922]: xv). No doubt a major driving force behind both of these statements was the spirit of his European age, in which severe doubts had emerged, particularly among intellectuals, concerning the relationship between the march of civilisation and the achievement of happiness. This scepticism was perhaps most memorably expressed by Durkheim: 'Is it true that the happiness of the individual increases as mankind advances? Nothing is more doubtful' (1960 [1893]: 241).

Questions about the qualities that may or may not have been lost through the relentless march of civilisation have been a paramount concern for anthropologists. The implication here is that the world is becoming a sadder place with the 'melting away' of some kinds of culture, and that anthropology in particular has every reason to be a sad discipline.

Lévi-Strauss's title *Tristes Tropiques* doubtless echoes, at least unconsciously, this kind of assumed sadness. He gives here a striking confession of his belief, shared with Rousseau, that it 'would have been better for our well-being' if mankind had stayed in the neolithic stage of evolution (1973 [1955]: 446). The chapter headed 'Virtuous Savages' complains of the 'wretchedness' of Indians living near peasant villages, and parades his aesthetic and moral admiration for Bororo, Nambikwara and other 'comparatively untouched' societies – representing them with pictures such as the naked adolescent girl captioned simply: 'A Nambikwara smile' (1973 [1955]: 234–35).

So Lévi-Strauss was interested in happiness and had some strong if absurdly under-theorised views on what makes people happy. Yet he wasn't interested enough in happiness to consider it worthwhile commenting, in that same chapter, on the morality of his act of selling a gun to a Bororo man, or on the morality of the extreme inequality in Bororo society, or on the men's use of rape as a punishment for women who stray too close to the men's house (1973: 247, 252). Gripped as he was by the powerful rhetoric of the lost Eden myth with which Malinowski had started *Argonauts*, Lévi-Strauss appears to have been incapable of standing back and offering serious analysis or empirical scrutiny of the myth of primitive happiness.

Perhaps the most famous 'lost Eden' text is Turnbull's *The Forest People* (1984 [1961]). The BaMbuti pygmies of the Ituri are portrayed here as happy people for whom nature and culture, people and their (BaMbuti) social and biophysical environments, are in harmony. They and their forest are introduced in positive evaluative terms. Their life is 'a wonderful thing full of joy and happiness and free of care'. Their knowledge of the forest is better than that of scientists. They 'have no fear, because for them there is no danger'. 'For them there is little hardship.' They are 'powerful and tough', less clumsy than their non-forest neighbours. They are 'simple, unaffected ... captivating' (1984 [1961]: 29, 18–19, 27). Turnbull himself grew to share the BaMbuti's 'complete faith ... in the goodness of their forest world' and their mystical appreciation of 'the presence of the forest itself' (1984 [1961]: 88), despite its evident dangers and shortcomings as a source of basic subsistence.

He indulges with gentle amusement the BaMbutis' stealing from neighbouring people and their racist disparagement of 'negroes' as 'animals'.

Still, wary perhaps of being labelled a romantic, Turnbull also says that 'the pygmies are no more perfect than any other people, and life, though kind to them, is not without its hardships' (1984 [1961]: 27). He wants us to fall in love with the carefree and pleasant and aesthetically pleasing BaMbuti, yet he admits that they are 'no more perfect' than their settled neighbours, the 'negro tribes' who are 'a rather shifty, lazy lot' (1984 [1961]: 36). Perhaps the BaMbuti are not even any better than the Ik of Uganda, who Turnbull later described as 'a people without life, without passion, beyond humanity' (1973: 243). Could the BaMbuti really be unaware of the real dangers and hardships they face, as Turnbull claimed? If so, then surely any insecure happiness they might achieve would hardly offer an enviable model for human flourishing. Not many of us would value happiness if it came at the cost of the most basic ecological awareness.

But which part do we believe: that Mbuti life has a 'full complement of hardships and problems and tragedies' or (continuing the same sentence!), that it is 'free of care' (1984 [1961]: 29)? Do we believe that 'for them there is no danger' or that elderly Mbuti people are terrified they will be left to die of starvation because everyone knows they 'may endanger the safety of the group' (1984 [1961]: 19, 38). Do we really believe that BaMbuti trust the forest, or should we suspect that they sing about the goodness of the forest, and flatter it with the metaphor of parenthood, because they are actually deeply conscious of its dangers and shortcomings?

Turnbull's unreliability may be an easy target that is already familiar to most anthropologists, but his work is interesting as an example of the difficulties that arise from our discipline's profound ambivalences towards evaluative responsibility. Tragically, despite being better than most anthropologists at capturing the public imagination, and braver than most in making explicit evaluative statements about the people he wrote about, Turnbull was unable to give his ethnographies even a veneer of scientific or moral credibility. Even the most rudimentary theorising of the quality of life and of the dimensions of happiness, could have helped him overcome those weaknesses while retaining the popular appeal of this books.

Another more recent and still-active populariser of the 'lost Eden' myth is Helena Norberg-Hodge. Her book *Ancient Futures* (1991) tells a story about how traditional Ladakhi culture had the secret of happiness, but that this happiness is now under threat from modern development. A chapter headed '*Joie de Vivre*' presents Ladakhis as the happy people: 'The Ladakhis possess an irrepressible joie de vivre. Their sense of joy seems so firmly anchored within them that circumstances cannot shake it loose' (1991: 83). She herself had been wrong, she argues, to assume that this was only a display of happiness, and 'that there were no significant cultural differences in the human potential for happiness':

'Realising the Substance of Their Happiness'

With so much of our lives [sic: that is, in the industrialised West] colored by a sense of insecurity or fear, we have difficulty in letting go and feeling at one with ourselves and our surroundings. ... I have never met people who seem so healthy emotionally, so secure, as the Ladakhis ... the most important factor is the sense that you are a part of something much larger than yourself, that you are inextricably connected to others and to your surroundings. (1991: 84–85)

Such passages offer unusually explicit analysis of links between culture and emotional well-being. Some of the examples and interpretations are certainly suggestive of important qualities of Ladakhi philosophies and attitudes that would be worth further study. But without an interpretive framework based on cross-cultural happiness theory, and with the comparative dimension relying on the crude rhetorical strategy of 'bad West' and 'bad modernity' versus 'good East' and 'good tradition', this kind of writing is hardly going to help anthropology gain a foothold in international happiness research.

The prize for the most influential analytical text in the 'lost Eden' category must go to Sahlins for his 'Original Affluent Society' essay. This was a bold but ill-conceived and morally irresponsible attempt to reinterpret hunter-gatherer culture through a metaphor of Zen Buddhism's want-limiting road to 'affluence'. This suggestion that people living in abject poverty are in some sense *choosing* poverty is rather chilling, and likening a hunter-gatherer underclass to the elite exponents of Zen is simply absurd. Zen was devised as a countercultural creed: followers chose to limit their material desires and consumptions as part of their ongoing struggle for social distinction, not as a livelihood strategy in a resource-poor environment. Still, this idea has for decades proved intuitively appealing enough to warrant the inclusion of that article on countless introductory anthropology courses. Generations of anthropology neophytes may have gained something by letting this essay persuade them that happiness lies in voluntary acceptance of material deprivation. But they have also missed important opportunities to assess contemporary hunter-gatherers' life quality in comparative and historical perspective. As I noted at the start of this essay, some authors have speculated that past hunter-gatherers may well have been happier than most of humanity is today. Portraying contemporary hunter-gatherers as 'affluent' stretches credibility to breaking point.

Strikingly, even ethnographies which emphasise pervasive violence and suffering can to some extent fall into the 'lost Eden' mould. In its 1992 edition, in response to mounting public criticisms, Chagnon changed his title from *Yanamamö: The Fierce People* (1968) to *Yanamamö: The Last Days of Eden* (1992). This is an interesting choice of terms, since Chagnon's gleeful cataloguing of grotesque levels of violence is somewhat at odds with the biblical Eden. A more interesting example, and certainly one that is more respected among academic anthropologists, is Michelle Rosaldo's book *Knowledge and Passion: Ilongot Notions of Self and Social Life* (1980), widely regarded as a classic in the anthropology of emotion. Like most of this school of anthropology, it focuses on adverse and dangerous emotion, rather than on happiness (her index lists over 50 references to the concept of *liget* [tension, anger] and just three to *sipe* [happiness]). 'Passion' seems to be understood here mainly in the original sense derived from the Latin *patere*, 'to suffer', although also more actively in the idea that anger is a key motive for action. Rosaldo states as a fact that in one community 65 out of 70 men over 20 years of age had killed and beheaded people. Given that she seems to have believed these statements, it is striking that her Preface waxes romantic about a glamorous world that was on the wane by the time she arrived:

I find myself overwhelmed with gratitude and nostalgia for a world that is typified by the warmth, consideration, and playfulness of people.... this book embodies my desire to celebrate these Ilongots in the context of political and economic developments that seem more than likely to crush them – developments that I have not learned how to change. (1980: xiv)

There is no mention here or anywhere else of any moral disgust at murder. She even appears to accept uncritically her informants' view that lopping off someone's head is 'not murder' (1980: 52). She disparages unreservedly the advent of modern development, refusing even to countenance the possibility that outsiders might be able to bring some material benefits and moral virtues which might help Ilongot people live happier, longer and less violent lives. Rosaldo's book offers fascinating, if brief, discussions of the relationships between anger and happiness in Ilongot culture:

To be happy for an Ilongot is to be light, clear-headed, healthy, and free of constraint. The happy heart is 'weightless'; it is 'fluttering' and 'vibrant,' – all conditions which come (for men) from releasing the 'weight' of anger, *liget*, by beheading someone. Happiness, for them, 'suggests activity and sociality, and has little to do with quietness, tranquility, or peace' but is 'born of liget and agitation. (1980: 51–52)

Potentially instructive though these vignettes may be for the cross-cultural study of well-being, it is hard to respect and trust them given Rosaldo's astonishing failure to develop an adequate moral and gender-balanced interpretation of the quality of Ilongot life.

In *Anthropology by Comparison*, Fox and Gingrich remind us of the sense of public responsibility that anthropologists felt in the 1920s and 1930s, part of which was to offer cultural comparisons which would be in the public interest. Since then, we have been neglecting cross-cultural comparison (2002: 1–3). A great deal of social writing has been *non-evaluative*: overwhelmingly, social science writing has been describing situations and analysing patterns without coming to explicit judgements about the good or bad quality of human experience. In multicultural studies, the influence of relativism has discouraged cross-cultural comparative moral judgements, resulting in a pervasive Panglossian optimism in anthropology. This adaptivism, as exemplified by the Bodley quote above, assumes that anything cultural or traditional (and especially if it is non-Western) must be benign and worth cherishing.

Edgerton argued in *Sick Societies* (1992) that anthropology remains largely non-evaluative due to the continued pernicious influences of both cultural relativism and adaptivism. The book seems dated because so much of it is taken up criticising 'lost Eden' mythologising that most anthropologists have long ceased to respect. In any case, the problem with 'lost Eden' myths is that they *do* take an evaluative stance, one which is embarrassingly naive, biased and not informed by any plausible theory of well-being. Still, there is a sense in which this hard-hitting book was needed: it is hard to deny that academic anthropology is still guided by an essentially negative code regarding evaluative judgement – that cultural traits and practices are mainly to be described and analysed but not judged in ethical terms since they must be assumed to make sense in terms of their cultural and biophysical contexts.

There are of course good reasons for not jumping too hastily to adverse and perhaps ethnocentric judgements. But what the adaptivist assumption lacks is a concept of human *flourishing*; instead, it is guided merely by a non-evaluative criterion of human existence. To the extent that we describe and analyse in non-evaluative terms, we are nowadays a surprisingly 'cold' discipline, despite our evolution from the 'hot' – emotional, tendentious, romantic attitudes of so many of our intellectual forebears. Ironically, given relativism's logical antipathy to evaluation, anthropology's penchant for Eden myths took hold as a rebound from the pathological critique of Western modernity. In the late twentieth century, pathologism then infected anthropology as an over-reaction to that earlier romantic relativism. As Colin Turnbull proved when he wrote the obsessively pathological *Mountain People* as a contrast to the absurdly romantic *Forest People*, it is even possible for an individual author to over-react against his own romanticism. Likewise, in Robert Edgerton's *Sick Societies*, which presents a catalogue of social ills, he admits that he includes his own earlier writing as part of the romantic relativism that he is responding to.

The lack of happiness anthropology is part of a broader pattern, affirmed in publications by Howell (1997) and Laidlaw (2001), namely the lack of explicit ethnographies and anthropological theorising on morality. Laidlaw has argued, reasonably, that 'there cannot be a developed and sustained anthropology of ethics without there being also an ethnographic and theoretical interest – hitherto largely absent from anthropology – in freedom' (2001: 311). Pursuing this argument, however, it is perhaps more important still to argue that *there cannot be an anthropology of ethics or of freedom without developing an anthropology of the ultimate goods which we might be free to choose.* Whether or not our philosophy puts happiness at the apex of all goods, it surely must feature in some form among our pantheon of ultimate goods. If there are other ultimate goods worth considering, we must be consider their relationships with happiness, that is, scrutinise the complementarities and trade-offs among the various ultimate goods which we value. It is embarrassing for the discipline to have professional codes of 'ethics' (for example, AAA 1998; ASA 1999), which pontificate on the good behaviour of anthropologists, and on their responsibilities towards the well-being of the people they study and of humanity in general, with no reference to any theories or empirical studies of well-being or happiness.

CLINICAL PATHOLOGISM IN THE SOCIAL SCIENCES

Purveyors of lost Eden myths write about happiness among pre-industrial people because they assume their readers will find such happiness remarkable. Generally, however, social scientists follow Tolstoy (in his famous declaration at the start of *Anna Karenina*) in finding happiness uninteresting. With apologies to Bourdieu, my suggestion is that in non-idyllic social science 'what goes *unsad* goes without saying'. In English, you can be unhappy but not unsad, unwell but not unill, unloved but not unhated, unhopeful but not unpessimistic. A negative tag can only be added to a word which refers to something normally taken for granted. You can be discontent, displeased or dissatisfied, because these are all marked departures from assumed norms. Most, though not all, adverse emotions are seen as abnormal: you can't be unangry or undepressed because you can't exceptionalise an already exceptional condition. Exceptionally positive emotions such as joy and elation are untaggable: you can't be unjoyful or unelated. *Social science's lack of interest in happiness, then, is part of its broader disinterest in normality.* Happiness is a default, unmarked category of experience. It is taken for granted, and conditions or experiences that depart from this norm are those that attract our attention and are 'marked' categories of condition and experience.

The muteness of the social sciences on happiness is part of the general pathologism of the social sciences – a lack of interest in the normal and the good that I have discussed at length elsewhere (Thin 2002). Edgerton's *Sick Societies* exemplifies this. Rhetorically pathological as an antidote to adaptivist ethnography, this important stepping-stone towards an evaluative anthropology of well-being is spoilt by its excessive focus on ill-being. Edgerton fails to consider what an 'adaptive' or 'well' culture might look like in theory, and offers no examples of good social institutions that promote well-being. More generally, social scientists in general focus on adverse experiences and evaluate the quality of life and of institutions and relationships in negative terms. While many have studied emotions and have written normatively about experiences and aspirations, they have written predominantly about sadness and suffering. When they have written about the distributions of desired goods they have focused much more on injustice than on all the work which every society does to achieve justice. Many social texts about morality, the emotions, and even those purportedly about well-being or quality of life, forget to mention happiness. These are shocking omissions.

My growing interest in the cross-cultural study of happiness is a logical progression from my 20 years as a development anthropologist. What good is planning if it isn't focused on optimising well-being? Like most developmentalists, however, I have succumbed to both pragmatism (looking at what can be delivered) and pathologism (looking at harm and its undoing, rather than at the production and reproduction of goods). Eldis, one of the best search engines on international development, finds only 23 references to happiness in its 30,612 records (December 2006). 'Suffering' scored 557 hits, 'violence' 987, 'poverty' 5615. 'Well-being' scores 1045 hits, but these are nearly all about ill-being (which itself scores only 57 hits). The 162 'Mental health' texts are all about mental illness.

Pragmatic pathologism can be defended by Popper's (1945) dictum of 'negative utilitarianism' (politicians should minimise suffering, not promote happiness), and by Murray's (1988) argument that the freedom to pursue happiness requires limited governance. But to emphasise only the reduction of poverty and reduction of human rights abuses is philosophically unsound, since even a minimal goods approach still needs to be informed by a theory of ultimate goods. On pragmatic grounds, it is contradictory to address poverty and suffering without trying, more generally, to promote collective efforts for social progress. In international development planning and analysis, the rise of the 'rights-based approach' as an alternative to 'needs-based' approaches is based on the argument that promoting 'rights' is less paternalistic than the charitable provisioning of goods to meet needs. These two should never have been seen as alternatives, but rather as complementary components in any sound development strategy. Both, however, exemplify a negative minimalism which arguably should be complemented by a third, 'happiness-based' approach.

Pathologism has a surprising hold even on texts supposedly about well-being. Arguably anthropology's most prominent enterprise in cross-cultural comparison and policy guidance on happiness, the huge report on *World Mental Health* (Desjarlais et al. 1995) focuses entirely on mental illness. Assuming we know what 'mental health' is, the authors forgot their own advice (1995: 7) that 'mental health is not simply the absence of detectable mental disease but a state of well-being'. Happiness is implicitly assumed to exist in the absence of problems. Mental health promotion is thereby reduced to preventing, alleviating and curing mental illness. Just as 'mental health' texts are invariably about mental illness, most academic and policy texts on 'well-being' (or 'welfare') are about ill-being and lack any serious attention to well-being. Texts on 'human rights' are about wrongs, and texts (and academic courses) on 'development' are about poverty and destruction, not usually about progress. Such counter-intuitive language usages have become so normalised that we rarely notice them.

Edgar and Russell's *The Anthropology of Welfare* (1998) forgets entirely the root meanings of welfare, focuses on pathologies and forgets well-being, and explores numbers and services rather than the experience and evaluation of the quality of life. Hollan and Wellenkamp's *Contentment and Suffering: Culture and Experience in Toraja* (1994) has a lot to say about culture and suffering (the index is replete with references to adverse emotions and processes such as anxiety, vulnerability, anger, conflict, sadness, shame, embarrassment, grief, crying, being upset, wailing, deceit, disturbing dreams, somatic complaints, suicide, mental disturbances, depression, disorder and dysphoria) but the 'contentment' theme is all but forgotten, figuring only in an assertion that, for Toraja, 'happiness and contentment can best be defined as the occasional and fleeting *absence* of suffering and hardship' and that they do not 'talk much about the ways of attaining happiness. Mostly, they talk of how to avoid distress' (1994: 28, 118).

Hollan and Wellenkamp's informants are mainly adults, who see adulthood as a time of suffering in contrast to a happier childhood (1994: 80–83). More generally, it seems possible that pathological bias in anthropology could derive from the tendency for transcultural ethnographies (where ethnographers have struggled with an unfamiliar culture and language) to be based mainly on talking to adults. Naomi Adelson's *Being Alive Well: Health and the Politics of Cree Well-being* (2001) was almost entirely based on discussions with adults whose holistic version of 'well-being' is told mainly in negative terms via a narrative of external incursions which have robbed them of their traditional way of life. It is quite likely that younger informants, eager users of the technologies and consumer goods of modern Canada, might have had utterly different stories to tell about their conceptions of well-being. Here, the 'lost Eden' mythologising combines with modern pathologism to ensure that the promised ethnography of well-being is undelivered.

PSYCHOLOGICAL ANTHROPOLOGY AND THE PROBLEMS OF CONSTRUCTIONISM AND COGNITIVISM

Anthropology's failure to develop happiness studies derives partly from its awkward relationships with the discipline of psychology. Our penchant for *social constructionism* has tended to position us in unhelpful opposition to psychologists' universalist assumptions about the psychic unity of humanity, making us reluctant to admit that an interest in humanity's universal genetic heritage could be relevant to our discipline. *Cognitivism*, which shares its roots in a suspicion of biological universalism, is not anti-psychological but it is anti-sentimental, resisting the incursion of emotional analysis into anthropology.

Happiness has cognitive aspects, concerned with thinking about the good life, and emotional aspects, also evaluative but more fleetingly so and concerned with the quality of experience. Despite some mainly North American exceptions, anthropology has proceeded largely without collaboration with psychologists and with remarkably little willingness to explore emotional experience. Most twentieth-century ethnographies described the social infrastructure of kinship arrangements, political structures and ritual in detail, complementing this with the kind of 'dry' interpretation you might expect for Egyptian hieroglyphics. Attention to symbolic patterning largely excluded attention to the ways in which diverse individuals might experience the institutions.

Needham's structuralist manifesto against psychologism, *Structure and Sentiment* (1962), epitomised this approach by declaring that 'making sense' of society means looking at 'structure' and not at 'sentiment'. Psychological interpretations of kinship systems are 'demonstrably wrong' (1962: vii–viii). Perhaps later in life Needham realised that no kind of account of kinship – whether it is descriptive, analytical or normative – can reasonably be proposed without reference to the ways in which people emotionally experience kinship systems, or to the roles of kinship criteria in people's conceptions of the good life. In 1981 he criticised anthropologists' failure to write about 'inner states' as understood through 'indigenous psychology' (1981: 56). Still a social constructionist, Needham then argued that anthropological neglect of psychology had derived from a naive belief that inner states are universal and therefore uninteresting.

Anthropologists since then have produced a great deal of interesting work on emotion, but this has been marred both by its pathological bias and by its often clumsy attempts to portray social construction as a better alternative to evolutionary psychology rather than as complementary to it (for good critiques, see Lyon 1995; Reddy 1997, 2001). Academic psychology departments are routinely kept separate from social sciences, despite the obvious common interests and interdependencies. British social anthropology courses and texts typically lack reference to any psychology texts, and seem particularly averse to mentioning the growing field of evolutionary psychology, which has produced some of the most promising recent texts on happiness and morality (see, for example, Buss 2000; Charlton 2000; Cosmides and Tooby 1997; Grinde 2002; Wright 1995).

Those social scientists who have paid attention to psychology have tended to be cognitivists, mapping out mental structures, patterns and representations while ignoring feelings. There have been far more texts on topics like rationality and cognitive processing than on happiness, love or hope. Those who have studied emotions have explored depression, anxiety, hate and anger far more than the positive emotions. Many have confined discussion to the cognitive, formally articulated, collective and public versions of emotions, and avoid speculation about private feelings. Denzin argued that we must ask 'How is emotion, as a form of consciousness, lived, experienced, articulated, and felt?' (1984: 1). Epstein's (1992) critique of cognitivism and constructivism in anthropology offers a landmark attempt to address these issues and deplores the inadequate attention to the emotions even in psychological anthropology. Yet he is mainly interested in adverse emotions.

THE MEANING OF HAPPINESS: UNIVERSALS AND VARIETY

Rather than defining happiness or specifying a particular approach to its analysis, I have assumed that readers will share common happiness-related concerns about well-being, motivation and morality. More specifically, we could explore ways in which anthropological sub-disciplines might engage with happiness studies. We could identify as essential engagements the anthropological analyses of morality, value, altruism, philanthropy and religion; of development, human rights and progress; of ill-being, poverty, suffering and harm; and of health and mental health (Thin forthcoming). A much longer list of desirable engagements could include anthropologies of politics, violence and peace-making, consumption, work and leisure, play and sport.

I have also argued (Thin forthcoming) that anthropologists should develop a set of semantic distinctions associated with the study of well-being, including:

positive versus *neutral* senses of well-being
residualist versus *constructive* approaches (well-being as default or as the product of effort)
short-term versus *long-term* orientations
this-worldly versus *other-worldly* orientation
experiential versus *conceptual* or *evaluative* orientation (feeling good or making assessments)
subjective versus *objective* accounts
aggregative versus *integrated* assessment
domain-specific versus *holistic/inclusive* assessment
physiological versus *metaphysical* assessment
egocentric versus *sociocentric* assessment
aroused versus *calm* forms of happiness

Psychologists are in reasonable agreement that three 'dimensions' of happiness are connected but independent: *positive feelings*; (avoidance of) *negative feelings*; and *life satisfaction*. Anthropologists' interests go well beyond assessment of individuals' happiness, so we might usefully begin with three broad reasons for including happiness in social analysis: to understand better people's *feelings*, their *evaluative meanings* and their *motives*. For anthropologists to seem uninterested in the feelings of the people they write about would be simply inhumane. We can helpfully relate information about feelings with analysis of how people evaluate their lives, other people's lives, and the moral quality of actions and institutions. If our informants leave feelings out of their accounts, we must try to understand why they do so. For example, if tradition or divine injunction is invoked as the moral basis for rules or behaviour we must see this as a form of indirection or discursive avoidance that requires explanation. In other words, it is not only anthropologists who find it strategically useful to avoid reference to people's feelings.

Finally, we must explore the ways in which people's motives are informed, but only partly so, by beliefs about how happiness is achieved, whether being happy is a good and noble way to be, and when it is good to display or conceal happiness. By discussing the meaning and status of happiness as a life goal, we can learn about how individuals and larger social entities rationalise and explain their cultures, structures and political choices. We can learn about how human nature and society are conceived, and how these

'Realising the Substance of Their Happiness'

concepts influence (or fail to influence) personal careers and development strategies. Even if people *avoid* mentioning happiness as they explain their rationales, anthropologists must see this avoidance as interesting and worthy of investigation. I hope I have shown that anthropological avoidance of happiness is not just reprehensible but also interesting.

REFERENCES

Adelson, N. 2001. *Being Alive Well: Health and the Politics of Cree Well-Being*. Toronto: University of Toronto Press.

AAA (American Anthropological Association). 1998. *Code of Ethics of the American Anthropological Association*. URL (consulted December 2006): http://www.aaanet.org/committees/ethics/ethcode.htm

Anthropological Index Online. URL (consulted December 2006): http://aio.anthropology.org.uk/cgi-bin/uncgi/search_bib_ai/anthind

ASA (Association of Social Anthropologists). 1999. *Ethical Guidelines*. URL (consulted December 2006): http://www.theasa.org/ethics.htm

Bentham, J. 1948 [1776]. *Introduction to the Principles of Morals and Legislation*. Oxford: Blackwell.

Bock, P.K. 1988 [1980]. *Rethinking Psychological Anthropology: Continuity and Change in the Study of Human Action*. New York: W.H. Freeman.

Bodley, J.H. 2007. Anthropology. In Microsoft® *Encarta®* (*Microsoft Online Encyclopedia*). URL (consulted June 2007): http://encarta.msn.com/text_761559816___57/Anthropology.html

Buss, D.M. 2000. The Evolution of Happiness. *American Psychologist* 55, 15–23.

Chagnon, N.A. 1992 [1968] *Yanomamö: The Last Days of Eden*. New York: Harcourt, Brace & Co.

Charlton, B. 2000. *Psychiatry and the Human Condition*. Oxford: Radcliffe Medical Press.

Cosmides, L. and J. Tooby. 1997. *Evolutionary Psychology: A Primer*. Santa Barbara, CA: University of California, Center for Evolutionary Psychology.

Denzin, N. 1984. *On Understanding Emotion*. San Francisco: Jossey-Bass.

Desjarlais, R., L. Eisenberg, B. Good and A. Kleinman (eds). 1995. *World Mental Health: Problems and Priorities in Low-income Countries*. New York: Oxford University Press.

Diener, E. and C. Diener. 1996. Most People are Happy. *Psychological Science* 7, 181–85.

Durkheim, E. 1960 [1893]. *The Division of Labour in Society*. New York: Free Press.

Edgar, I. and A. Russell (eds). 1998. *The Anthropology of Welfare*. London: Routledge.

Edgerton, R. 1992. *Sick Societies: Challenging the Myth of Primitive Harmony*. New York: Free Press.

Eldis Gateway to Development Information. URL (consulted December 2006): http://www.eldis.org

Epstein, A.L. 1992. *In the Midst of Life: Affect and Ideation in the World of the Tolai*. Berkeley: University of California Press.

Evans-Pritchard, E.E. 1956. *Nuer Religion*. Oxford: Oxford University Press.

Fox, R.D. and A. Gingrich (eds). 2002. *Anthropology by Comparison*. London: Routledge.

Frazer, J.G. 1978 [1922]. Preface. In B. Malinowski, *Argonauts of the Western Pacific*. London: Routledge.

Grinde, B. 2002. *Darwinian Happiness: Evolution as a Guide for Understanding Human Behavior*. Princeton, NJ: Darwin Press.

Harré, R. and W.G. Parott. 1996. *The Emotions: Social, Cultural and Biological Dimensions*. London: Sage.

Hollan, D.W. and J.C. Wellenkamp. 1994. *Contentment and Suffering: Culture and Experience in Toraja*. New York: Columbia University Press.

Howell, S. (ed.). 1997. *The Ethnography of Moralities*. London: Routledge.

James, W. 1902. *The Varieties of Religious Experience: A Study in Human Nature*. London and New York: Longmans.

Laidlaw, J. 2001. For an Anthropology of Ethics and Freedom. *Journal of the Royal Anthropological Institute* 8, 311–32.

Lévi-Strauss, C. 1973 [1955]. *Tristes Tropiques*, trans. John Weigthman and Doreen Weightman. New York: Washington Square Press.

Liedloff, J. 1986. *The Continuum Concept: In Search of Happiness Lost*. New York: Addison Wesley.

Lyon, M. 1995. Missing Emotion: The Limitations of Cultural Constructionism in the Study of Emotion. *Cultural Anthropology* 10(2), 244–63.

Malinowski, B. 1978 [1922]. *Argonauts of the Western Pacific*. London: Routledge.

Marshall, A. 1890. *Principles of Economics*. London and New York: Macmillan.

Mathews, G. and C. Izquierdo (eds). forthcoming 2007. *The Good Life: Anthropology of Wellbeing*. Oxford: Berghahn.

Mill, J.S. 1863. *Utilitarianism*. URL (consulted December 2006). http://www.constitution.org/jsm/utilitarianism.txt

Murray, C. 1988. *In Pursuit of Happiness and Good Government*. New York: Simon & Schuster.

Needham, R. 1962. *Structure and Sentiment*. Chicago: University of Chicago Press.

—— 1981. *Circumstantial Deliveries*. Berkeley: University of California Press.

Norbeck, E. 1965. Review of David Plath, *The After Hours. American Anthropologist* 67(2), 535–36.

Norberg-Hodge, H. 1991. *Ancient Futures: Learning from Ladakh*. London: Rider.

Popper, K.R. 1945. *The Open Society and its Enemies*, vol. 1: *Plato*. London: Routledge & Kegan Paul.

Rapport, N. and J. Overing. 2000. *Social and Cultural Anthropology: The Key Concepts*. London: Routledge.

Reddy, W.M. 1997. Against Constructionism: The Historical Ethnography of Emotions. *Current Anthropology* 38(3), 327–34.

—— 2001. *The Navigation of Feeling: A Framework for the History of Emotions*. Cambridge: Cambridge University Press.

Reining, C.C. 1962. A Lost Period of Applied Anthropology. *American Anthropologist* 64, 593–600.

Rosaldo, M.Z. 1980. *Knowledge and Passion: Ilongot Notions of Self and Social Life*. Cambridge: Cambridge University Press.

Rousseau, J.J. 1754. *The Discourse on Inequality*, trans. G.D.H. Cole. URL (consulted December 2006): http://www.constitution.org/jjr/ineq.txt

Sahlins, M.D. 1977. *The Use and Abuse of Biology: An Anthropological Critique of Sociobiology*. Ann Arbor: University of Michigan Press.

Schwartz, G.M., C. White and A. Lutz (eds). 1992. *New Directions in Psychological Anthropology*. Cambridge: Cambridge University Press.

Segall, M.H., P.R. Dasen, J.W. Berry and Y.H. Poortinga (eds). 1999. *Human Behavior in Global Perspective: An Introduction to Cross Cultural Psychology*, 2nd edn. London: Allyn & Bacon/Longman.

Thin, N. 2002. *Social Progress and Sustainable Development*. London: ITDG Publications.

—— forthcoming. Good Feelings and Good Lives: Why Anthropology can Ill Afford to Ignore Well-Being. In G. Mathews and C. Izquierdo (eds) *The Good Life: Well-being in Anthropological Perspective*. Berghahn.

Tolstoy, L. 2000 [1884]. *Anna Karenina*. Modern Library.

Turnbull, C.M. 1984 [1961]. *The Forest People*. London: Chatto & Windus.

—— 1973. *The Mountain People*. London: Jonathan Cape.

Veenhoven, R. 1997. Correlational Findings. In *World Database of Happiness*. Rotterdam: Erasmus University. URL (consulted December 2006): http://worlddatabaseofhappiness.eur.nl

—— 2005. Apparent Quality-of-life in Nations: How Long and Happy People Live. *Social Indicators Research* 71(1–3), 61–86.

Wright, R. 1995. *The Moral Animal: Evolutionary Psychology and Everyday Life*. London: Little, Brown & Co.

8 THE INTENSION AND EXTENSION OF WELL-BEING: TRANSFORMATION IN DIASPORA JAIN UNDERSTANDINGS OF NON-VIOLENCE

James Laidlaw

The purpose of this volume is to consider how anthropology might benefit from, and contribute to, debates around the concept of 'well-being', as developed recently by economists, moral philosophers and political theorists.[1] As Alberto Corsín Jiménez observed in convening the conference from which the volume derives, these debates have been conducted without much anthropological input. This is surprising, since a good deal of the interest in 'well-being', as distinct from more straightforwardly utilitarian measures such as 'happiness' or 'affluence', has been expressed in terms of its greater inclusivity and conceptual breadth. As Corsín Jiménez (2003: 2–3) puts the matter in his position paper for the conference, it is of interest, in part, because it may be 'stretched' beyond the merely economic and beyond the human individual, to include collective life and also divergent conceptions of a good life (and so to allow for cultural diversity), to include also past and future generations; and it may be extended beyond the human species to include other animals, ecosystems and the global environment.

However, notwithstanding these hopes, expressed to differing degrees by Griffin (1986), Sen (1993, 1999, 2002), the contributors to Nussbaum and Sen (1993), Dasgupta (2001), Clark (2002) and Nussbaum (2006), it is nevertheless fair to say that, in all this literature, the imagined constituents of human flourishing are more or less consensually taken for granted. It is not just that debate about how best to characterise and measure the good life takes place within a consensus of left-liberal egalitarianism, although that is also true, but more substantively there is ready agreement on the necessity and centrality to well-being of a repertoire of human values and capacities – physical robustness and longevity, psychological health (including feelings of self-worth and dignity), freedom from bodily and mental suffering, privacy, personal autonomy and responsibility, family life and relationships, civic inclusion, political enfranchisement, and so on. I have no interest in questioning the value of either this repertoire or any of its constituents. My concern instead is with the apparent assumption that the often-expressed wish to broaden the *extension* of the concept of well-being may be accomplished without consequences for its *intension* or meaning. So my point is not merely the one made so eloquently in a different context by Asad (2003), that to take cultural diversity seriously involves accommodating forms of life in which human flourishing is imagined as being distinctly different from this. I shall indeed be taking, as my starting point, just such a form of life. But its interest lies not in the mere fact of its being different, nor in its being, as it happens, uncongenial to contemporary Anglo-Saxon left-liberal sensibility, but rather in what it suggests about the relation between ambitions to broaden the scope of well-being and its content.

JAINISM AND THE WELL-BEING LITERATURE

Although interest in the concept of well-being has been fuelled by dissatisfaction with more strictly utilitarian measures, its proponents' departure from utilitarian thinking is in some respects very limited. Discussion remains rooted in a consequentialist conceptual framework – a framework, that is to say, in which actions, events or processes are judged good or bad on account of their overall net effect. The notion of utility is replaced with one that is more congenial to multiculturalist, environmentalist and other interests, but the work that concept is expected to do intellectually, and the framework within which it does it, remain basically the same. So, for instance, Sen's reasons for diverging from utilitarian measures of 'happiness' are not objections of meta-ethical principle but are themselves consequentialist in form: observations or conjectures about the effects of using different measures such as happiness or welfare as a guide for policy, such as unintended consequences and perverse incentives.

The literature in general is coloured by a desire to make not just descriptive or explanatory but also evaluative judgements, and to influence public policy with proposals and measurable targets. Without the language of objective measurement and consequentialist reasoning, it is difficult to connect with and inform government or NGO policy and planning, or to make claims for the use of state power or funds. Those who are interested in basing policies for poverty alleviation, animal welfare or environmental protection upon notions of 'well-being' wish to make use of these resources. And yet, the hope seems to be that the notion is sufficiently capacious to be able to transcend the 'culture-blindness' that is traditionally associated with utilitarianism, and also to transcend its specifically Western, individualist and humanist or 'species-ist' origins.

In the light of these hopes, it might be instructive to consider the case of Jainism – a South Asian religious and ethical tradition. On the face of it, the Jains provide both a profound challenge to, and at the same time rather striking support for, the idea that actions, policies or states of affairs might be assessed in terms of their impact on 'well-being', very broadly conceived.

The apparent challenge comes from the fact that Jainism is a tradition of renunciatory asceticism. It is, indeed, perhaps the most consistent and uncompromising soteriology of all the major religions. Jainism is an instance of the kind of religious viewpoint that sees the world as irredeemably polluted, corrupted or fallen. True self-realisation is possible only through escape from this world, and the first step towards that is learning to resist material comfort, sensual pleasure and sociality. On this view, these and all other manifestations of well-being, as the authors cited above have conceived it, are not a sensible measure of how well our affairs are arranged, but are rather traps and temptations that make it harder to achieve real salvation.

Jainism presents an extreme example of this – it devalues worldly well-being to the extent of institutionalising, and recommending for the spiritually advanced as a *telos* of religious life, the practice of fasting to death (Laidlaw 2005). Progress towards enlightenment involves realising that life's apparent goods and values, including not only success, renown and wealth, but also skills and accomplishments, and personal and family loves and loyalties, are all ties that bind one to a necessarily miserable and degraded embodied existence. The soul's natural state is eternal omniscient tranquillity, but to attain this it must permanently escape embodied existence, which is to say that the human being whose soul it is must die, in the right state and circumstances so that it will not be reborn again; and to do this it must relinquish and resolutely dissociate itself from everything that goes by the name of 'well-being'. No degree of mere broadening of the concept could accommodate this.

On the other hand, Jainism apparently gives equally dramatic support for an ethics based on a 'stretched' well-being. When Jain religious teachers stress that non-violence, or *ahimsa*, is the centrepiece of their religion, they invariably insist that it applies to all living things, and that it is not just a negative injunction. We should practise *ahimsa*, not only towards other animals but also insects, plants and invisible living things in the soil, water, fire and the air. They all can suffer, they all desire to live, and we have a positive obligation to attend to their interests and well-being. Furthermore, they are all interconnected, in ways that mean that in harming them we in fact harm ourselves.

These aspects of Jain teaching, and the well-known lengths to which Jain renouncers in particular go to avoid harming even the tiniest living thing, have inspired increasing numbers of Jains, especially in the diaspora and especially in Anglo-Saxon countries, to argue that Jainism does or should occupy a special place in global movements for animal rights and liberation, and in promoting care for the environment.

Until the nineteenth century, Jainism remained confined to peninsular India, where it is a small but disproportionately affluent and influential religious minority. Lay Jains first moved in any numbers to East Africa, in parts of which there remain small but flourishing Jain communities; and then, following the expulsion of Asians from some of the countries in that region in the 1970s, to the UK, Canada, Australia and the United States.[2] Like other mobile and commercial communities of South Asians, such as the Sindhis (on whom see Falzon 2004), Jains outside India maintain extensive networks of family and commercial connections with those in other parts of the globe. In each of these countries there are now many cities with established local Jain communities, and other Jain households are dispersed across these and other nations, linked increasingly by national and international organisations, as well as their own networks of connections.

An increasing and vocal number of Jain spokespersons, together with some vocal non-Jain admirers (for example Tobias 1991, and the same author's 1989 PBS film, *Ahimsa*), argue that the insights of contemporary ecology and animal liberation theorists were anticipated, and acted upon, in this ancient Indian tradition: that Jainism not only teaches but realises in practical terms – though of course it will need updating – an ethic of care for the well-being of the planet. They claim that Jainism is the only long-established tradition that sees every living thing as morally important – not just selected 'sacred' animals, as in Hinduism (Jaini 2000a: 10) – and that understands the interdependence of living things in something like the same way as contemporary 'deep ecology'.[3] A defining moment occurred in 1990, at a reception at Buckingham Palace, when, on behalf of Jain organisations from India and the UK, an eminent Indian jurist and later Indian High Commissioner in London (1991–97), Mr L.M. Singhvi, issued the 'Jain Declaration on Nature'. Jainism, this document declares, has been all along, 'a cradle for the creed of environmentalist protection and harmony' (Singhvi 2002 [1992]: 222). It 'defines the scope of modern ecology while extending it further to a more spacious "home"' (Singhvi 2002 [1992]: 219). This text has been widely reproduced in Jain websites and magazines; it has set the agenda for subsequent publications and also many conferences and gatherings of Jain organisations, and its claims have been incorporated into their educational programmes and self-presentation.

So we are presented with an apparent paradox. Is it really the case that a tradition that devalues the well-being, ordinarily understood, of its own followers so far as to recommend that the best of them take their own lives, also teaches a kind of universal mutual care and sympathy, based on a unique insight into the value and interconnectedness of all living things? Implausible as it might seem, this is indeed the case.

I shall attempt to explain why this is only an apparent paradox in soteriological Jainism. But I shall also show why the conclusion that at first sight seems to follow – that Jainism has a natural place in the vanguard of the international environmental and animal-liberation movements – is a good deal less certain. As we shall see, recent attempts to align the soteriological tradition's understanding of *ahimsa* with those international movements involve a definite shift of emphasis in ethical style,[4] from virtue-ethical forms of reasoning and practice towards consequentialist ones.[5] They also have consequences for the range of species to which the concept is in practice applied. This material supports the conclusion that the extension of core ethical concepts such as well-being and non-violence will not normally be able to vary independently of their intension, and that the hope that the current left-liberal discourse on well-being would survive unchanged the radical 'stretching' envisaged by some of its advocates is misplaced.

AHIMSA IN SOTERIOLOGICAL JAINISM

The Jain tradition is a first cousin to Buddhism.[6] Both crystallised in the Ganges valley in north India in the fifth to fourth centuries BC, the last of Jainism's 24 founding saints or Jinas, Lord Mahavir, being almost certainly an elder contemporary of Gautam Buddha. Today, as then, relatively small numbers of men and women take life-long vows to renounce their families and possessions. These renouncers live and travel in small single-sex groups, observing a strict code of ascetic conduct, and teaching their lay followers the importance of non-attachment, the renunciation of sensual pleasures and the practice of *ahimsa*, or non-violence. The lay followers, who are mostly in trade, retail or finance, but also fairly numerous in the educated professions, are enjoined to emulate the renouncers as far as they are able, and also to support them by providing alms and shelter, as well as maintaining temples and preaching halls, and supporting charitable institutions. These include hospitals and refuges for sick animals, and even shelters for rodents and insects.

The rule for renouncers illustrates what, traditionally, concern for the well-being of other living things has been held logically to entail. They have no home, and no possessions other than those they carry with them as they move from place to place. They travel only by walking barefoot. While walking they brush the ground gently to remove insects in their way. Also, to save insects and other creatures in the air, they should never wave their arms about or move suddenly, and they should lie completely still as they sleep. Since fresh water is full of living things, they are not allowed to bathe. They may not use electric fans or light, since these too are a danger to the invisible 'air bodies' that Jain teachers, from the earliest times, have claimed are omnipresent in the air. Since soil is also home to innumerable life forms ('earth bodies'), they should avoid digging or otherwise disturbing the earth; and fire being also a medium for living things, they should neither light nor put out fires.

Jains are not merely vegetarian; they avoid also a range of vegetables, on the grounds that they contain a large number of separate living things, or that they excite the body, and therefore incline those who eat them to carelessness. Renouncers never prepare food themselves – cooking involves cutting and using heat. Instead, they collect alms from lay households. So while lay Jains are not bound by the same strict dietary requirements as renouncers, it is important that a large number of them do approximate those rules, so that food they prepare is acceptable to the renouncers. It must not have been specially cooked for them, but made to be included in the family meal. Renouncers collect a small amount at a time from a number of families, so that no one will be deprived, and so that no one will cook more food to replace what is given. If they did, then the renouncers would be responsible.

The image used for this concern is that the renouncer subsists as does a honey-bee, taking only a little sustenance from a large number of plants. The idea that preparation of food and eating involve violence helps explain the importance of fasting, and Jainism has an extensive repertoire of fasts, which involve omitting certain foods, or else all foods, including water, for varying periods. Fasting is also important in teaching that one can get by with little to eat, and in developing capacities to resist the pleasures of food and the force of hunger.

These ascetic practices, and many more besides, are underwritten by a vision of the world, parts of which are articulated even in the very earliest canonical texts, as comprehensively inhabited by uncountable millions of living things, from single-sensed earth or air bodies and what Jains nowadays call 'germs',[7] to five-sensed animals, humans and gods. Each has an immortal soul that is fundamentally like that of any other. Of course, the number of senses with which a living thing is endowed affects the range of sensations it can experience. But all need sustenance and suffer if deprived of it. Even those with only the sense of touch feel pain, and all have a desire to live. Plants as well as animals are born and grow. They feel pain if cut or injured. They grow old and they die. This is happening all around us, all the time. The world we live in is literally filled with sentient creatures, constantly being born, living and dying: a never-ending cycle of pain and suffering.

Much Jain teaching and practice is concerned with developing this vision of the world we live in, and making it compelling and experientially present. It is an important element of what the Jains call the Right View (*samyak darshan*), requiring Right Knowledge (of the existence of invisible creatures and so on) but also, beyond this, one should learn actually to experience the space around one as inhabited. So, for instance, a lay teacher one day interrupted a discourse he was giving me on Jain philosophy and drew to my attention the scene in the street outside, which was knee-deep in monsoon rainwater. 'You see only rain outside, and people rushing to get to work', he said, 'but Jain religion sees much more than that. Today there is much violence being done.' All those people wading about were heedlessly killing the creatures living in the water. Jain renouncers would all stay indoors that day, he said. I should reflect on this until, like him, I learned imaginatively to see the living things and therefore the violence around me.

Two related ideas build from this vision, to give the Jain doctrine and practice of non-violence its distinctive character. First is the Jain version of the pan-Indic idea of rebirth. Each living thing has already lived many times, as many different kinds of creature. The most primitive one-sensed form of life, called *nigodas*, are believed to exist indefinitely, as a sort of reserve army of souls from which the universe is gradually populated. Generally, when these die and are born in another form, they begin a long and by no means unidirectional journey through many other life forms. Only a privileged few ever take a human birth, and only from this is it possible, by following Jain teachings, permanently to escape this cycle of suffering. So probably each of us has in the past been an insect, a plant, a microbe, a beast of burden, a wild animal.[8] This doctrine might have been invented to give psychological support to the arguments put forward by Western animal liberation activists, such as Peter Singer (for example, Singer 1997 [1975]), who argue on utilitarian grounds that once we have overcome inter-species prejudice we shall treat suffering by any sentient creature as morally equivalent. Jainism teaches that, whenever one thinks of harming any of these creatures, one should reflect that, in the past, I too have been just such another creature. Such a thought helps to make harm to other species seem genuinely equivalent to harm to other humans.

The second idea is also a distinctive Jain version of a more general pan-Indic notion, in this case that of *karma*. This idea of moralised causality, that our good or bad actions will rebound on us and we will gain or suffer in consequence, provides a further sense in which, in harming another creature, one is harming oneself. According to Jain renderings of this idea, each action causes inanimate matter to attach to the soul, matter that is different in character depending on the action in question and which attaches to the soul with a tenacity that derives from the emotion with which the action is performed. It is this karmic matter that binds the soul to embodied existence, and determines (indeed in a complex way constitutes) the body in which the soul is condemned to live and suffer. Progress towards enlightenment and release involves painfully 'burning' this matter from the soul, either through the involuntary sufferings that life in this world inflicts upon us, or, and ultimately, through voluntary asceticism. Violence committed in anger, greed or lust is particularly harmful and its effects on the self are difficult to undo: thus the emphasis in Jain teaching, from the canonical *Acaranga Sutra* (Jacobi 1964 [1884]) onwards, on the point that in harming others one is actually harming oneself.

A NEGATIVE SUM GAME

This then is indeed, as proponents of 'Jain ecology' argue, a powerful image of the interdependence of all living things. But it differs profoundly from environmentalism and animal activism. These latter movements are reformist, focused not only on reforming the behaviour of their signed-up enthusiasts, but also on proselytising, and on promoting political and other practical measures that will induce, compel or otherwise cause the population at large to behave differently, the justification being that the outcome will be altogether better for all concerned: a world in which man will happily coexist in mutually beneficial relations with other species and the rest of the natural environment. Yet, as we shall see, there is in the soteriological Jain vision no image of happy coexistence – however much we humans might mend our ways.

The standard Jain rite of confession is *pratikraman* (see Laidlaw 1995: 204–15). Jain renouncers perform this twice each day; devout lay Jains less often but still regularly. Any even remotely observant Jain performs a long version of it annually, on the most important day in the religious calendar. In all these forms, it involves a lengthy series of recitations and prayers, and adopting bodily postures indicative of self-examination, repentance and penance. One confesses and repents for the harm one has caused to all kinds of living things. These are enumerated in the recitations. There are 8,400,000 different species, and the chants specify that this includes 700,000 different kinds each of one-sensed earth bodies, water bodies, fire bodies and air bodies; 2,400,000 different kinds of plants, and so on for two-, three-, four- and five-sensed animals, creatures in heaven and in hell, and 1,400,000 different, as it were, 'species' of human being: persons of different castes, religions, nations, and so on. One confesses to having harmed *all* these, because you do not know just what harm you might have caused or to whom. Just by being alive you must have caused some. And indeed the rite includes confession and repentance for violence committed during the performance of the rite itself, just by breathing and moving about. The sense that violence is practically inescapable, except in the end by escaping from embodied existence altogether, is therefore powerfully reinforced.

This idea, that life is a ruthlessly negative sum game, that not only animals but all forms of life must harm other living things merely in order to sustain themselves, is found in canonical texts such as the *Acaranga Sutra*, where we learn that trees, in order to draw sustenance from the soil, harm and kill the earth bodies that live there. So if, as that text also tells us, insects, plants and microbes all feel pain and pleasure, the conclusion cannot be that the world could be made a better place overall, by arrangements or changes in behaviour that would increase everyone's pleasure and diminish their pain. The world could not be reshaped in this fashion. Instead, the only way any living thing can permanently escape suffering is by ridding its own soul of *karma* and so escaping rebirth. And this is achieved only through suffering, including and especially voluntary asceticism. The more contact and interaction there is between living things, the more mutual harm there will be.

So the injunction to attend to the well-being of all living things arises from the most profound possible rejection of the value of any such embodied life, and of any kind of well-being that is possible within it. We have a duty not to harm them. But this is not because their lives are particularly admirable (they themselves do not practise non-violence, for instance), nor because they and we might together create an ongoing way of life that is peaceful, productive, happy or sustainable. Embodied life just is transient and painful and will always be based to some extent on harm done to others (an idea that is anathema to animal liberationists, cf. Singer 1995 [1975]: 209ff). In renouncers' sermons, religious narratives and publications for children, this conception of an everything-eat-everything world is stressed in a whole variety of ways, and, as my Jain friend who invited me to see violence in the rain-soaked scene from the window was demonstrating, Jains are encouraged actively to cultivate a sense of the world as being so.

So, although Jainism has a powerful sense of the causal interconnections between living things, there is nothing here to support the kind of more or less mystical holism of much contemporary environmentalism, nor the idea that, if only humans changed the way they behaved, some kind of natural harmony between species could be attained or recovered. The traditional Jain recognition of the claims to consideration of all living things derives from a clear ontological dualism – 'souls' distinguished from inanimate matter – and from an equally clear metaphysical individualism. Each soul is a distinct entity that preserves its identity through innumerable rebirths. The interconnections between living things are close, but they are causal relations between forever-separate entities, not the holism of deep ecology. In addition, the tradition is unanimous in describing cosmic cycles of time not unlike those in Hinduism, in which, over long periods, the condition of the world, and with it the physical and moral quality of its inhabitants, progressively improves and degenerates. We are currently low on a degenerative phase in the cycle and therefore, as Dundas points out, the degradation of the world environment is from this point of view inevitable, a powerful reason to renounce worldly life and seek individual release, but none at all to try to act to arrest the process (Dundas 2002b: 96–97).

Jain literature and art do contain images of moments of peaceful coexistence. When a great Jain saint achieves enlightenment and begins to preach, not only humans but also gods and animals gather to listen. Representations of these moments, when lion and lamb lie down peacefully together, plainly do recognise non-human animals, at least potentially, as soteriological agents, consistent with the doctrine of the transmigration of souls. They are also important evocations of the transformative power of Jain teaching, but they remain miraculous moments. Insofar as they have a dynamic significance, this arises when a creature at the assembly is so affected by the saint's message that it thereupon adopts the Jain way. What this means is illustrated by a very famous story – it is included in innumerable children's books and illustrated on the wall of almost every temple – of a previous incarnation of Lord Mahavir. In this life, the soul that is eventually to be Mahavir is living as a lion. By chance he hears two Jain monks preaching and is miraculously persuaded by their message. What Mahavir gains from their sermons is not any particular factual knowledge but the Right View, including understanding of the intrinsic violence of embodied existence. This insight, once achieved, means that eventually, perhaps after many lives, the soul will achieve liberation. For a carnivorous wild animal, the only thing to be done having gained this understanding is to fast to death, and this indeed is what the lion does. It is reborn in heaven and eventually, after several more rebirths, as the Jain saviour.

There is another almost equally famous story of moral action by an animal (for other such stories see Jaini 2000b). There is a forest fire and the animals in the jungle flee to the banks of a lake. They are crowded together there, pressed up against each other with not an inch to spare. An elephant lifts a

The Intension and Extension of Well-Being

foot to scratch itself and a hare runs into the now-vacant space. Moved by compassion for the small helpless creature, the elephant, instead of putting its foot back down and crushing it, continues to stand on three legs. It takes days for the fire to subside. By the time it does the elephant's leg is paralysed. It becomes ill and dies, but as was the case with the lion, it is rewarded with a good rebirth, this time as a prince who lives at the same time as Lord Mahavir and becomes one of his disciples.

In both stories, moral and religious insight and agency are portrayed as possible for an animal, but equally as incompatible with continued life – let alone well-being – as such. And in most Jain narrative, it should be added, rebirth as an animal figures as the karmic punishment for sin, most typically violence of some kind, an equivalent of which violence the perpetrator will in turn suffer during life as an animal.

WELL-BEING IN QUARANTINE

Of course Jainism, as I have said, as well as being the path followed by a few dedicated renouncers, is also the long-lived tradition of a flourishing lay community, so resolute world renunciation of the kind I have described cannot be the whole story about Jain social and cultural life. Since the mid 1980s a substantial body of ethnographic description of Jain communities has appeared.[9] All this work has emphasised the coexistence, alongside the ascetic soteriology, of institutions and practices that give sustained expression to quite contrasting values. One author (Cort 2001), for instance, sums this up by distinguishing what he calls two 'realms of value' within Jainism: the *moksh-marg* ideology – the ascetic path to liberation – and the 'realm of value of well-being'. The latter involves celebration of health, fecundity and harmony in the family, wealth and good social connections, and public regard, this last especially from support for religious institutions and hospitality. Now, as all the ethnographers have commented, while lively, the institutions and practices where these values are expressed in Jain communities are not explicitly valorised or theorised by Jain authors or in public discourse among Jains, and they draw heavily on themes that Jainism shares with other South Asian social groups. Indeed, much of it is more widespread than that, and some of it is well-nigh universal. In these senses it is not specifically Jain. For these reasons, it is only half of the truth to describe it as a 'realm of value' distinct from renunciatory ethical thinking. Insofar as Jainism institutionalises this worldly conception of well-being, which it certainly does, it consists of such ideas of health, opulence and so on, not in themselves but only insofar as they are in a proper relation to asceticism. This proper relation is firmly subordinate, and also dynamical.

For instance, there is the practice of temporary adoption of asceticism, either on holy days or for longer periods. This produces rather dramatic aesthetic counterpoints between episodes of sparse austerity and others of lavish celebration. The juxtaposition of fast and feast is of course common in other world religions. Perhaps the most distinctive thing about the Jain sensibility is just the extent to which this technique of aesthetic counterpoint is developed (see Laidlaw 1995: ch. 12). Routinely, in festivals and also on occasions such as the initiation of renouncers, the pattern is the same: movement between asceticism and opulence.

A common instance of this is when someone completes a lengthy fast. Many young Jain women, especially in socially conservative business families, undertake a fast of up to a month at the age when their families are looking for husbands for them, or in some cases shortly after marriage. The successful completion of these fasts is celebrated with a grand procession through the streets of the neighbourhood, and a public feast thrown by the family. Obviously several things are going on here. It is common for these feasts to be used as an occasion for the male head of the family to announce a religious donation. So there is the idea of heroic asceticism being marked and celebrated by display of worldly wealth. Well-being and the ascetic pursuit of release are contrasting but mutually supporting. But there is also another idea in play. One of the things the young woman is doing is showing, to her in-laws especially but also to the world at large, that her enjoyment of material plenty and sensual pleasure is under command. By the exercise of ascetic will and effort she can control her desires. The wealth, reputation and well-being of her conjugal family will not be put at risk by extravagance or sexual incontinence. In a world where the senses and enjoyment of worldly goods are a constant source of temptation to self-destructive un-mindfulness, worldly well-being is a precarious achievement. It exists only insofar as it is kept under command by disciplined asceticism.

This protection and preservation of well-being happens partly by as-it-were magical means. Great saints generate, by means of their asceticism, the power to perform miracles. But much more importantly, as I show below, asceticism protects the well-being lay Jains achieve because it is the way they learn to keep the destructive forces of the natural world at bay, or, perhaps better, to keep themselves under restraint so that they hold themselves back from unnecessary contact with the natural world.

EFFECTS AND VIRTUES

Jain renouncers are permitted to drink only boiled water, and many pious lay Jains do the same, especially when they are fasting; more routinely, as a less time-consuming measure, they fix muslin filters over their drinking water taps. The reason for both practices is that fresh water contains millions of tiny living things. So drinking it is violence. Now, of course, these creatures are killed when the water is boiled or filtered just as surely as they would be if it were drunk. So what is the point? For a consequentialist ethic, such as utilitarianism, this seems like an empty gesture. It is certainly a counter-intuitive way, at first sight, to attend to the rights or the welfare of those creatures, and is unlikely to find its way into the policy proposals of the global animal liberation movement. If it were merely a case of one person boiling the water for someone else to drink, then we could explain it as the first sinning so that the other need not, and indeed lay Jains do boil the water for renouncers. But this is not all that is going on, because they also do so for themselves.

The point of the practice is clear when we see that soteriological Jain asceticism is not principally a consequentialist moral system, but a set of practices that develop certain virtues in a human subject – a bodily and personal training or ascesis. From this point of view, what matters is not the question of whether or not the creatures in the water die. They, and millions like them, are dying every minute of every day, and nothing that anyone does can change that fact. What matters is that you learn so to comport yourself that this violence does not cause further *karma* to ensnare you further in the world. You must disengage yourself from it, not be a proximate cause of it. You must be constantly mindful of it, and adapt your conduct in the light of this mindfulness. This is why Jain non-violence is in many ways what I have called 'an ethic of quarantine' (1995: 153–59). Rather than trying to prevent violence from happening, it is about separating the self from violence that is going to happen anyway. For the same reason, Jaini observes (2000a: 5): 'The orientation of the Jaina discussion on *ahimsa* thus proceeds from the perspective of one's own soul and not so much from the standpoint of the protection of other beings or the welfare of humanity as a whole.'

If humans, in their greed, passion and carelessness, are a danger to other living things and indeed to the environment generally, as ecologists maintain, and if soteriological Jainism endorses that judgement, it is from the Jain point of view equally true, and equally important, that other living things and the environment generally are supremely dangerous to humans, for they are the medium through which we perpetuate our bondage and prolong our own suffering.

Several other practices required of renouncers make sense only in these terms. I mentioned above that renouncers do not bathe. They may not use flushing lavatories, and, although they should avoid disturbing the ground, they must also cover their bodily waste with sand or dry soil. After collecting alms, a group of renouncers who live and travel together will share the food they have severally been given. Between them, they must ensure that they eat all this food, in one sitting. They may never store or throw any away. The rationale for all these practices is the same. Renouncers must not create or be the cause of an environment in which 'germs' will grow. Just as they cannot accept food that has been prepared specially for them, since then they would be the occasion for violence and karmically responsible for it, so here too they avoid being the occasion for violence. But the 'violence' they are required to avoid consists not only of the destruction of life but also its creation: seen from within the sensibility Jains are enjoined to cultivate, these are the same thing.

With such a comprehensive conception of the destructive mutual dependence of living things, such that all activity of any kind involves violence, how does one choose what to do? How to choose between different courses of action? Jain thinkers, both in conceptualising the path to liberation and in issuing guidance for the laity, have generally resolved such questions not principally by asking what will cause fewest deaths or save most lives – though instances of such reasoning are not unknown – still less by asking what will be the effect on an abstractly conceived 'environment', but rather by evaluating what will be the effect on the agent's own spiritual development.

This can be seen as a continuity running through otherwise changing attitudes, over the long term in Jain history, as described by Dundas (2002b). In the early period, when the texts we have were all clearly addressed to renouncers, violent acts are rejected even where the rationale is that by taking one life many more might be saved. An example is a group of ascetics, described as rivals to the Jains, who, it is said, instead of collecting alms, themselves kill an elephant and then consume it, living off it for as long as possible. Apparently taking seriously the Jain view that all living things contain ultimately equivalent souls, they reason consequentially that killing this one animal is better than the death of all the many plants they would receive as alms in its stead. They are cited in the Jain text described by Dundas only to have their views roundly condemned.

In later writings, questions of conduct among the laity are specifically addressed. Dundas cites a seventeenth-century text that discusses the building of temples and making of material offerings. These activities involve violence, and some Jain teachers had argued that they are all on that account unacceptable, and indeed new Jain sects, including some that exist today, were founded on just this basis. But in the mainstream traditions these activities have been justified because and insofar as they promote the spiritual development of the lay worshipper. Consequential reasoning is not absent – and not only in the sense that spiritual development is itself one causal outcome – but it is firmly subordinate to the project of cultivating ascetic virtues. There are rules for reducing loss of life. Flowers offered in worship should, for preference, be those that have fallen naturally rather than being plucked for the purpose, and so on. And renouncers themselves are expected to be so spiritually advanced that they do not need material forms to aid them in worship, but they are nevertheless permitted to attend rites of worship in which material offerings are made, and to lead the singing and recitation.

In both these writings described by Dundas, the reasoning as to what is and is not acceptable is structured by concern for the cultivation of ascetic virtues of mindfulness, restraint and devotion to ascetic exemplars.

This is, of course, fundamentally different from the central concerns of contemporary global movements for animal liberation and from conventional environmentalism. These movements are both essentially consequentialist.[10] The animal liberation movement in the Anglo-Saxon world aims explicitly to reduce the suffering of animals,[11] and the environmental movement aims, as it puts it, to save the planet. The apparent similarities between important

The Intension and Extension of Well-Being

elements of traditional Jain teaching and central dogmas of these movements notwithstanding, they are profoundly different kinds of enterprise.

DIASPORA JAIN REFORMISM

Yet, as I have said, some intelligent and thoughtful Jains, both in India and even more energetically in the diaspora, are portraying their religion as an ancient precursor and natural ally of these movements, and arguing that just this is the contemporary relevance of Jainism, and the reason young Jains should remain committed to it. What they are attempting is a rather dramatic transformation and it is unclear to what extent it will be successful, but it is not surprising that it should be happening.

One reason diaspora Jainism must be different from its Indian progenitor derives from the fact that Jain renouncers are forbidden from travelling other than on foot. Except in the case of a very few radical innovators, none of them has ever gone abroad, so communities in the diaspora do not have among them on a routine basis living embodiments of the project of ascetic self-fashioning in terms of which the soteriological tradition's understanding of *ahimsa* makes sense. The absence of renouncers weakens Jain sectarian identity, which, since the differences between Jain sects very largely relate to rules of conduct for renouncers, for lay Jains is very largely a matter of who are 'their' renouncers (Banks 1991, 1992, 1995; Vallely 2002b).

Those few renouncers who have travelled overseas have therefore been atypical – radical, not publicity-shy and actively seeking a forward-looking image. These globetrotting figures are the subject of intense interest even in orthodox circles in India (where their claims still to be Jain renouncers are not universally acknowledged), although they represent only very few direct disciples.

Of more institutional importance are the *samans* and *samanis* of the Svetambar Terapanthi order. The Terapanth is the most centralised of the main Jain orders, being under the authority of a single Acarya, and it is the only one that has an existing profile as socially and politically engaged (see Vallely 2002a for a study of this tradition). The 'Anuvrat Global Organization' or Anubhava, started by the order's late leader Acarya Tulsi to bring about social improvement through the personal spiritual development of its members, has branches in several countries in Europe and the English-speaking world, and these have embraced the ecological agenda with some enthusiasm. The Terapanthi centre, at Ladnun in Rajasthan, now runs courses on 'Ecology and Environmental Science' and has taken the environment as the topic of several of its conferences. The current leader, Acharya Mahaprajna, has incorporated environmentalist language and themes into his speeches – harmony with nature, controlling consumption and development, and so on.

Only a small proportion of Jains are formally or by family tradition Terapanthi followers, but the order achieves prominence beyond its numbers, especially overseas, because it has created the office of *saman* or *samani*, for men and women respectively who live under regular monastic authority and take vows to observe the ascetic disciplines of full renouncers, excepting only those that prohibit or render impractical international travel (they are allowed to have food cooked for them, when necessary, for example). Thus they escape the widespread suspicions of laxness and heterodoxy that attach to the dissident renouncers. The fact that the Terapanth has found a way to make present to overseas Jains figures who are very like renouncers, yet who do not substantially lose authority by travelling, has given that order, and its preference for social engagement and self-consciously modernist style, a prominence that is greater proportionally than it has in India.

The absence of renouncers has also given scope to lay people to speak and act on behalf of Jainism. Mr L.M. Singhvi, over whose name the 'Jain Declaration on Nature' was issued, is an example. A rather different figure (though their views on Jainism as ecological appear to be very similar) is Satish Kumar, who was a Jain monk in childhood but as a young man escaped for a life as a political activist. He now lives in England, where he runs a school named after E.F. Schumacher, the father of 'intermediate technology', and edits a spiritually inclined ecological magazine. He was one of the leading lights of the international Jain magazine, *Jain Spirit*, which, until it closed in 2006, put forward a particularly vigorous and uncompromising vision of a reformed Jainism that would be fully part of the environmentalist, animal liberation, and generally anti-globalisation and anti-capitalist movements. Kumar is creative in devising new ecological rationales for traditional Jain practices. So a traditional prohibition on eating some fruits, in which the seeds are inseparable from the flesh, becomes an injunction to save and plant seeds, so as to replenish the environment (Kumar 2002: 183), although planting seeds is something renouncers are forbidden from doing. And the injunction to walk barefoot is given a New Age twist: 'The minerals of the earth enter the body through the soles of our feet and heal our souls' (2002: 184).

To the extent that these various 'eco-Jains' are successful in persuading diaspora Jains and others that their interpretation represents a valid future for the religion (and, as they also claim, a rediscovery of its true meaning), they will have accomplished a change from a tradition organised around a project of ethical self-fashioning and cultivation of ascetic virtues, whose *telos* is extraction of the individual from an irredeemably violent world, to one guided by ideas about how that world might be changed for the better. This is a change of emphasis in ethical reasoning, then, from a virtue ethics towards a consequentialist morality. It is not, of course, that environmentalists and animal liberationists, Jain or otherwise, do not engage in self-fashioning. Both these latter movements (they overlap, obviously) admit of quite thoroughgoing ascesis for those for whom they become self-defining concerns. The difference is that, unlike an orientation to renunciation, these projects require that one contribute to effecting changes not only in one's own but also, for the effect to be worthwhile, in other people's conduct. Consequentialist reasoning about the effect of one's decisions and actions beyond the shaping of the self are thus essential to them. Equally, renuciatory Jainism does not lack reasoning about or judgement of actions in terms of what their consequences might be. Nor do eco-Jains entirely lack respect for traditional asceticism. But the basic difference in orientation and the change that is involved, as one is re-shaped into the other, are clear enough. The attempt to retain the uniquely wide extension of the application of *ahimsa* in Jainism, but at the same time to reshape its intension from world-renouncing to world-affirming concerns and values, entails reversing the subordination I mentioned above, of what Cort calls 'the realm of value' of worldly well-being to that of soteriology.

The central focus of Jain asceticism, as compared to its Christian counterparts, has always been food rather than sex. But still, like most asceticisms, Jainism has traditionally required celibacy (fairly strictly interpreted) from its renouncers, and has enjoined sexual restraint on its lay followers. The latter involves not only the idea that legitimate sexual relations be restricted to marriage – even within marriage restraint is recommended. Lay Jains should refrain from sexual relations during fasts or other austerities. And on auspicious Holy Days, when married Hindus of child-bearing age are virtually enjoined to have sexual relations, because children conceived on these days will have good fortune, Jains are enjoined to abstain. Recall also that renouncers bury bodily waste, so as not to feed insects and bacteria. In the 'Jaina Declaration on Nature' these desiderata appear in somewhat altered form, as the idea that Jains, 'must not procreate indiscriminately lest they overburden the universe and its resources' and the claim that Jainism 'declares unequivocally that waste and creating pollution are acts of violence' (Singhvi 2002 [1992]: 223–24). The latter is true, but seems much less conventionally 'ecological' when it is recalled that the avoidance of 'waste' is to prevent, in one's own interests, 'life' from being created, sustained and multiplying rather than to prevent its being destroyed.

THE SCOPE OF COMPASSION

One can see this change reflected, for example, in the use of the word '*karuna*' (and some near-synonyms) in the discourse of these reforming environmentalist Jains. '*Karuna*' is used to describe the feeling of sympathy that should arise when contemplating the lives and deaths and sufferings of living things. Traditionally, this is a feeling a practising Jain should cultivate (Wiley 2006), and in eco-Jain writings it is cited to show how Jainism has always led its followers to attend to the well-being of fellow creatures. But the stress is crucially different. In the canonical traditions in India, dominated by renouncers, *karuna* is stressed and *most* valued when it arises from contemplating the sufferings of creatures we cannot even see and for which we have no natural sympathy – microbes, insects, and so on. And most important is to learn to feel that one has oneself lived as creatures such as these oneself, so that one will experience 'disgust' with the world (*vairagya*) and for the prospect of continuing to live in it in any form at all.

In the writings of eco-Jains, by contrast, the idea is that, from contemplating the sufferings of other creatures, there should arise a desire to care and make life better *for them* in some way. One consequence is that the emphasis is not on microbes and cockroaches, but instead, as with conventional Anglo-Saxon environmentalism and the animal welfare movement, the emphasis is on species that are closer to humans and for which it is easier to feel affection and sympathy. Thus, as Valley has observed (2002b: 205), the Western notion of veganism (vegetarians who avoid not only meat but all animal products including dairy foods and leather), which has no real constituency among Jains in India, is gaining popularity among young Jains in North America and the UK. Spokespersons for organisations that promote veganism, such as People for the Ethical Treatment of Animals (PETA), are given prominent space in Jain magazines and at conferences and gatherings.

Now it is not, of course, that soteriological Jainism ignores attractive mammals, but the general view is that sympathy for them is easy to achieve and therefore of comparatively little importance or value. It does not require the counter-intuitive revealed knowledge of the Jain tradition, is not unique to Jainism (unlike concern for single-sensed creatures), and does not lead to an understanding of embodied existence as necessarily violent and so to 'disgust with the world'. It is therefore not dynamically related to the pursuit of ascetic virtues. In the emerging diaspora tradition, this quality of disgust with the world hardly figures at all. Yet it is an absolutely central concept in Jain moral psychology and provides the crucial turning point in the life stories of all Jain saints. It is this that underpins the uniquely general and comprehensive interpretation in Jain tradition of the injunction to attend to the well-being of absolutely all living things. The irony, of course, is that it is this uniquely stretched idea of morally relevant well-being that is the basis in the first place of the idea of Jainism as uniquely concerned with the environment and other species.

That is not to say that this new eco-Jainism, if it becomes more widely established among Jains both in India and elsewhere, will lose all distinctiveness. But it is difficult to see how it can really maintain *this particular* distinctiveness. As Valley has insightfully pointed out (2002b), shorn of the ascetic renunciatory project and the 'ethic of quarantine', the suffering of living things loses its soteriological significance. Instead it becomes simply regrettable: no longer a reason to withdraw in disgust from all contact and interaction with nature, but a reason instead for a newly intensified engagement to take action to improve things. But seen this way, the sufferings of invisible and not very attractive creatures lose the *special* importance they have in the ascetic tradition, and practices that make sense in terms of this – such as boiling water before you drink it – appear incomprehensible or beside the point. It is therefore unsurprising that eco-Jain writers and campaigners portray such practices as arcane, outdated customs that ought to be reformed (which generally means abolished).

Every concrete religious movement, if it is going to achieve any very useful degree of doctrinal coherence, relies on more or less aggressively selective quotation from its scriptural texts. One can tell a lot about eco-Jainism by observing the kinds of selection it routinely involves. Below are two examples.

There is a passage in the Shvetambar Jain canonical text, the *Uttaradhyayana Sutra* (19.61–74: see Jacobi 1964 [1895]), in which a prince describes his former lives. A Western scholarly enthusiast for an ecological interpretation of Jainism cites this passage as an example of the capacity Jainism gives its followers to feel the intense suffering of other species, and of 'the importance and urgency of taking an ecological perspective in thought and action'. The passage is cited as follows:

> From clubs and knives, from stakes and maces, from broken limbs,
> have I hopelessly suffered on countless occasions.
> By sharpened razors and knives and spears have I these many times
> been drawn and quartered, torn apart and skinned.
> And as a deer held helpless in snares and traps,
> I have often been bound and fastened and even killed.
> As a helpless fish I have been caught with hooks and nets,
> scaled and scraped, split and gutted, and killed a million times ...
> Born a tree, I have been felled and stripped, cut with axes and chisels
> and sawed into planks innumerable times.
> Embodied in iron, I have been subjected to the hammer and tongs
> innumerable times, struck and beaten, split and filed ...
> Ever trembling in fear; in pain and suffering always,
> I have felt the most excruciating sorrow and agony. (Koller 2002: 32)

Now the narrative background to this speech is that the young prince, taking a break one day while spending time with his wives, looks out from the jewel-encrusted balcony of his palace, and sees a Jain renouncer. Gazing at him, the prince is granted the miraculous gift of remembering all his former lives. This knowledge produces in him a desire to relinquish his kingdom and become a renouncer. His parents try to dissuade him, pointing out how difficult the life of a renouncer is. His reply is that these difficulties are indeed great, but they are nothing compared with what he now knows he has suffered before in his former lives and will inevitably have to suffer again, unless he takes the ascetic path: hence the description of life as a deer and a fish and a tree and as iron. In Jain didactic literature of this kind, the revelation of knowledge of one's former lives always serves as a provocation to disgust with the world and so to a decision to renounce. But the passage as quoted omits two of the sources of the sufferings the prince has gone through in former lives, because the circumstances of these, although central to traditional ascetic Jainism, and therefore to the concerns that animate the original text, are not really assimilable to its eco-variant.

The first is life in hell. This is described in the original text in some detail, as it is depicted in countless didactic paintings in Jain temples throughout

India. Hairy and dark-skinned demons inflict a pretty inventive range of tortures on those who are born in hell, suspending them over fire, sawing and hacking them to pieces, crushing them in presses, and so on. All this is omitted from the passage quoted, as it is in general from the internet postings and glossy magazines, partly of course because belief in hell is old-fashioned and superstitious, partly because of discomfort with the implication that the religion somehow approves the deliberate cruelty this involves, and partly because authors who see the point of Jainism as making the world a happier and less violent place miss the positive value which these sufferings have within the project of asceticism. The tortures of hell are horrible and to be avoided, but the only way really to avoid them is instead to inflict suffering on oneself. So one of the omitted verses of the *Sutra* goes: 'An infinite number of times have I been crushed like sugar-cane juice in presses, shrieking horribly, to atone for my sins, great sinner that I was.' Eco-Jainism, like environmentalism and animal liberation, concentrates pretty well exclusively on suffering caused by humans, whether to other humans or animals or plants.

A second class of misfortunes that gets omitted from this text, therefore, consists of those caused by other animals. The original has a verse between the prince's life as a fish and that as a tree. In this, 'As a bird I have been caught by hawks, trapped in nets, and bound with bird-lime.' In another, also omitted, he was torn to pieces by 'black and spotted wild dogs'. Such references are omitted, not, of course, because eco-Jains and their supporters are unaware that some animals eat other animals, but because, not being committed by humans with moral choice (soteriological Jainism unblinkingly says they will nevertheless have to suffer from the bad *karma* of doing so), this is not violence that is amenable to 'reform'. Insofar as it is, they do try, by campaigning, for instance, for pet cats and dogs to be kept on vegetarian diets. But otherwise, unlike soteriological Jainism, violence other than by humans does not figure in their moral imagination.

What most conspicuously distinguishes eco-Jainism from its ascetic counterpart, and links it instead with animal liberation and environmental activism more generally, is faith that the world can somehow be made good, that suffering can be, if not eradicated, at least very significantly reduced. The young prince described in the original Jain text, explaining to his parents why he proposed to leave behind his family and his responsibilities as king, would not have been much gripped by this ideal. He would have replied that suffering is not a contingent or tractable but an essential quality of the world, as it is and as it ever could be. That precisely is the lesson he learned from his millions of former lives.

A second example is from the writings of Sadhvi Shilapi (one of the jet-setting unorthodox renouncers mentioned above). She briefly tells the story of how Lord Mahavir sent his chief disciple, Gautam Swami, on a mission to prevent the (Hindu) Brahmin ascetic Agnisharma from staging a massive sacrificial ritual involving the death of thousands of animals. Gautam Swami was successful in his attempt, but the traditional importance

The Intension and Extension of Well-Being

of this story lies in the fact that Mahavir knew when he sent him to do this, but did not tell Gautam Swami, that he himself was about to attain release (*moksh* or *nirvan*), so his devoted disciple would miss his departure from the world and the opportunity to say 'goodbye' to him. Here is how the Sadhvi glosses this fact.

> When Lord Mahavira sent Gautam to prevent Agnisharma's act of violence, he himself was about to attain *nirvana*, the final death, after which Mahavira would not be able to give any more lessons about perfection to his disciples. Certainly, Gautam would not get the chance to sit at the feet of his master. Yet, Mahavira preferred to take a step that was more universal, a feeling more concerned about the life of others – nonhuman others – than to work further toward the spiritual benefit of one single individual. Thanks to the efforts of Indrabhuti Gautam, the slaughter of animals was stopped, and Agnisharma took a vow not to kill animals in the future. (Shilapi 2002: 163)

This is a very popular story, told especially at the festival of Diwali, at which time of year the events it describes occurred (see Laidlaw 1995: 384–87). I have heard it told many times in India by renouncers and lay Jains of various ages and walks of life, but never with the utilitarian interpretation given here. The point of the story is usually a different one. Gautam Swami was a wonderful teacher, in many ways the paradigm of a guru. All his disciples had attained omniscience, but he had not, and the reason was the depth of his affection and therefore attachment to Mahavir. Mahavir reveals to him that in their previous lives, as gods in heaven and humans on earth, they have been bound together by affection, and explains that even after release they will not be separated. He devotes his last sermon to trying to persuade Gautam to relinquish his attachment, but this does not succeed. The ruse of sending Gautam away is to spare him the anguish of watching his friend die, and because Mahavir knows that when Gautam recovers from his grief this will help him finally to overcome his attachment. In the eco-Jain version of the story, as Sadhvi Shilapi recounts it, this story of love surviving as the very last human emotion, right to the point of the final extinguishing of earthly life, is replaced by the stern, puritanical morality of the political activist and the impersonal utilitarian values of Mrs Jellyby. The compassion Mahavir acts upon in the Sadhvi's version is certainly 'stretched', much wider than the close personal relation that is the concern of the traditional tale, but its content is also quite radically changed. In this case, it might also be fair to say the content is here stretched thin.

CONCLUSION

In some influential circles, especially in the diaspora, Jainism is being reconfigured away from a resolutely world-renouncing vision and orientation. As it undergoes this change, and insofar as it is reorganised around a consequentialist concern with the alleviation of suffering, not only is the positive moral significance which suffering has in the ascetic project being lost, but also the uniquely broad range of the forms of living thing whose well-being is held to be morally significant, is narrowing. Concern with insects and microbes, and stress on bodily practice relating to them, are seen as ritualistic and outdated. The practices that encourage and enable ascetic Jains actually to experience care of the self as being dependent on care for unseen creatures around them are being abandoned. Although the idea of Jainism as uniquely concerned about such creatures remains emblematic, eco-Jainism in fact proposes nothing distinctive to be done about them. *Jain Spirit*, in 2001, was adding its voice to the campaign in the UK to ban hunting and reprinting articles from the *Guardian* newspaper urging a boycott of Nike shoes, and others by PETA spokespersons recommending veganism, but not proposing to non-Jain environmentalists or activists any distinctively Jain projects of its own. The insects and invisible creatures Jains are traditionally enjoined to attend to do not actually figure in the policies eco-Jainism proposes, any more than they do in the programmes of other animal welfare or environmental campaigns.

Both soteriological Jainism and the advent of its eco-variant illustrate the interconnection of the intension and extension of 'well-being'. I began by noting the hope that its advantage over other measures of moral and political virtue might be in its expandable extension. I drew attention to the apparently paradoxical coexistence in ascetic Jainism of concern with the well-being of all living things as its highest ethical imperative on the one hand, and on the other its uncompromising devaluation of one's own life and well-being, which one is enjoined actively to renounce. What the changes we see in diaspora Jainism illustrate is that, far from being in tension, these features depend upon each other. Jainism's expansive application of well-being, which at first sight resembles the sensibility we find in ecological activism, turns out to be an entirely different and indeed incompatible phenomenon, which, when its marriage to the latter is attempted, in fact loses its distinctive purposes and power – and, as my last example indicates, on some occasions also its surprising capacity for human sympathy. Eco-Jainism's change towards consequentialist reasoning with respect to 'well-being', is leading, surely against its proponents' desires, to a contraction in its effective extension in their hands. Their assumption that the soteriological tradition's wide understanding of non-violence would be preserved through 'modernisation' of content has proved unfounded. Since the hopes with which we began, of the expansion of existing programmes for, at present, merely human betterment, rest on parallel assumptions, this might serve as a cautionary tale.

NOTES

1. Earlier versions of this chapter were delivered at the 2004 'Well-Being' conference, and subsequently at the Senior Seminar at the Department of Social Anthropology, University of Cambridge. I am grateful to Alberto Corsín Jiménez for his invitation to the Manchester conference, and to participants in both gatherings for their comments.

The Intension and Extension of Well-Being

I should also like to thank the following for their comments: Peter Allen, Susan Bayly, Matei Candea, Joanne Cook, Alberto Corsín Jiménez, Caroline Humphrey, Jonathan Mair and Anne Vallely.
2. For analysis of the Jain diaspora, see Banks (1991, 1992, 1995), Radford (2004) and Vallely (2002b, 2004).
3. On 'deep ecology' see Drengson and Inoue (1995). For a sympathetic comparison between 'Jain ontology' and 'Gaia theory', see Chapple (1993: 68–72).
4. I have learned a great deal and draw freely here from Anne Vallely's excellent essay 'From Liberation to Ecology', and I agree with her persuasive conclusion that the embracing of ecology by diaspora Jains represents 'a fundamental reinterpretation of Jainism's ethical orientation' (2002b: 194). Vallely describes the new orientation as 'sociocentric'. I have attempted a different, or perhaps rather a complementary characterisation.
5. I follow Hursthouse (1999) in regarding virtue ethics and consequentialism as variously differing but connected and overlapping constellations of problematics and forms of reasoning, rather than mutually exclusive types of ethical theory.
6. The best single-volume introductions to Jainism are Jaini (1979) and Dundas (2002a [1992]).
7. For obvious reasons, Jains have adopted vocabulary deriving from scientific microbiology with enthusiasm, hailing it as late confirmation of ancient Jain teachings.
8. An exception proves the rule. Marudevi, mother of Lord Adinath (the first Jina), was born directly from life as a *nigoda*. After her son attained enlightenment she too renounced and attained liberation. Thus she is popularly said to have been the only living thing never to have lived as an insect, plant, or animal – a distinctively Jain variant of the theme of Immaculate Conception?
9. The principal ethnographic monographs and collections are Reynell (1985), Mahias (1985), Carrithers and Humphrey (1991), Banks (1992), Folkert (1993), Humphrey and Laidlaw (1994), Laidlaw (1995), Babb (1996), Cort (2001), Kelting (2001), Vallely (2002a) and Flügel (2006).
10. Although the expression 'animal rights' is used routinely, and although a few theorists have formulated their case in strictly rights-based terms (Regan 1983), these arguments provide much weaker claims than activists generally want. They are rejected roundly by the most influential spokespersons (for example, Singer 1987). The routine political invocation of the concept of rights by animal liberationists is basically instrumental. Compare, on 'human rights', the explicit recommendation of an instrumental (thus knowingly done, it would perhaps be better to call it cynical) use of the vocabulary of rights by Dembour (1996).
11. This is clear in the work of Singer (for example, 1997 [1975]: 177), an avowedly utilitarian theorist who is perhaps the most influential individual on the animal liberation movement. He explicitly favours measures to maximise the impact on animal suffering *for the minimum human inconvenience*.

REFERENCES

Asad, T. 2003. Reflections on Cruelty and Torture. In *Formations of the Secular: Christianity, Islam, Modernity*. Stanford, CA: Stanford University Press, pp. 100–24.
Babb, L.A. 1996. *Absent Lord: Ascetics and Kings in a Jain Ritual Culture*. New York: Columbia University Press.
Banks, M.M. 1991. Orthodoxy and Dissent: Varieties of Religious Belief among Immigrant Gujarati Jains in Britain. In M. Carrithers and C. Humphrey (eds) *The Assembly of Listeners: Jains in Society*. Cambridge: University Press, pp. 241–59.
—— 1992. *Organizing Jainism in India and England*. Oxford: Clarendon Press.

—— 1995. Jain Ways of Being. In R. Ballard (ed.) *Desh Pardesh: The South Asian Presence in Britain.* London: Hurst, pp. 231–50.
Carrithers, M. and C. Humphrey (eds). 1991. *The Assembly of Listeners: Jains in Society.* Cambridge: Cambridge University Press.
Chapple, C.K. 1993. *Nonviolence to Animals, Earth, and Self in Asian Traditions.* Albany, NY: SUNY Press.
Clark, D.A. 2002. *Visions of Development: A Study of Human Values.* Cheltenham: Edward Elgar.
Corsín Jiménez, A. 2003. Well-being: Anthropological Perspectives. Unpublished proposal for an international symposium held in September 2004.
Cort, J.E. 2001. *Jains in the World: Religious Values and Ideology in India.* New York: Oxford University Press.
Dasgupta, P. 2001. *Human Well-being and the Natural Environment.* Oxford: Clarendon Press.
Dembour, M.-B. 1996. Human Rights Talk and Anthropological Ambivalence: The Particular Context of Universal Claims. In O. Harris (ed.) *Inside and Outside the Law: Anthropological Studies of Authority and Ambiguity.* London: Routledge.
Drengson, A. and Y. Inoue (eds). 1995. *The Deep Ecology Movement: An Introductory Anthology.* Berkeley, CA: North Atlantic Books.
Dundas, P. 2002a [1992]. *The Jains,* 2nd edn. London: Routledge.
—— 2002b. The Limits of a Jain Environmental Ethic. In C.K. Chapple (ed.) *Jainism and Ecology: Nonviolence in the Web of Life.* Cambridge, MA: Harvard University Press, pp. 95–117.
Falzon, M.-A. 2004. *Cosmopolitan Connections: The Sindhi Diaspora, 1860–2000.* Leiden: Brill.
Folkert, K.W. 1993. *Scripture and Community: Collected Essays on the Jains,* edited by J.E. Cort. Atlanta, GA: Scholars Press.
Flügel, P. 2006. *Studies in Jaina History and Culture.* London: Routledge.
Griffin, J. 1986. *Well-being: Its Meaning, Measurement, and Moral Importance.* Oxford: Clarendon Press.
Humphrey, C. and J. Laidlaw. 1994. *The Archetypal Actions of Ritual: A Theory of Ritual Illustrated by the Jain Rite of Worship.* Oxford: Clarendon Press.
Hursthouse, R. 1999. *On Virtue Ethics.* Oxford: Clarendon Press.
Jacobi, H. 1964 [1884]. *Jaina Sutras, Part I.* Delhi: Motilal Banarsidass.
—— 1964 [1895]. *Jaina Sutras, Part II.* Delhi: Motilal Banarsidass.
Jaini, P.S. 1979. *The Jaina Path of Purification.* Berkeley: University of California Press.
—— 2000a. Ahimsa: A Jaina Spiritual Discipline. In *Collected Papers on Jaina Studies.* Delhi: Motilal Banarsidass, pp. 3–19.
—— 2000b. Indian Perspectives on the Spirituality of Animals. In *Collected Papers on Jaina Studies.* Delhi: Motilal Banarsidass, pp. 253–66.
Kelting, W.M. 2001. *Singing to the Jinas: Jain Women, Mandal Singing, and the Negotiation of Jain Devotion.* New York: Oxford University Press.
Koller, J.M. 2002. Jain Ecological Perspectives. In C.K. Chapple (ed.) *Jainism and Ecology: Nonviolence in the Web of Life.* Cambridge MA: Harvard University Press, pp. 19–34.
Kumar, S. 2002. Jain Ecology. In C.K. Chapple (ed.) *Jainism and Ecology: Nonviolence in the Web of Life.* Cambridge, MA: Harvard University Press, pp. 81–90.
Laidlaw, J. 1995. *Riches and Renunciation: Religion, Economy, and Society among the Jains.* Oxford: Clarendon Press.
—— 2005. A Life Worth Leaving: Fasting to Death as Telos of a Jain Religious Life. *Economy and Society* 34(2), 178–99.
Mahias, M.-C. 1985. *Délivrance et convivialité: Le système culinaire des Jaina.* Paris: Maison des Sciences de l'Homme.
Nussbaum, M. 2006. *Frontiers of Justice: Disability, Nationality, Species Membership.* Cambridge, MA: Harvard University Press.

Nussbaum, M.C. and A. Sen (eds). 1993. *The Quality of Life*. Oxford: Clarendon Press.

Radford, M.A. 2004. (Re)Creating Transnational Religious Identity within the Jaina Community of Toronto. In K.A. Jacobsen and P.P. Kumar (eds) *South Asians in the Diaspora*. Leiden: Brill, pp. 23–51.

Regan, T. 1983. *The Case for Animal Rights*. Berkeley: University of California Press.

Reynell, J. 1986. Honour, Nurture and Festivity: Aspects of Female Religiosity among Jain Women in Jaipur. Unpublished PhD dissertation, University of Cambridge.

Sen, A. 1993. Capability and Well-being. In M.C. Nussbaum and A. Sen (eds) *The Quality of Life*. Oxford: University Press, pp. 30–53.

—— 1999. *Development as Freedom*. Oxford: University Press.

—— 2002. *Rationality and Freedom*. Cambridge, MA: Harvard University Press.

(Sadhvi) Shilapi 2002. The Environmental and Ecological Teachings of Tirthankara Mahavira. In C.K. Chapple (ed.) *Jainism and Ecology: Nonviolence in the Web of Life*. Cambridge, MA: Harvard University Press, pp. 159–67.

Singer, P. 1987. Animal Liberation or Animal Rights. *The Monist* 70, 3–14.

—— 1997 [1975]. *Animal Liberation*. London: Pimlico.

Singhvi, L.M. 2002 [1992]. The Jaina Declaration of Nature. In C.K. Chapple (ed.) *Jainism and Ecology: Nonviolence in the Web of Life*. Cambridge, MA: Harvard University Press, pp. 217–24.

Tobias, M. 1991. *Life Force: The World of Jainism*. Berkeley: Asian Humanities Press.

Vallely, A. 2002a. *Guardians of the Transcendent: An Ethnography of a Jain Ascetic Community*. Toronto: University of Toronto Press.

—— 2002b. From Liberation to Ecology: Ethical Discourses among Orthodox and Diaspora Jains. In C.K. Chapple (ed.) *Jainism and Ecology: Nonviolence in the Web of Life*. Cambridge, MA: Harvard University Press, pp. 193–216.

—— 2004. The Jain Plate: The Semiotics of the Diaspora Diet. In K.A. Jacobsen and P.P. Kumar (eds) *South Asians in the Diaspora*. Leiden: Brill, pp. 3–22.

Wiley, K.L. 2006. Ahimsa and Compassion in Jainism. In P. Flügel (ed.) *Studies in Jaina History and Culture: Disputes and Dialogues*. London: Routledge, pp. 439–55.

9 WELL-BEING IN ANTHROPOLOGICAL BALANCE: REMARKS ON PROPORTIONALITY AS POLITICAL IMAGINATION

Alberto Corsín Jiménez

In 1691, when Johannes Vermeer's *Woman in Blue Reading a Letter* was sold at auction in Amsterdam, the catalogue noted: 'the charming light and dark suggest a splendid well-being'. The idea that well-being could be a matter of shadows and light is very distant from our twenty-first-century concern with material and moral standings; the softness and suppleness of Vermeer's aesthetics very far from our current economic and political preoccupations. In this chapter I would like to suggest that there may be, however, a sense in which well-being is still today a matter of appropriate illuminations, a matter of finding the right balance between the visible and invisible elements of social life. In thinking about the place of well-being in human life, I have come to realise some of the current deficiencies of social theory. Finding an analytical place for well-being in social theory is a two-fold provocation: a realisation of the limits of our theoretical tools, and a call for an imaginative way forward. For well-being throws into relief how difficult it is to talk about social life and human virtues simultaneously. It seems that our analytical vocabularies are good for one task or the other, but not for working on both at once. We have not yet quite found the right proportion between social analysis and a theory of ethics. My aim in this chapter is to volunteer one such model of proportional ethics. In fact, I would like to suggest that one possible way out of this ethical-cum-sociological impasse may well lie in the idea of proportionality itself. It may turn out that proportionality, the image of the rightful balance, may work too as an analytic of sociological righteousness. But this first entails unpacking the kind of 'proportionality' that has figured centrally in Western political thought. This chapter is an attempt to sketch out such a recursive analytic, by playing off the classical notion of proportionality as 'ethical balance' against an assessment of the 'proportions' of Euro-American social thought.

AGGREGATION

Perhaps the single most important issue confronting economists and moral philosophers when devising indices of well-being is that of aggregation. The question of aggregation emerges at almost every juncture of the well-being problematic. It points to the fundamental question about well-being, which is about its size, and the location of this size. ('What is well-being?' is so thorny an issue that is probably best left unanswered, and in a sense is contained in the first question, as I hope to show below.) James Griffin has expressed the metric nature of well-being in the following terms: 'When speaking of well-being, we all resort to quantitative language. We speak of "more" and "less". At times we aim to "maximize" well-being' (1986: 75). Hidden in the question about the size of well-being there is also the question about its location: where is well-being to be found? Is well-being located in individual persons or in collectivities? Is it a matter of individual happiness, interpersonal relations or transcendental values? The question about the location of well-being is therefore expressly an anthropological question, for it calls for a theory of the workings of society, and indeed of the very terms that social groups employ to think of themselves. To put it bluntly: we need to know how to look for society if well-being is to be found in one or another of its expressions.

The distribution of society, that is, the mechanisms through which society becomes itself, will therefore determine the size of well-being, and its location therein. Aggregation is part and parcel of this analytic because whatever and wherever society is, well-being can only emerge as the concrete articulation of bits and pieces otherwise distributed across the social. Aggregation is the tool used to bring these bits and pieces together, which would otherwise probably not be on speaking terms with one another. Happiness and life expectancy, for instance, might both be elements of social well-being, but they refer to different moments and values of sociality, and as such are located and run along different social pathways. This diverse and plural occurrence of well-being raises the issue of scale. Social well-being is often assumed to be the sum of personal well-beings (health, happiness, freedom); and personal well-being is in turn taken to be an aggregate of plural forms of well-being, all found at the level of the individual (different people want different things from life).[1] The personal-to-the-social scale thus refers to the remit of well-being, to its location within one of many possible social worlds – this is a question about numbers, about how many units of intra and interpersonal well-beings ought to be taken into account in our calculations: one individual or one million.

But there is another way in which the concept of scale works and this is when referring to the nature of the values that are summoned in the name of well-being: happiness and life expectancy are different sort of indices, as noted above, and each makes sense within its own scale. They may both be constituents (or determinants) of well-being, but they point to different dimensions of it – this, then, is a question about orders of knowledge. Say that our society is made up of 1 million people. The personal-to-the-social scale might tell us the numbers that we have to compute (1 million) to come up with an aggregate for well-being. But this kind of scale will not work very well, or will not do enough, if it turns out that what makes half our population happy makes the other half miserable. We need to know, then, not only whom to count (a question of numbers), but also on what basis to count (a question of orders of knowledge). Making different kinds of scales work together is not always easy, which is why aggregation is so important. I return to the notion of the size or scale of well-being in the conclusion.

Aggregation, then, appears in many guises when considering the relations of sociality to well-being. In line with the above, we would expect there to be different modalities of aggregation, and for different aggregations to play a different part in the imagination of well-being. An issue that is implied by this vision is that well-being will vary with the workings of society. That is, not with the kind of society we live in, but with the way in which we think about the social. This is the main point of this chapter and I will return to it on a number of occasions. Suffice to say now that moral philosophy and economics have favoured a consequential view of well-being, where the latter is a consequence of particular social orderings. This, in my view, is clever economics but flawed social theory, for it works uniformly with one single model of society. It sets out to measure well-being by adding or taking social bricks away from a ready-made model of society; but it makes no attempt to rethink the nature of the construction materials employed by society in the building of its own changing edifice. This means that when we set out to measure or think about well-being what we are in effect doing is measuring and reifying a particular notion of society, and of the ways in which people make themselves available to the social body. We come up with a number but lose track of the social; we end up focusing on the units that are aggregated and not on the mathematics of aggregation. Society, in sum, disappears behind the fiction of its measurement.

This is a gloomy picture and, in a sense, an unfair representation of the analytical powers of aggregation. Much recent work on the social foundations of well-being is expressly addressed at correcting this fiction and does so by enlarging our perspective on the infrastructure of well-being, looking at 'the quality of the transactions in which the individual can take part, which means taking an interest in a background of inherited possibilities' (Douglas and Ney 1998: 61–62). Mary Douglas and Steven Ney have recently reviewed these attempts at taking account of the social and institutional structures of well-being, and have in turn developed a model of the person that aims to redefine social theory around these measuring refinements. But there is another way in which the work of economists may in fact be of use to social theory, though it involves a rather imaginative application of the notion of aggregation. I want to suggest that the concept of aggregation (and its reverse, disaggregation or distribution) may have formidable analytical mileage if used as a social analytic, one that allows us to move away from

Well-Being in Anthropological Balance

worn-out models of society and that further allows us to substantiate the political purchase of well-being. Let me explain how.

DISTRIBUTION

The question of aggregation is at the heart of an old agenda in economics, namely, social choice theory. In its programmatic form, social choice theory was laid out by Kenneth Arrow in 1951. It was motivated by the following central issue: how can it be possible to arrive at cogent aggregative judgments about, say, social welfare, collective interest, or aggregate poverty (Sen 1999b: 349)? Perplexed by these summative difficulties, Arrow's pioneering work concluded by stating the impossibility of social choice. More recently, on occasion of his Nobel Prize in Economic Sciences lecture, Amartya Sen took up the task of discussing some of the challenges and foundational problems of social choice theory and concluded on a more positive note, by advocating the need for broadening the informational basis of social choices, such as the use of interpersonal comparisons of well-being and individual advantage (Sen 1999b). In a nutshell, Sen's vision is that the predicament of well-being is best confronted if we substitute the problem of distribution for the problem of aggregation (if we 'open up' our image of society, with more information, for instance), and if we further look beyond distribution to the entitlements or capabilities that allow people to make claims on the goods to be distributed and on their own development as human persons. Let me look at this transition more closely.

A crucial starting point of social choice theory is the analytic that it employs to conjure up an image of society. Sen makes the point succinctly when asking: 'How can we judge how well *society as a whole* is doing in the light of the disparate interests of its different members?' (Sen 1999b: 350, emphasis in the original). Marilyn Strathern has brought the same question home to anthropology when arguing that:

To think of society as a thing is to think of it as a discrete entity. The theoretical task then becomes one of elucidating 'the relationship' between it and other entities. This is a mathematic, if you will, that sees the world as inherently divided into units. The significant corollary of this view is that relationships appear as extrinsic to such units: they appear as secondary ways of connecting things up. (Strathern 1990: 5)

The question of society's 'wholeness', then, raises three questions: about the idea of society as a whole or entity; about the parts that make up a whole; and about the mathematic (that is, the analytic) that we use to think about the social. The three are related, but I address them in turn.

For much of the twentieth century, welfare economics was concerned with the issue of how to make appraisals of the ordering of social states. If everybody in society A is happy and everybody in society B is not, then one ought to be able to find the factor that makes the social order in A preferable to that in B. For many years, economists and moral philosophers used *utility* as a measure of such factor, and social states were ranked in terms of the sum-total of utilities that their respective orderings yielded. (Many measures of utility were employed. I use the term here loosely to refer to them all.) Utility, then, became a proxy for society, which thence ceased to exist as an idea and assumed the semblance of a whole number instead. This is the question of *social wholes*, where society or its proxies are imagined as numerical units and are made to work analytically as such.

Economists and philosophers know as well as anthropologists that 'wholes' are useful fictions. They serve a purpose, though they are also very murky analytical tools. Take the infamous case of 'society': where does a society start and end? In a friendship, a generation or an economic stream of inter-generations? What counts as a whole is a question whose pragmatics will bounce back with a vengeance – however we count, we are bound to leave some people out, or take people in for the wrong reasons (that is, reasons that are not the same for all). Now economists have tended to deal with the complications of wholes by means of the concept of 'distribution'. In relation to well-being, Partha Dasgupta explains it thus:

To speak of social well-being is to speak in aggregate terms. There is, however, a danger that by an 'aggregate' one understands some sort of *average*. This isn't the way I am using the term here. The kind of aggregate I have in mind reflects a comprehensive notion of aggregate well-being, including as it does not only average well-being, but also other features of the distribution of well-being, such as its variance, skewness, and so forth. In common parlance, features other than the average of the distribution of a thing are called the 'distributional features' of that thing. (Dasgupta 2001: 19)

Distribution is a useful notion because, although it preserves the fiction of wholes, it inflects the latter with a sense of heterogeneous weights, thus observing that not all wholes have the same make-up. (Two societies may have identical measurements of well-being, but whereas in one society one person is the sole contributor to social well-being, the others being destitute, in another society well-being is evenly distributed amongst all its members.) The heterogeneity to which distribution is a remedy has two moments: an allocational or institutional one, and a social one.

Allocational distribution is what economists have largely been concerned with: coming up with weights that make up for the inequalities of society. There are many such weights, some focusing on the commodity *determinants* of well-being (potable water, food, education, etc.), some on its *constituents* (health, freedom, happiness). A distributional weight may point and aim to correct my lack of access to food; but it will not be very effective if it does not call out at the same time my inability to vote out of office the people who are deliberately keeping the food away from me in the first place. The latter points to the question of 'negative freedom': freedom from arbitrary interference, and is the trademark of Dasgupta's important refinement to Sen's deservedly famous capabilities approach to well-being (Dasgupta 1993; Sen, 1999a). Allocational distribution, then, has nothing or very little to say about society;

it is solely concerned with the institutional mechanisms that make sure that society works fine, and with making sure that people feel comfortable with such working arrangements. In allocational models, society is in place, and one allocates and makes decisions *against* it.

My larger point here is that allocational distribution must be a variant of social distribution, which antecedes and informs it. When economists make up for ill-distributed well-being what they are in effect doing is compensating for a social distribution already in place; that is, they are redistributing the social. Society comes into being in distributive episodes, one of which is awakening to the fact that we should rethink our social distribution. An early anthropological advocate of this vision was Stephen Gudeman (1978). Though his approach at the time was essentially allocational, looking at the question of the origin and use of a society's 'surplus value' or 'output allocation', it is still the case that for him distribution operates relationally: 'distribution as a meaningful system, distribution in light of social forces, and distribution as a structure' (Gudeman 1978: 374) – that is, a structure of social choices and social values, or a reflection of how, in its distributive episodes, a society stretches and branches out as it chooses its future image.

The idea of social distribution, or of the distribution of the social, is perhaps best presented in the work of Marilyn Strathern (for example, Strathern 1988). Most famously, the language of distribution takes form in her notion of 'distributed personhood', where persons emerge as social beings in moments of relational efficacy, like when they make themselves available to others in acts of ceremonial gift-giving. This is why, in a book aimed to engage an economic audience, Mary Douglas has observed that 'When Strathern says ... that for "person" one could write "gift," she is not being flippant' (Douglas and Ney 1998: 9). If persons emerge as moments of distribution – distribution of themselves in others and others in themselves – then what we need to look out for are the values or idioms through which a society decides to conduct its own branching-out. This is where the idea of the distributed person meets the theory of economy, and in particular of moral economy. If the person becomes an element in, or even the carrier of society's distributional base (Gudeman 2001), then it is only legitimate to suggest that persons make the social good (that is, well-being) available to others in their capacity of distributing themselves in a certain fashion (Strathern 1981). How they become available is therefore a matter of the quality of the relations that they set up with others.

This introduces us to the second question about the wholeness of a society: the relationship of the parts to the whole, or what Dasgupta, in the quote above, calls the 'distributional features' of things. Our habit of aggregating parts into wholes is emblematic of what linguists call a partonomic mode of classification. John Davis has observed that partonomies are just one way in which people establish links with other people and things, other ways being pairing and taxonomic classifications (Davis 1992: 34–37). What appears to be distinctive about partonomies, however, is that they are very good at making explicit the logic behind material transactions. Davis's own examples capture it nicely:

> Gifts between friends should more or less balance; gifts exchanged between parents and children should be unequal. Altruists should expect no return, while alms-givers may quite legitimately hope for a supernatural reward. All these are different appropriate relations between income and outgo.... In summary, an intended exchange is a balance of two partonomies. (Davis 1992: 40–1)

Note the language in which Davis explains the relations between transacting partners: 'balance', 'return', 'equality', 'appropriateness'. Exchange relations are qualified by a controlled give-and-take, a measured equilibrium that makes sure that things do not get out of proportion, as they do in potlatch ceremonies, for instance. As Mary Douglas has noted, a 'community works because the transactions *balance out*' (1986: 74, emphasis added).What is brought into balance is a measure of the portion of society that we want to make available to others; and so the gift, by obviation, signals also the size of society that is not available for distribution. The part that we give is an indication of the whole that is not given – what you see (the gift) is what you do not get (the larger social whole). Gift-giving is thus an expression and effect of proportionality.

Economic proportionality can be useful to think about other forms of sociality too. The imagery is for instance at the heart of Marilyn Strathern and Roy Wagner's writings on fractality, where relations self-replicate across different orders of magnitude. The paradigmatic case here is the individual vs. society dichotomy, for however we define society, individuals will always be seen as a fraction or proportion of the social whole (Strathern 1992a, 1992b). But individuality itself is of course also subject to fractal partitioning, as in the image of the pregnant woman or, for that matter, in the potential for future relations that all people carry within. Fractality is thus not unlike Davis's partonomic model of classification, except that in the former parts and wholes work across and within different scales, so that there will always be a scale where any part will figure as a whole and any whole will stand as a part (Strathern 1991, 1995). To pursue a flippant analogy: if a gift signals the invisible size of society, an individual works as a proportional 'remainder', as was noted in the Introduction to the volume. That is, individuals are what Euro-Americans give away to keep their social wholes (that is, 'society') at home.

This may all sound of little empirical relevance to the problem of well-being were it not for the question with which I opened this chapter: where is well-being located? We saw that, to be fair to the distribution of well-being in society, we first had to disaggregate the concept and look to its emergence in distributive episodes. These were in turn defined by the qualities of relations, which came together in the carrying capacities of persons. But these carrying capacities work differently at different orders or scales of sociality. Individuals may be good carriers of society and thus a good place where to locate well-being. However, we ought to remember that individuals are just proportional factors of society, and that for some purposes, or in some circumstances, a society will afford a much fairer and even distribution of well-being if it uses a different proportional model. Take the case of intergenerational well-being. If we use the individual as the site and carrier of well-being, the soon-to-be-born child of a pregnant woman – let alone the child's child – will not be factored into our calculations of social wealth – future generations are not part of an individual's whole. In order to take future generations into account we need to modify our aggregational and distributional model. And so it is that one is tempted to locate well-being not in wholes but in proportions, for it is ultimately in a proportional manner that we decide what to factor in and what to leave out (Strathern 1996). This brings me to the last question about the wholeness of society, namely, the type of mathematic that we use to think about the social.

PROPORTIONS

The use of terms like 'individual choice', 'subjective' and 'objective' measures of well-being, or even the use of market frameworks as models of social interaction, belies the relational analytic that underpins current work on the measurement of well-being, such as Amartya Sen's capability approach or Partha Dasgupta's generation-relative ethics (see also Offer 1996). Their focus on interpersonal comparisons, intergenerational streams of wealth and sustainable development, shows that theirs is not a mathematic of social wholes but of relations, even if their descriptive language suggests otherwise. True, their use of relations is methodological, not analytic – it informs their efforts at measuring well-being, not their social theory. But decades of work on the problem of well-being by economists and political philosophers has shown that aggregation and the ensuing problem of distribution are factorial in how one thinks about the social good. So integral is their resolution to the question of well-being that one is tempted to think that they may in fact be part and parcel (part and whole) of the very workings of society – that is, the very way in which the social apportions itself.

Social apportionments are of course distributive episodes, and as such are informed by a relational analytic. But unlike relations, which only tell you *how* to disaggregate, apportionments tell you *what* to disaggregate into. Apportionments are relations of magnitude and thus carry with them a value judgement (cf. Griffin 1996). The relational work they do is inflected by this magnitude and shows up in the final allocation. In other words, the apportionment is the form the relation takes when it emerges as a consequence; or to say it somewhat differently, when it works as a proportion (Corsín Jiménez 2003). I go back to the problem of disaggregating intergenerational well-being. Parents care for the well-being of their children, so it is in their own interest to make the necessary provisions to pass on to them a 'good-enough world'. The question is, good enough for whom? For it is clear that eventually their children will face the same concern, and so will their grandchildren, and so on. Good-enough-for-whom, then, entails a decision on how many futures will the current generation discount when making up their minds on the current valuation of well-being. Not only that, but also whether all futures are worth the same or some are worth more than others. Accounting for the well-being of the 400th generation down from ours may not only be burdensome but of little avail altogether, for there are just too many imponderables getting in the way of our predictions. So a concern with intergenerational well-being presupposes a relational analytic, but this is ultimately of little help in understanding how people work out their life-projects. People care a lot for their children, yes; but they might find it just a little too difficult to take account of the care for their great-great-grandchildren. Relationships, then, are not worked out linearly but proportionately, and it is towards the elucidation of a proportional model of sociality that we should strive.

PROPORTIONAL SOCIALITY

A model of the workings of society based on the idea of proportional distribution may look like an unlikely pill to swallow. Unlike individuals, or even relations, proportions are difficult to visualise, or so it would seem. This may simply be a matter of perspective, however. I would like to suggest that not only are there good analytical reasons to take up the model, but that there are also firm historical foundations to support it, which have also, in the process, inflected our theories of political ethics. It may be that history has kept its perspective on proportions hidden from view, a point recently raised by Jonathan Israel (2001) *apropos* the contribution of Spinoza's geometrical thought to the fashioning of philosophical modernity.

I realise that this is of course no place in which to sketch a history of the idea of proportional sociality; but I would nevertheless like to point to some historical uses of the image of the proportion, for I believe it can illuminate some aspects of the current political purchase of the concept of well-being in liberal societies. In a nutshell, my argument is that social theory is strongly geometrical (that is, proportional) and that it is important to acknowledge the mechanical principles of our theoretical toolkit if we are to put our models to full and good use. Not to do so is to fall for a political conception of social well-being that is disembedded from how people relate to one another. It is to look for well-being where it is not, and to demand social responsibilities where they do not apply.

In one sense, the idea of proportionality is as old as political thought itself. It is for instance a fundamental premise of Greek political theory, for it is to be found at work within its metaphysic, from where it informs much of its cosmology and politics. This is particularly evident in the thought of Plato. Like all classical Greek thought, Plato's political vision is founded on principles of cosmological correspondence: political relations grow out of the application of the same rules that organise the cosmos, which hence figures as the all-encompassing scale. All relations have a place in the cosmos and nest within it in varying orders of hierarchy. Nature, man and society are to be 'adjusted' (*dike*) in one ethical and cosmic relation, and if carried out properly (if relations are properly apportioned) this justification produces *nómos* or custom. In a state of tradition or equilibrium, the virtues of man mirror the virtues of the *politeia*, though each is worked out on a different scale and the cosmic principle of 'just apportionments' (*dike*) is what keeps the correspondence in place. One may call this order of correspondence a fractal ordering, for all relations contain within themselves the wider cosmological equilibrium towards which they contribute. The notion of fractality was, however, foreign to Greek thought; but proportionality, of which fractality is a more sophisticated expression, was not, and in this light the model may be seen as one of cosmological proportionality (or just apportionment).

There is another way in which the imagery of proportionality was at work in classical Greek thought, one that addresses directly the analytical tools that we use in economic anthropology. This is Aristotle's metaphysic of exchange relations. Upon confronting the problem of exchange, Aristotle's underlying aim was of course to remain faithful to the model of cosmological correspondence (which is why his discussions of exchange are to be found in the *Nicomachean Ethics*). But as soon as he starts to work on the problem of exchange, he is struck by the mystery of commensurability: how can things that are by nature of a different kind be brought into exchange equations? How can shoes be exchanged for houses? Aristotle was of course the first to make the distinction between use and exchange values, and in his mind the problem of commensurability is the problem of the transformation of value: of one thing being exchanged, and therefore changed, for another. Scott Meikle has studied Aristotle's economic thought and has uncovered the proportional imagery that guides his understanding of this transformation:

Aristotle takes the first step towards defining the particular form of reciprocity that is appropriate in the context of exchange. He says it is 'reciprocity ... on the basis of proportion, not on the basis of equality'. The reciprocity must be of proportions of things, not the 'simple reciprocity' of Rhadamanthys, which would mean giving one thing for one thing. It would not be fair for a builder and a shoemaker to exchange one house for one shoe, because a house is too great or too much to give for a shoe. So they must exchange in proportions, so many shoes to a house. (Meikle 1995: 10)

Aristotle never quite resolved the paradox of proportional commensurability. He studied the logic of barter and the development of money, but in the end was incapable of explaining satisfactorily how use values become exchange values. The problem, however, remained crucial to him, for he thought that it was on the basis of reciprocal relations that larger political associations flourished. Whatever it was that brought people to exchange, proportional reciprocity enabled the 'holding together' of the *polis* (Meikle 1995: 35–37).

Aristotle worked within the horizon of the good life. Proportional commensurability and the 'holding together' of society were foundational bricks of the good life, which was accomplished if and only if there was a proper distribution of relations in the *polis* – that is, if the relations of exchange, and the relations of political obligation that were built upon these, were allowed to develop into and assume their natural *telos*. The good life was a metaphysical possibility of the good society, which was in turn a metaphysical development of fair exchange. Fairness was a metaphysical postulate of Aristotle's political theory.

It is important to keep in mind the metaphysical assumptions behind Aristotle's political theory, and in particular his metaphysic of exchange relations or proportional commensurability, for it is these assumptions that were viciously attacked by Hobbes in the wake of the seventeenth century's scientific revolution. Hobbes, unlike Aristotle, saw no reason why one should emphasise the distributive fairness of relationships. The nature of exchange, he argued, was arithmetic, not geometric; there were no good reasons for upholding proportional equivalences in exchange. A shoe is a fair exchange item for a house, if people want it to be so. What Hobbes was in effect saying was that the terms of political association should not be qualified by a fictitious distinction between 'ought' and 'is' (Macpherson 1962: 70–87): what people do is what ought to be done, and contractual agreements entered into freely by free, desirous agents are exemplary of fair justice:

Justice of Actions, is by Writers divided into *Commutative* and *Distributive*: and the former they say consisteth in proportion Arithmeticall; the latter in proportion Geometricall. Commutative therefore, they place in the equality of value of the things contracted for; And Distributive, in the distribution of equal benefit, to men of equall merit. As if it were Injustice to sell dearer that we buy; or to give more to a man than he merits. The value of all things contracted for, is measured by the Appetite of the Contractors: and therefore the just value, is that which they be contented to give. (Hobbes 1991 [1651]: 105)

Hobbes's critique of distributive justice was part of the post-Reformation and anti-Aristotelian movement that culminated in the birth of the *nuova scientia* in the late sixteenth and early seventeenth century. Hobbesian political thought was itself the foundation of what C.B. Macpherson (1962) has called 'possessive individualism', a theory of political organisation that sees the individual as the proprietor of his own person and capacities, and that is at the root of modern liberal-democratic theory. My reading of Hobbes is somewhat different, however, and although I have no contention with Macpherson's lucid diagnosis of the origins of possessive individualism, I would like to suggest that, despite his best efforts at repudiating Aristotelian metaphysics, Hobbes remained faithful to the model of proportional sociality that informed Aristotle's politics. Working tacitly or explicitly within the Hobbesian and Aristotelian models, the lubricant of social organisation is always a mechanism of proportional sociality.

Well-Being in Anthropological Balance

The source of Hobbes's proportionalism is to be found in his Galilean baggage, what, following Peter Machamer (1998b), I call his Archimedean vision of the workings of the world. Machamer has argued that Galileo's work and scientific orientation was premised on a model of intelligibility based on the image of the Archimedean balance: 'The principle to be noted is that for Galileo the whole schema of intelligibility becomes putting a question in the form of an equilibrium problem: What is the cause of (or force that causes) something becoming unbalanced? Where is the balance point?' (Machamer 1998a: 60). In order to solve such problems of equilibrium, seventeenth-century scientists turned to the construction of mechanical models. These mechanical models fulfilled their aspirations for 'demonstrative proof', which, as Hobbes put it, 'was understood by them for that sort of ratiocination that placed the thing they were to prove, as it were before mens eyes' (cited in Machamer 1998b: 15). Perhaps more significantly, the preferred form of such representations was taken to be spatial displays, and in particular those based on proportional geometry, which replicated the workings of the world as being founded on the balance of magnitudes and the general relational measurement (ratios) of things. In the writings of Galileo this concern with proportionality is even used as a metaphor for clear thought, as when he writes that 'Human understanding or reason (ragione) is having the correct measure (ratio) for things' (cited in Machamer 1998a: 63). For seventeenth-century scientists, then, the mechanics of the world were proportional, and both the epistemology and method of our enquiries were supposed to mirror these mechanics of ratiocination.[2]

It is to this proportional natural philosophy that Hobbes bowed. His theory of man and social relationships was a theory of motion, of the balance of forces that moved people to associate or fight with one another. For Hobbes, men were 'automated machines', 'self-moving' and 'self-directing' (Macpherson 1962: 31). He explained everything, from free will to social interaction, by resorting to a mechanics of pressure and bodily push: perception, for instance, had its origin in the diffusion of species that foreign bodies emitted and their pressing on the eye of the observer. Likewise, motivation and action were the outcome of excitement and the pressure of the appetites, or their aversion, towards different objects. Man, in sum, was an arithmetical creature: 'the whole *summe* of Desires, Aversions, Hopes and Fears, continued till the thing be either done, or thought impossible, is that we call DELIBERATION' (Hobbes 1991: 44, emphasis added). This is why J.W.N. Watkins called *Leviathan* 'the political expression of the Galilean theory of motion' (1955: 129), a thought that finds its echo in Hobbes's own capitulatory expression, 'Life it selfe is but Motion' (1991: 46).

It is well known that Hobbes's model of possessive individualism became the standard formulation of liberal-democratic society (Macpherson 1962), and in this sense his mathematics of society, based on the arithmetic of individual volitions, has become common stock in social theory, and especially so in economic theory. The model did not remain unchallenged, of course, and perhaps the most famous of the neo-Aristotelians was Marx himself (see, for example, Meikle 1994). Neo-Aristotelianism is another word for a mathematic of society that comes to terms with its own aggregative structure, with its own varying shapes and 'geometric justice': that is, a model of social interaction that takes stock of, and makes the effort of actualising itself through, the distribution of its 'parts'.

It is this history also, the history of the idea of social justice as an expression of proportionality, that Derrida (1995) has recently resurrected in his reading of Heidegger's philosophy of justice. Following Heidegger, Derrida (1995: 37) recognises the analytical purchase – and yet problematic nature – of the original Greek term *dike* (the image of proportionality and balance; the principle of 'just apportionment') for re-centring and making the political rest on the dynamic of gift relationships. Echoing Hamlet's famous sentence, 'The time is out of joint', Derrida ascribes a quality of 'out-of-jointness' to all social life, and thus to the very possibility of human justice. For Derrida, gift-giving and debt-honouring are both paradigmatic expressions of the necessary asynchrony of human sociality (1995: 40). They are both indicative of a form of life that is always, existentially, out-of-synch with itself: a shadow of its own condition. In this view, social life is always falling short of itself, gesturing towards its own disproportion, because of its own phenomenology as a process of becoming. With Derrida, then, I want to suggest that it is the irresolvable nature of this asynchrony – the paradox of proportional incommensurability – that works as the engine of social life everywhere. It is the confusion of not knowing how and which orders of knowledge have to be made commensurable, or the realisation that commensurability, when accomplished, is frail and temporary, that makes social life continuously re-dimension itself.[3]

CONCLUSION

Earlier in the chapter I used the expression 'social mathematic' to point to the ways in which we think about the social. We have seen that different authors use different categories to build their images of society. The word 'society' itself is strongly associated with a mathematic of wholes, for once we talk about society it is difficult not to reify it as an entity. Economists in particular have had much difficulty resisting the temptation of working arithmetically with these wholes. Much of the recent work on the problem of well-being by Amartya Sen or Partha Dasgupta may be read as a heroic effort to refashion the economic corpus with the use of geometric models of society. The analytics of aggregation and distribution, for instance, are tools devised to help economists move away from a social theory that takes society for granted. They allow economists and moral philosophers to de-objectify the social and work with its moments of articulation instead.

Anthropologists, on the other hand, have long had an interest in these moments of articulation, to which we have traditionally referred to as 'social

Well-Being in Anthropological Balance

relationships'. But I think it is fair to say that we have now arrived at a point where anthropology is close to fetishising its own analytic, doing with social relationships what economists once did with the 'individual' and 'society'. In drawing attention to the different analytical vocabularies of economists and anthropologists, my aim has been to emphasise the importance of rethinking our conceptual imaginaries, a task to which I dare say some economists have been dedicating themselves with far greater passion and urge than most anthropologists. Of particular interest are the methodological efforts that economists have made to disaggregate society. In this chapter I have singled out two such tools: aggregation and distribution. I have suggested that both methodologies may be put to formidable analytical use if applied to help us disentangle the workings of social forms. I believe that, if used as analytical categories, aggregation and distribution can tell us a great deal about how people relate to one another; in particular, they can help us qualify our traditional relational analytic, pointing us to the forms that relationships take. That is, they can tell us how a relationship becomes a proportion.

In the language of classical political theory, a proportional model of sociality is neo-Aristotelian[4] and geometric: it discusses how people measure and distribute their choices, and how the possibility of choice refashions and resizes people's self-conceptions. It shows that all choices, even the choices made by a Hobbesian automated agent, are proportional choices: a measure of the capacity of 'society' to make itself available to its members through certain forms of proportional distribution. Put somewhat differently, proportionality tells us the effort that people have to make, to extract their own self-image as distributive and capable agents.[5]

In the Hobbesian model of liberal self-extraction, the effort people have to make is scant: it affects only them, for they are the sole yardstick of their measured actions – the ratio of the proportion is a flat zero. It is not, then, that there is no proportionality at work, but rather that it has been bracketed off: the part and the whole are one and the same thing; the individual is the measure of society.

In contrast, in, say, Melanesian societies, where personhood takes a distributive fashion, the pain that people have to go to is considerable, for it stretches out from, and has sources of agency outside, the individuated person: people are what their relations to others makes them be (for example, Strathern 1988). Now, the trouble with the Melanesian model is that although proportionality is not zero, it is nevertheless a constant, and it is therefore assumed that people always relate in the *same* fashion – a relation is a relation is a relation. But:

> ... [o]ne person cannot suffice as the measure of another, but reflects only that part which is invested in the relationship in question. Thus from others one ever only gets a partial perspective on oneself. In the same way, one's own external presentation remains *out of proportion* to one's internal disposition. (Strathern 1992a: 132)

A full model of proportional sociality, then, is one that takes into account the different ways in which people inflect and qualify their relationships. Proportional sociality tells us the factors by which the stretching out of the social takes place. It talks about how people re-scale their biographical projects.

This brings me to the question with which I opened the chapter, about the location and the size of well-being. It is clear that if different people factor their relationships in different and varying proportions, the size of their social interactions will vary; that is, the kind of sociality they set in motion will have different weights or dimensions. The consequence of this is rather obvious, and that is that not everything that people do is directed towards the enhancement of their well-being. Heidegger once said that the crucial ontological question was: 'Why is there Being, and not simply Nothing?' The same could be said about well-being. A notion of well-being is by default a notion of a lack – of something that there is, but not quite in the proportion that we would like it there to be. This is of course why the economic idea of *measuring* well-being is not entirely a misguided notion, for if social life had reached its full potential (call it happiness, well-being, virtue, whatever), then there would be nothing to measure well-being against – indeed, the very idea of well-being would be incomprehensible. My larger point is that the project of an anthropology of well-being demands inexorably a model of proportional sociality, for however we define well-being, it will always need to be something less than perfect social life: it will always entail a 'remaindering of life' (Lear 2000). It will always therefore have a size and will always need to be expressed in one kind of social scale or another[6] – and the location of this size and scale will always be the person.

Our awareness of topological re-dimensioning, of social forms continuously changing size and effects (that is, of their inherent re-scaling properties), provides us with an extraordinary tool with which to enhance our category of the person. It allows for a novel and stronger theory of personhood, where people emerge as the proportional factors and carriers of social life. Mary Douglas and Steven Ney (1998) have recently pointed out the extent to which the social sciences have taken the person for granted. Social life has been seen to work upon persons, or from them, but not *through* them, as their own sizing projects. An analytic of social life that focuses on the *size* of sociality, however, will necessarily have to point, too, to the shape that human life takes in the form of biographical and historical projects. Persons are not simply agents, or actors, or rational decision-makers. They are the site where social life becomes strong because it becomes their own. Persons are social life writ small, expressed in emerging forms of proportional (that is, biographical) sociality.

To conclude, my aim in this chapter has been to sketch the foundations of a social theory that will live up to the efforts that moral philosophers and economists have invested into tackling the problem of the estimation of well-being. I have tried to show that an analytic that accommodates some of their very important contributions requires us to reformulate our social theory, and in particular that it requires us to rethink some of the basic categories through which we make up our images of the social. I have suggested that one such model of sociality may be founded on the idea of proportional sociality, for the notion of proportional relationships seems to have underpinned the political thought of scholars from the Classical period to our age. Perhaps more importantly, the notion of proportional sociality appears well suited to the task of addressing the problem of well-being because it accommodates itself to the distributional and aggregational tactics of economic models. It learns from economics, but it also points to where the social theory of economists has gone wrong. Last, a model of proportional sociality allows us to make a case for a stronger theory of personhood, where people become themselves so long as they have the capacity to hold and envision their own projects of virtue ethics. And it is perhaps in the nature of such intellectual engagements (between economics, moral philosophy and anthropology, between the factual and the possible) that an enquiry into the nature of a problem as intractable as that of well-being may obtain new and refreshing sources of impetus.

ACKNOWLEDGEMENTS

My warm thanks to Marilyn Strathern for her intellectual stimulus and generosity in engaging with my work. Thanks also to Carlo Caduff, for his detailed and insightful reading of the chapter, which provided suggestive avenues for further thought.

NOTES

1. This is debatable, although the literature tends to be unanimous on this point; Dasgupta is representative: 'Not only is the socio-economic personal, the political is personal too: it is the individual that matters' (2001: 13).
2. Cohen has observed how the application of the imagery and vocabulary of the natural sciences to the social sciences reached a dead end with the development of Newtonian natural philosophy:

    The reason is that the Newtonian system of the world, the application of Newtonian rational mechanics, does not lend itself to a mechanical model or visualization in the human mind that can easily be transferred to an image of society at large or to economics. (Cohen 1994: 61)

    This may be why most social theory works within a Galilean paradigm, and why recent innovations in our sociological vocabulary echo those of topological mathematics, whose development finally allowed overcoming the intractability of the three body problem in (Newtonian) physics. Examples of the use of topological metaphors in sociology can be found in the work of John Law (for example, 1999), and in actor-network theory more widely (Law and Hassard 1999). An early anthropological use can be found in Leach (1961).
3. I thank Marilyn Strathern for prompting me to think about the different origins of perspectives (orders of knowledge/reality) and their reconciliation, or not, in proportional encounters.

4. I use the term incautiously, almost provocatively. But I still find it appropriate, especially on two fronts. First, an Aristotelian model of sociality points to the extent to which social life emerges in distributive episodes, and in particular to the structure of these episodes as moments of proportional equivalence, however frail and transient these equivalences may be (see note 2, above). Second, it is strongly ethical, envisioning social life through the lens of robust projects of virtue ethics played out *at the level of the person* (for example, Hursthouse 1999; MacIntyre 1985; Nussbaum 1996). As it happens, this ethical tradition is congenial with Amartya Sen's capability approach (Nussbaum 1988) and, I believe, offers wonderful new opportunities for anthropological theory.
5. My vocabulary is not gratuitous: the Latin etymology for 'choice' is traced to the word *elegire*, which was originally used to denote the capacity to cultivate and extract whatever the fertility of the land could afford. The imagery of *extraction* is of course also present in Roy Wagner's (1975) account of the forms that the emergence of social life takes.
6. I use the term 'scale' in a double sense: scale as size and scale as idiom . The image is, once again, Archimedean: one category presses and gets translated into another category, and the translation brings forth its own effects. If the natural environment is the modern scale of well-being, then environmentalism will necessarily have to change the size of society. The environment can only be factored into society if society is re-proportioned and changes size. Scales are therefore orders of knowledge that carry forth their own magnitudinal effects. This may be why 'the global' is Euro-American society's current proportional self-descriptor.

REFERENCES

Arrow, K.J. 1951. *Social Choice and Individual Values*. New York: Wiley.
Cohen, I.B. 1994. Newton and the Social Sciences, with Special Reference to Economics, or, The Case of the Missing Paradigm. In P. Mirowski (ed.) *Natural Images in Economic Thought: 'Markets Read in Tooth and Claw'*. Cambridge: Cambridge University Press.
Corsín Jiménez, A. 2003. The Form of the Relation, or Anthropology's Enchantment with the Algebraic Imagination. Unpublished manuscript: University of Manchester.
Dasgupta, P. 1993. *An Inquiry into Well-being and Destitution*. Oxford: Clarendon Press.
—— 2001. *Human Well-being and the Natural Environment*. Oxford: Oxford University Press.
Davis, J. 1992. *Exchange*. Minneapolis: University of Minnesota Press.
Derrida, J. 1995. *Espectros de Marx: el estado de la deuda, el trabajo del duelo y la nueva internacional*. Madrid: Editorial Trotta.
Douglas, M. 1986. *How Institutions Think*. Syracuse, NY: Syracuse University Press.
Douglas, M. and S. Ney. 1998. *Missing Persons: A Critique of the Social Sciences*. Berkeley, CA: University of California Press.
Griffin, J. 1986. *Well-being: Its Meaning, Measurement and Moral Importance*. Oxford: Clarendon Press.
—— 1996. *Value Judgement: Improving Our Ethical Beliefs*. Oxford: Clarendon Press.
Gudeman, S. 1978. Anthropological Economics: The Question of Distribution. *Annual Review of Anthropology* 7, 347–77.
—— 2001. *The Anthropology of Economy: Community, Market, and Culture*. Malden, MA: Blackwell Publishers.
Hobbes, T. 1991. *Leviathan*. Cambridge and New York: Cambridge University Press.
Hursthouse, R. 1999. *On Virtue Ethics*. Oxford and New York: Oxford University Press.
Israel, J.I. 2001. *Radical Enlightenment: Philosophy and the Making of Modernity 1650–1750*. Oxford: Oxford University Press.
Law, J. 1999. After ANT: Complexity, Naming and Topology. In J. Law and J. Hassard (eds) *Actor Network Theory and After*. Oxford: Blackwell Publishers/The Sociological Review.

Law, J. and J. Hassard (eds). 1999. *Actor Network Theory and After*. Oxford: Blackwell Publishers/The Sociological Review.
Leach, E.R. 1961. *Rethinking Anthropology*. London: University of London/Athlone Press.
Lear, J. 2000. *Happiness, Death, and the Remainder of Life*. Cambridge, MA: Harvard University Press.
Machamer, P. 1998a. Galileo's Machines, His Mathematics, and His Experiments. In P. Machamer (ed.) *The Cambridge Companion to Galileo*. Cambridge: Cambridge University Press.
—— 1998b. Introduction. In P. Machamer (ed.) *The Cambridge Companion to Galileo*. Cambridge: Cambridge University Press.
MacIntyre, A. 1985. *After Virtue*. London: Gerald Duckworth & Co. Ltd.
Macpherson, C.B. 1962. *The Political Theory of Possessive Individualism: Hobbes to Locke*. Oxford: Oxford University Press.
Meikle, S. 1994. Was Marx an Economist? In P. Dunleavy and J. Stanyer (eds) *Contemporary Political Studies 1994*. Belfast: Proceedings of the Political Studies Annual Conference.
—— 1995. *Aristotle's Economic Thought*. Oxford: Clarendon Press.
Nussbaum, M.C. 1988. Nature, Function, and Capability: Aristotle on Political Distribution. *Oxford Studies in Ancient Philosophy*, suppl. vol., 145–84.
—— 1996. *The Therapy of Desire: Theory and Practice in Hellenistic Ethics*. Princeton, NJ: Princeton University Press.
Offer, A. (ed.). 1996. *In Pursuit of the Quality of Life*. Oxford: Oxford University Press.
Sen, A. 1999a. *Development as Freedom*. Oxford: Oxford University Press.
—— 1999b. The Possibility of Social Choice. *American Economic Review* 89, 349–78.
Strathern, M. 1981. Self-interest and the Social Good: Some Implications of Hagen Gender Imagery. In S.B. Ortner and H. Whitehead (eds) *Sexual Meanings: The Cultural Construction of Gender and Sexuality*. New York: Cambridge University Press.
—— 1988. *The Gender of the Gift: Problems with Women and Problems with Society in Melanesia*. Berkeley: University of California Press.
—— 1990. For the Motion (I). In T. Ingold (ed.) *The Concept of Society is Theoretically Obsolete*. Manchester: Group for Debates in Anthropological Theory, Department of Social Anthropology, University of Manchester.
—— 1991. *Partial Connections*. Savage, MD: Rowman & Littlefield.
—— 1992a. *After Nature: English Kinship in the Late Twentieth Century*. Cambridge: Cambridge University Press.
—— 1992b. Parts and Wholes: Refiguring Relationships in a Post-plural world. In A. Kuper (ed.) *Conceptualizing Society*. London: Routledge.
—— 1995. *The Relation: Issues in Complexity and Scale*. Cambridge: Prickly Pear Press.
—— 1996. Cutting the Network. *Journal of the Royal Anthropological Institute* 2, 517–35.
Wagner, R. 1975. *The Invention of Culture*. Englewood Cliffs, NJ: Prentice Hall.
Watkins, J.W.N. 1955. Philosophy and Politics in Hobbes. *Philosophical Quarterly* 5, 125–46.

NOTES ON CONTRIBUTORS

Alberto Corsín Jiménez is lecturer in the anthropology of organisations at the University of Manchester. He carried out fieldwork amongst the nitrate mining communities of the Atacama Desert in Chile. He writes mainly on the political and ethical formations of contemporary capitalism, and in particular on the institutionalisation of values and knowledge. His current interest is the political and economic organisation of research as a public good. He is editor of *The Anthropology of Organisations* (Ashgate 2007).

Ian Harper trained as a medical practitioner, worked in hospital medicine and general practice in the UK, before working for six years in public health and community health programmes in Nepal and India and subsequently 'retraining' in social anthropology. He is a lecturer in social anthropology at the University of Edinburgh where he teaches medical anthropology. Currently he is researching as part of a multidisciplinary team into issues around the pharmaceutical industry in South Asia. His publications, which range across public health and anthropology, can be accessed at: http://www.sps.ed.ac.uk/staff/harper.html

Eric Hirsch is Reader in Social Anthropology at Brunel University. He has a long-standing interest in the ethnography and history of Melanesia and he has also conducted anthropological research in Greater London. He recently co-edited *Transactions and Creations: Property Debates and the Stimulus of Melanesia* (Berghahn 2004) and a special edition of the journal *History and Anthropology* on the theme of 'Ethnographies of Historicity' (2005).

Wendy James is professor of social anthropology at the University of Oxford, and a Fellow of St Cross College. She has carried out research in the Sudan and Ethiopia intermittently over four decades, and has long-standing academic links with universities and other institutions in the region of north-eastern Africa. She is a Fellow of the British Academy and has served as President of the Royal Anthropological Institute. She has published widely not only on Africa but on the history and current scope of anthropology, as well as acting on various occasions as a consultant to the UN and associated agencies. Her most recent books are *The Ceremonial Animal: A New Portrait of Anthropology*

(2003), and *War and Survival in Sudan's Frontierlands: Voices from the Blue Nile* (2007 in press), both Oxford University Press.

James Laidlaw is a University Lecturer in the department of social anthropology at the University of Cambridge, and is a Fellow of King's College, Cambridge. He has conducted research in India, Inner Mongolia and Taiwan, and publications include *The Archetypal Actions of Ritual* (1994, with Caroline Humphrey), *Riches and Renunciation* (1995), *The Essential Edmund Leach* (2000, jointly edited with Stephen Hugh-Jones), and *Ritual and Memory* (2004, jointly edited with Harvey Whitehouse). His most recent publication is *Religion, Anthropology, and Cognitive Science* (2007, also jointly edited with Harvey Whitehouse). He is currently working on a book on the anthropological study of ethical life, and directing a collaborative research project on the ethics of self-cultivation in East Asian Buddhism.

Michael Lambek is professor of anthropology at the London School of Economics and at the University of Toronto, where he holds a Canada Research Chair. He is the author of *Human Spirits: A Cultural Account of Trance in Mayotte* (1981); *Knowledge and Practice in Mayotte: Local Discourses of Islam, Sorcery and Spirit Possession* (1993); and *The Weight of the Past: Living with History in Mahajanga, Madagascar* (2002) as well as editor of *A Reader in the Anthropology of Religion* (2002) and co-editor of several works, including *Tense Past: Cultural Essays on Trauma and Memory* (1996) and *Illness and Irony: On the Ambiguity of Suffering in Culture* (2003).

Bryan Maddox is a social anthropologist working on literacy, language and education in South Asian contexts. He studied at the Sussex University and King's College London. He teaches in the School of Development Studies at the University of East Anglia. He has undertaken ethnographic fieldwork in Nepal and Bangladesh in rural areas including research on literacy in farming and fishing communities and on religious literacies. His current research interests are interdisciplinarity, and the links between literacy, human capabilities and well-being.

Nigel Rapport has recently held the Canada Research Chair in Globalization, Citizenship and Justice at Concordia University of Montreal, and was a founding director of the Centre for Cosmopolitan Studies. He is Professor of Anthropological and Philosophical Studies at the University of St Andrews; and he has been elected a Fellow of the Royal Society of Edinburgh. His research interests include: social theory, phenomenology, identity and individuality, conversation analysis, and links between anthropology and literature and philosophy. His recent books include: *The Trouble with Community: Anthropological Reflections on Movement, Identity and Collectivity* (Pluto Press 2002); *'I am Dynamite': An Alternative Anthropology of Power*

(Routledge 2003); and (as editor) *Democracy, Science and the Open Society: A European Legacy?* (Transaction 2006).

Griet Scheldeman completed her PhD on young people with diabetes at the University of St Andrews, Scotland. Her current research interests centre on how people creatively pursue their well-being in and through diverse aesthetic engagements with landscape(s). She is working as a Teaching Fellow at the Department of Anthropology, University of Aberdeen.

Neil Thin is senior lecturer in social anthropology in the School of Social and Political Studies at the University of Edinburgh. His advisory work for international development agencies focuses on social development policy and poverty reduction, and his publications include the book *Social Progress and Sustainable Development* (2002 ITDG Publications).

INDEX

Compiled by Sue Carlton

adaptivism 138, 142, 146–7, 148
Adelson, N. 150
Adorno, T. 1, 24, 25
Agamben, G. 15–16, 18, 26, 44
agency 8–9, 36, 72, 74
aggregation 181–3, 193, 195
ahimsa (non-violence) 158, 159, 160–2, 166–8, 174, 176
aid 41, 45, 71, 75, 76–7
Alma Ata, Declaration of (1978) 39
amede (Fuyuge chief) 19, 55, 56, 59
Anthropological Index Online 137
anthropology 121–2
  and happiness 135, 136–48, 150–3
  and psychology 150–1, 152
  and relativism 23, 49, 127–8, 138, 142–8
anti-hedonism 138, 138–42
anti-psychologism 138, 151
anti-utilitarianism 138–9, 140–1, 157
Anuvrat Global Organization 169
Appenzell Ausserrhoden, Switzerland 124
apportionments 187, 189
  dike (just apportionment) 189, 192
Arendt, H. 11, 13–16, 24, 26
Aristotle 8, 10, 11–14, 16, 118, 123–4, 130, 189–90
Arrow, K.J. 183
Asad, T. 157
Auschwitz 13, 107
Azande 20, 74

BaMbuti pygmies (Ituri) 143–4
bare life 15, 16, 18, 24, 44
Batase 37
Bateson, G. 95, 96, 101
Bateson, M. 95
Bentham, J. 117, 141
Betsimisaraka (Madagascan people) 128
Blue Nile State 78

Bobbio, N. 10
Bodi (son of Kol Usi) 53–4
Bodley, J.H. 142, 146
body
  as metaphor 38–9
  see also embodiment
Bonga refugee scheme 76, 78
Bororo 143
Buddhism 160
Burghart, R. 46

Canada, and quality of life 122
Canovan, M. 13
capabilities 7, 8–9, 21, 23, 48, 120, 183, 184
capacities 23, 24, 59, 64, 109, 128, 156, 190
  carrying 186–7
  exercise of 11, 117–21, 122, 123–4, 126, 127, 130
  and judgement 128
  killing 55–6
  measurement of 127
  relational 19, 20
Castoriadis, C. 26
Chagnon, N.A. 145
choice 9, 91–2, 93, 106, 116, 121, 174, 187, 193
Clark, D.A. 156
clinical pathologism 138, 148–50
  see also pathologisation
cognitivism 138, 150, 151
Collier, S. 16
Collingwood, R.G. 20, 75
communitarianism 6, 7, 20
Community Health and Development Programme (CHDP) (UMN) 37
Community Medical Assistants (CMAs) (Nepal) 41–2
Community Services schemes (UN) 76–7

Index

Community Services in UNHCR: An Introduction 76–7
Comte, A. 136
Condorcet, Marquis de 136
conflict, conditions of 73–4
constructionism *see* social constructionism
contemplation 12–13
Corsín Jiménez, A. 69, 73, 92, 109, 115, 116, 156
Cort, J.E. 171
Csordas, T. 81

Darfur, Sudan 75–6, 78
Dasgupta, P. 156, 184, 185, 187, 192
Davis, J. 185–6
democracy 117–19, 121, 190, 191
Denzin, N. 151
Derrida, J. 192
diabetes 21, 80–93
  and blood tests 82, 84, 85, 924
  and embodiment 81–2, 89
  and health carers 90–2
  management routine 82, 83–5, 86, 92
  see also insulin pump
Diagnostic Statistical Manual (DSM III) 43
dike (just apportionment) 189, 192
Directly Observed Therapy Short-course (DOTS) programme 18, 40
Disability Adjusted Life Year (DALY) 18, 39
disease 18, 49–50
  illiteracy as 45–6
  and the norm 38–9
  and the state 39–40
distribution 3, 6, 183–7, 193, 195
  allocational 184–5
  distributive justice 3, 4–7, 16, 17–19, 190
  social 185
Dome Resources 62
Douglas, M. 10, 182, 185–6, 194
Doyal, L. 108
Dreze, J. 48
Duffield, M. 78
Dundas, P. 164, 168
Durban Roodeport Deep Limited 62–3
Durkheim, E. 129, 136, 141, 143

eco-Jainism 25, 170, 171, 172–3, 176
Eden *see* 'lost Eden' mythology

Edgar, I. 149
Edgerton, R. 147, 148
embodiment
  bodily subjectivity 81
  and diabetes 81–2, 90, 93
  and hospital porters 99–100
  and Jainism 158, 163, 164, 172, 173
Epstein, A.L. 151
equality 4–10, 17, 121
  see also inequality
Erikson, E. 128
Ethiopia, refugee camps 20–1, 76–7
eudaimonia 10, 116
  see also happiness
Evans, Pritchard, E.E. 1–2, 123, 140

Farmer, P. 44, 47, 49
Feuchtwang, S. 26
Filer, C. 63
Fillmore, C. 106
Finkielkraut, A. 18, 44
Foucault, M. 16, 45
Fox, R.D. 146
fractality 186, 189
Frazer, J.G. 138–9
freedom 2, 7–9, 10, 116, 120, 121, 130
Freire, P. 45
Freud, S. 129, 136
friendship 12–13
functionings 8–9, 15, 18, 48, 120, 139
Fuyuge 19, 20, 54–64
  gab ritual 20, 53, 55–6, 58, 61, 64
  good ways 19, 53–4, 55, 56, 59, 60–4
  and land ownership 60, 61–2
  and law 19, 54, 55–60, 64
  living standards 60–1, 62
  and murder 58
  and patrols and police camps 57–8, 59
  personhood 20
  and resource extraction 60–4

gab ritual 20, 53, 55–6, 58, 61, 64
Galileo Galilei 191
gift-giving 185–6, 192
Gingrich, A. 146
Gisu (Uganda) 74
good life 2–3, 15, 24, 116, 118, 123, 127–9, 138, 151, 190
  and diversity 156
  and tradition and modernity 126

good ways (*mad ife*) 19, 53–4, 55, 59, 60–4
Gough, I. 108
Griffin, J. 156, 181
Gudeman, S. 185
Gupta, A. 38
Gurung, H. 47
Gywali, D. 41

ha u bab 19, 55–6
Habermas, J. 126
happiness 1, 23, 129–30, 134–53
   Aristotle's concept of 10, 11–13, 130
   and contemplation 130
   and motives 152–3
   negative approach to 149–50
   studies of 136–8
   ways to study 151–3
Haraway, D. 49
Harper, Ian 18, 37, 40, 42
Harsanyi, J. 6
health care, Nepal 18, 35–41
Hega, Alphonse 53, 63
Heidegger, M. 24, 192, 194
Hirsch, E. 18–19, 20, 109
Hobbes, T. 4, 190, 191, 193
Hollan, D.W. 149–50
hospital porters 95–111
   ailments of 103–4
   attitude to job 110–11
   and contact with patients 102–3
   and death of colleague 104–7
   and hospital administration 98
   managing attendance at workplace 100–2
   and patient careers 97
   professional well-being 21–2
   and sickness absence 100, 101–2
   tricksterish role 99–100
   ways of moving around hospital 98–9
household (*oikonomia*) 14, 15, 16
Howell, S. 147
human condition 10, 11, 13–14, 15–16, 17, 26, 129
Human Development Index (UNDP) 2, 8, 18
humanitarianism 16, 18, 44–5, 48, 71
Hungarian Revolution (1956) 13

Ik (Uganda) 144
Illich, I. 45

illiteracy
   as social pathology 45–8
   see also literacy
Ilongot (Philippines) 145–6
individualism 11, 117, 121, 191–2
inequality 7, 46–7, 119, 120, 143
   see also equality
insulin pump 80–93
   and control 87, 89
   effect on everyday life 83–4, 86, 89–90
   experience of young people with 81–90
   and freedom 82, 84, 85, 89, 89–90, 93
   need to count carbohydrates 83–4, 86
   problems with 85, 89
   and relations 88–9
International Consortium for Mental Health Policy and Services 43
Israel, J. 188

Jackson, M. 87, 88, 89
Jain Spirit 170, 176
Jains/Jainism 24–5, 157–76
   and animal rights movement 158, 159, 162, 166–7, 168–9, 172, 174, 176
   and compassion (*karuna*) 171–5
   and confession 162–3
   diaspora 158–9, 169–70, 172
   eco-Jainism 25, 170, 171, 172–3, 176
   and embodied existence 158, 163, 164, 172, 173
   and environmentalism 158, 159, 162, 164, 168–75, 176
   and ethic of quarantine 24, 165, 172
   and fasting 158, 161, 165–6, 171
   interconnectedness of living things 25, 159, 163–4
   and non-violence (*ahimsa*) 25, 158, 159, 160–2, 166–8, 171, 174, 176
   and rebirth 161–2, 163, 164
   reformism 169–71, 175–6
   and renunciation/asceticism 24–5, 157–8, 160–1, 163, 165–6, 167, 169–70, 170–1
   Right View 161, 164
   and sexual restraint 171
James, W. 20–1, 109, 136
John Hopkins 40
justice 4–10, 73, 117, 128, 148, 190
   distributive 3, 4–7, 16, 17–19, 190
   political 10, 16
   social 4, 11, 141, 192

Index

Kambisi 58
karma 162, 163, 167, 174
kibbutz 122–3
Kol Usi 53, 55, 59, 63
kula exchange 123–4, 139–40, 141
Kumar, S. 170

labour 11, 14–15, 119–20, 122–3, 139
Ladakhis 144–5
Laidlaw, J. 24–5, 140, 147, 158
Lain Entralgo, P. 24
Lakoff, A. 16
Lambek, M. 23, 69, 92, 93, 139
Landesgemeinde 124
law
   distribution and scale 57, 59
   Fuyuge and 19, 54, 55–60, 64
Lear, J. 12, 13, 23, 129
Leder, D. 81–2
leisure 12, 72, 125, 129, 152
Levi, P. 107
Lévi-Strauss, C. 143
Liedloff, J. 142
limit 25–6
   notion of 4, 26–7
literacy
   programmes 18, 46
   and well-being 47–8
   see also illiteracy
Lock, M. 38
Locke, J. 136
'lost Eden' mythology 41, 141, 142, 143, 144–6, 147, 148, 150

Machamer, P. 191
MacIntyre, A. 123, 130
Macpherson, C.B. 23, 117–21, 123, 127, 129, 130, 190
Maddox, B. 18, 109
magic 20, 74, 139
Mahavir, T. 160, 164, 165, 174, 175
Malcolm, N. 129
Malinowski, B. 123, 138–41, 142–3
Malthus, T. 136
Maoists 37, 45
Marshall, A. 136
Martin, E. 38, 101–2
Marx, K. 117, 119, 136, 192
Mauss, M. 124
Mayotte 124, 128
Melanesian societies 54, 61, 193
Merlan, F. 54, 56

Mill, J.S. 141
Montesquieu, Baron de 136
Murray, C. 149
Murray, Hubert 54–5

Nambikwara 143
Ndembu, village life 125
Nebilyer Valley 54
Needham, R. 151
needs 36, 57, 64, 71, 76–7, 116, 121, 123, 149
   basic 4, 7, 76, 108
   see also primary goods
   intermediate 108
Nepal 18, 35–50
   corruption 41
   health 36–41
      Community Medical Assistants (CMAs) 41–2
      drugs 40
      mental health 42–4
      training for traditional healers 37–8, 42
   illiteracy 45–8
   language policy 47
   pathologisation of 35, 36, 40, 41–2, 43
   social pathologies 41–8
   and violence 39–40
Nepal Chemists and Druggists Association 40
Ney, S. 182, 194
Nielssen, H. 128
non-evaluation 23, 135, 146–7
Norberg-Hodge, H. 144
normal, concept of 38–9
Nozick, R. 6, 10
Nuer 1–2, 27, 123–4, 140, 141
Nussbaum, M. 156

Ononge 53, 58
Overing, J. 136

Papua New Guinea (PNG) 19, 53–64
   and colonial past 54–5, 56
   resource extraction 57, 60–2
   see also Fuyuge
Parry, J. 124
partonomic mode of classification 185–6
pathologisation 18, 35, 49–50
   see also clinical pathologism; social pathologies

People for the Ethical Treatment of Animals (PETA) 172
personhood 6, 9, 20–2, 194, 195
　distributed 185
Pigg, S. 37
Plath, D. 140
Plato 13, 188
political morality 2, 3, 5, 7, 11, 16–17, 44, 45
political thought 9, 10–17
Popper, K.R. 149
Port Moresby 59–60
Poverty Reduction Strategies 41
pragmatic pathologism 148–9
primary goods 4, 5, 7, 10, 121
　see also needs, basic
proportions/proportionality 4, 22–6, 180, 186, 187–92, 193
　proportionate sociality 188–92, 194, 195

quality of life 2–3, 21, 108–9, 122–3, 125, 127–9, 148–9
　and freedom of choice 93, 121, 125, 129
　and insulin pump 80, 81, 84, 87, 91, 92
　see also happiness

Rapport, N. 21–2, 93, 136
Rawls, J. 3, 4–7, 10, 21, 73, 121
Reed, A. 59–60
refugee camps 20–1, 72–3, 76–8
relativism 23, 49
　cultural 127–8
　moral 138, 142–8
renunciation see Jains/Jainism, renunciation/asceticism
resource extraction
　distribution and scale 60–3, 64
　environmental consequences 63, 64
　and Fuyuge living standards 60–1, 62, 64
Roche 40
Rosaldo, M.Z. 145–6
Rousseau, J.-J. 4, 136, 142, 143
Rumsey, A. 54, 56
Russell, A. 149

Sahlins, M. 117, 140–1, 145
Sakalava 124–5
samans/samanis 169–70

Sandel, M. 6
Sapkota, S. 42
Scanlon, T. 10, 17
Scheldeman, G. 21
Scheper-Hughes, N. 38
Schumacher, E.F. 170
Scott, J. 39
Sector Wide Approaches 41
Sen, A. 7–9, 14, 73, 116–17, 120–1, 156, 183, 192
　literacy 47–8
　patients and agents 36, 63–4
Shilapi, S. 174–5
Shklar, J. 9
Singer, P. 162
Singhvi, L.M. 159, 170
Smith, Adam 136
social choice theory 4, 183–4
social constructionism 138, 150, 151
social pathologies 43–4
　and body politic 41–5
　illiteracy 45–8
society 11, 13, 14–15, 182, 184, 192–3
　and individual 4, 5, 38, 73, 76, 121, 186–7, 193
Spencer, H. 136
SPLA (Sudan People's Liberation Army) 78
Strathern, M. 183, 185, 186, 193
Street, B. 48
Sudan 75–8

Tauade (PNG) 58
Taylor, C. 126, 128
technology, human-machine relation 87, 88, 89, 90
teleology 11, 13, 14, 15
Terapanthi order 169–70
Thapa, H.B. 41
Thin, N. 3, 23–4, 36, 109
tidibe 55, 64
time-keeping, attitudes to 53–4
Tolstoy, L. 148
Tolukuma mine 62
Tolukuma Times, The 62–3
Trias, E. 13, 26
Trobrianders 139, 141
Tulsi, Acarya 169
Turnbull, C.M. 143–4, 147
Turner, V. 125
tyranny 13

Index

UNESCO, Asian Cultural Centre poster 45
United Mission to Nepal (UMN) 37
United Nations Development Programme (UNDP) 2, 8, 18
USAID (US Agency for International Development) 40
utilitarianism 6, 7, 24, 39, 71, 73, 75, 175, 183–4
  anti-utilitarianism 138–9, 140–1, 157
  and culture-blindness 158
  negative 149
Uttaradhyayana Sutra 173–4

Vallely, A. 172
Veenhoven, R. 137
veganism 172, 176
Vermeer, J. 126, 180
Virchow, R. 44
vitamin A capsule distribution programme 18, 40

Wagner, R. 186
Weber, M. 126, 136
Weiner, J. 27
welfare 20–1, 69–73, 74, 76, 149
well-becoming 96, 110–11
well-being
  and characteristics of different societies 121–5
  concept of 69–76, 95, 108–9, 116, 156–7
  emergence of concept 2
  and intervention 115
  measuring/evaluating 127–9, 157, 194
  and political philosophy 10–17
  relevance of ethnography 2, 23
  and self-knowledge 75–6
  sense of 22, 72, 88, 96, 102, 104, 107, 109, 110–11
  size of 181–2, 194
  and social changes 125–6
  and universal standards 126–7
  in workplace 95–111
Wellenkamp, J.C. 149–50
Werbner, R. 109
Williams, B. 4, 6, 9–10, 20, 23, 27
Wittgenstein, L. 129–30
women, and agency 8–9
Woolf, V. 95, 96, 107, 110
World Bank 39
World Database of Happiness 137
World Health Organization (WHO) 2
World Mental Health: Problems and Priorities in Low-income Countries 43–4, 149
Wundt, W. 136

Yavu Inoge 55

Zen Buddhism 145
Žižek, S. 22
ZOA Refugee Care 77